THE ARABS IN ISRAEL

The Arabs in Israel

Ori Stendel

sussex
ACADEMIC
PRESS

2 4 6 8 10 9 7 5 3 1
First published in English in 1996 by

SUSSEX ACADEMIC PRESS
18 Chichester Place
Brighton BN2 1FF, United Kingdom

Distributed in the United States by
International Specialized Book Services, Inc.
5804 N.E. Hassalo St.
Portland, Oregon 97213-3644
USA

British Library Cataloguing in Publication Data
A CIP catalogue record for this book is available from the British Library.

ISBN 1–898723 23 0 (hardcover)
ISBN 1–898723 24 9 (paperback)

Printed and bound by Biddles Ltd, King's Lynn and Guildford

Contents

Foreword

Moshe Ma'oz

The Israeli Arabs are a unique and complex minority, unlike any other in the world. It is a minority with psychological convictions of a majority, due to Israel's position in the midst of the Arab World. It is a minority living close, yet at the same time far removed from, the consciousness of the bulk of Israel's Jewish population.

Its young people are Israelis, who speak fluent Hebrew, read the Hebrew press and watch Hebrew television. Yet, they seclude themselves in their villages, in towns like Nazareth, or among their fellow Bedouin of the tribes in the northern Negev. Even in the few mixed towns, their residential quarters sometimes seem as if closed by a wall.

Young Israeli Arabs dress and behave like their Jewish Israeli peers. Yet, they jealously preserve their Arab identity and take pride in their nationalism. They aspire to equality, yet will not give up their right to be different.

Israeli Arabs are both Israelis and Palestinians. Moreover, their old ties with their *hamulah* (clan), tribe and religious community persist. These affinities are not always complementary. Israeli Arabs may therefore find themselves torn between conflicting loyalties; while struggling with the Jewish majority to ensure for themselves both equality of rights and the freedom to remain different, they also face a grave crisis within their own Arab community.

Ori Stendel's book is a fascinating attempt to deal with the subject from all angles. It is an enquiry into the key factors of the Arab Israelis' existence. It probes how they are being integrated into the State of Israel and how, at the same time, they face dilemmas of identity. For almost every question that arises, the author provides the relevant historical background and distinguishes features shared with, or different from, the developments in Arab countries.

The political map of the Arab minority is at the heart of this book, but there are extended chapters on demographic trends, geographic distribution, the configuration of the religious communities, evolving social conditions, the status of women, Arabic-language literature in Israel, the Arabic press, the legal status of the minority, government policies, and the relations of Israeli Arabs with those of the occupied territories and with the PLO. All these aspects are brought together here for the first time in a volume combining factual description with in-depth analysis.

This is a comprehensive basic book of a kind not found until now. Ori Stendel has been engaged in Israeli Arab affairs since 1962, when he first lectured on the subject. There followed two periods of work in the Prime Minister's office during which he served for a time as deputy to the Prime Minister's Adviser on Arab Affairs. His legal training has stood him in a good stead in bringing out some sections of the present book in sharper relief.

The book is well organized and clearly written, and despite its academic standard, is easily readable. The reader will sense that it is a result of many years of labor.

Professor Moshe Ma'oz
Department of Islamic and Middle Eastern Studies
The Hebrew University, Jerusalem

In the Midst of Change

The Starting Point: The Armistice Demarcation Lines

Since the establishment of the State of Israel in 1948, Israeli Arabs have had to contend with an internal contradiction that has defied solution, while constantly striving for self-definition. They are a national minority groping to find a way between contradictory currents, in a state that is, by its own definition, Jewish and dedicated to an in-gathering of the exiles, while at the same time aiming toward equality of all its citizens, regardless of religion, race, and sex. Israel's Declaration of Independence, written during the fateful battles of 1948, states: "We call, even in the midst of this bloody onslaught, which has been carried out upon us these past months, to the sons of the Arab people who are residents of the State of Israel, to maintain peace and to take part in the building of the State, on the basis of full and equal citizenship, and on the basis of appropriate representation in all its institutions, provisional and permanent."

This was a declaration of the People's Council, a special body constituted under historical, non-recurring circumstances, amidst the storm of the war for Jewish independence. The life of the state, only just born, still hung in the balance, yet its founders set out to determine the state's relationship with the Arabs destined to live within its borders, as a basic principle of its system of values. The armies were still locked in combat but the Arabs of Israel were changed in one fell swoop from a majority to a minority. Throughout the period of "Jewish statehood in the making" they had remained convinced that they would continue to rule over the entire country; their leaders, unwilling to compromise, exhorted the Arab population to take up arms, but those same leaders were the first to flee when the tide of war favored the Jews and they could not keep their promises of annihilating the Jews.

After the fighting subsided, the Arabs found themselves in the minority, reduced in numbers and almost totally devoid of a social elite: the large landowners, merchants, industrialists, engineers, doctors, judges, lawyers, religious leaders, writers and journalists all fled, and with them vanished all focal points of economic and social activity. Thus took place the mass exodus of some 600,000 Arabs from territories which came to be included within the borders of the State of Israel.

The urban Arab population struggled with spreading unemployment and economic hardship. Peasants faced hunger, while searching frantically for credit. Cultural activity died, religious institutions ceased to function. Many found themselves in new places within the country to which they fled in the whirlwind of events in search of shelter. They were the *uprooted*, as opposed to *refugees*, who fled further afield, to the "West Bank," to Arab countries, or even overseas. In those days, which now seem so far off, the Arabs of Israel struggled for basic existence, anxious to decipher the components of their new reality. Their defeat came upon them so unexpectedly that they could not easily grasp its ramifications. Israeli rule materialized too suddenly, abstractly, for them to react in a political way. They could not, at first, reconcile themselves to the very existence of Israel in a land that was intended for them, a land that for thirty years had been called Palestine, *their* Palestine. For a long time they referred to the State as *maz'uma*, the "so-called" or "make-believe" state; for them it was not real; it was a mirage. Arabs likened the Israeli state to the Crusader state, which, despite its military superiority at a given moment in history, was destined not to survive because it lacked roots in the region. They awaited the day of redemption. Women vowed not to use make-up or comb their hair, or even wash, until relatives who fled returned and the foreign state vanished as if it had never existed.[1]

But there slowly emerged a feeling that it was impossible to deny completely the existence of the Jewish state which in this early period seemed threatening, hostile, watchful. Israel's Arabs felt isolated, shut off from their world; they lacked reliable information about current events. In this void, contradictory rumors were spread, which only increased the confusion. Their only reality was that they had become a minority overnight, leaderless, not knowing what the morrow would bring; this was their only point of reference.

By late 1948, the war had almost ended. Israel, albeit established as a nation state in the eyes of the world, was yet without borders. The cease-fire lines were being negotiated. Discreet contacts with King 'Abdallah of Jordan were soon to commence. Other hostile states began joining the talks at Rhodes, and by the autumn of 1949 the armistice agreements had already been signed, giving form to the State within the "Green Line."[2] The borders were estranged and strange, contorted in shape, artificial. Under the terms of the agreement with the Hashemite Kingdom of Jordan, the "Little Triangle,"[3] which had not been captured by the Israel Defense Forces (IDF), was annexed; its inhabitants discovered that they, a population of 31,000 souls, were Israelis.

During this period, 35,550 Arab refugees returned to Israel: some returned under family reunion arrangements, while others infiltrated back illegally, but later received permission to remain. Israeli policy was intended as a goodwill gesture aimed at blunting the sharp edge of confrontation, but it went unrequited in the face of the hostility of the Arab states. According to the 1949 census, the Arab population within the "Green Line" numbered some 156,000 persons. In the early years, the border seemed unclear, maps were not definitive. The meandering border was manned by barbed wire fences, whitewashed rocks, trees or rocky hills. Children on both sides were warned not to cross it. They had trouble understanding the proscription. Exchanges of fire in the middle of the night brought home the reality of the buffer zone from time to time, but despite the "blurred political wall," there was a common saying that crossing the border was simpler than crossing a street where, heaven forbid, one could get run over . . .

Such reality was well reflected in the village of Barta'a, in the Samarian hills. This small village was split by a line on the map, which nearly "swallowed" the dot that indicated its existence. Under the terms of the armistice agreement, the wadi through the center of the village marked the border, which the local people disregarded at their pleasure. People on the Jordanian side of Barta'a quickly learned the advantages of the Israeli doctor, who frequently visited *there*, and who was much closer to them than any Jordanian clinic. For a long time children in the "Jordanian sector" studied at the Israeli school, without noticing they were being brought up by the "enemy." Barta'a women on both the Israeli and Jordanian sides continued going each evening to the same well, as they had gone from time immemorial. Neither did the border impinge on the standing of the *mukhtar*, of the Kabaha family, whose members dwelt throughout the village. Until 1954, he continued as the joint *mukhtar* of both parts of the village, unintentionally creating an historic precedent, controlling areas situated in both countries, recognized in both, despite the state of war between them.

It is told that the *mukhtar* had two wives, one in Israel and one in Jordan, and that he was wont to cross the border lightheartedly from one wife to her rival. He was finally caught by the Arab Legion, the Jordanian army, while engaged, among his other activities, in smuggling (according to the dictates of supply and demand). Barta'a Israeli inhabitants took up a collection to pay for a Jordanian lawyer, Anwar Nusseiba, who later became the Jordanian minister of defense.

Neither was the border obvious to two Jordanian educational inspectors from Jenin, who went on a tour of schools in their area in 1964. They reached the "Green Line" in their car, failed to notice it was green, and went on to the Israeli Arab village of Muqibla, next to Kibbutz Jezreel. "Wein el-madrasa?" (Where is the school), they asked, and were directed to it and entered. "Wein el-mudir?" (Where is the headmaster), they inquired. He came and asked who they were. "Inspectors from the ministry of education." They failed to add "Jordanian."

The school's headmaster received them in his office "in their official capacity" and spoke at length with them. While arranging for coffee to be served, they were left for a few minutes alone in the office; as they looked around, behind them they saw the photographs of Israeli President Zalman Shazar, Prime Minister Levi Eshkol, and Chief of the IDF General Staff Yitzhak Rabin. There was no photograph of King Hussein. It was then that the inspectors realized they exceeded their authority somewhat and quickly left. I was able to locate them after the Six Day War, and they told me about that exciting experience, and on this occasion took plenty of time to sip coffee.

In the summer, the Information Center would send crews to screen movie pictures in Arab villages out-of-doors. The screen would be placed in an open field before viewers on benches, and pictures would soon flicker across the screen. More than once a shout would be heard from over the border, "For God's sake, move the screen. *We* can't see!"

Many are the "border stories" which bear witness to its lack of distinctness, yet over the years a deep meaning was distilled into it. At the outset, a "military government" existed in the Arab sector. Proximity to the border created the need for a night-time curfew. Limitations on freedom of movement were placed upon Israeli Arabs during daytime as well. A regime of licenses cast a heavy shadow over their lives, inhibiting their development. They were suspect because of their very nationality.

The matter was not left strictly in the realm of security. It quickly took on a political coloration. Arab leaders fought for abolishment of the military regime as a sharp symbol of discrimination. On the right of the political spectrum, Herut[4] saw it as a means for the ruling party to control the Arab vote. Gradually, its sharpness was blunted, its embrace slackened. Pressure to abolish it faced the implacable demand of the prime minister, David Ben-Gurion, to continue it at all costs.

Despite the victory won in the Knesset – Israel's parliament – by supporters of the military government, it became obvious that its perceived necessity was doubted by many. Its proscriptions became fewer. The Israeli economy cried out for working hands from the Arab villages, and they did much to undercut the ethos of the military government. In the meantime, Ben-Gurion resigned. Levi Eshkol took the opposite track, and in 1966 the military government was officially abolished, although the Emergency Defense Regulations, under which it had been implemented, remained on the books. A new stage commenced in the development of Israeli Arabs, in the midst of a far-reaching socioeconomic change.

Minority or Majority? Integrated or Alien?

Israeli Arabs are undeniably a unique minority, without parallel among national minorities elsewhere in the world. They ponder their identity, feel conflicted and question their essence: are they a minority within Israel or an inseparable limb of the large Arab majority in the Middle East? Israelis or Palestinians? Devout Muslims or citizens of the western world, believers in progress?

From the beginning of their experience in 1948, the ties with their kin who became refugees have defined their status. Someone is missing from every Arab home: a cousin, brother, mother or father who fled the country and are today considered "absentee." These people live in refugee camps scattered all over the Middle East.

The Arabs of Israel are a minority that had once been a majority. Extremist elements among them fan the flames of a vision in which the wheel of fortune will change direction, the circle come round, and Israeli Arabs will again become an absolute majority. The high birth-rate, the fading of the "Green Line," minimal Jewish immigration until 1989 when the Soviet Union opened its gates – all these nourished an expectation, fed by the ongoing battle for the "right of return" of these refugees, which figured prominently in the Palestinian Declaration of Independence in Algeria on November 15, 1988: the solution as envisaged by the PLO includes the return of hundreds of thousands of refugees who fled during the 1948 war, together with their whole families.

The Oslo agreement, reached in secret in the summer of 1993, does not deal with the PLO demand that the refugees from the 1948 war return, but the demand has not vanished. From time to time Palestinian leaders mention the "right of return" to Israel in the same breath as the demand for the right of those displaced in the Six Day War to return to their homes in the West Bank or Gaza Strip. The subject is clearly a rumbling volcano that will erupt as the peace process progresses, jeopardizing the entire process. There is a virtual consensus in Israel that refugees from Haifa, Jaffa, Beersheba, and elsewhere must not be permitted back, as the return of hundreds of thousands of refugees from 1948 would mean one thing: the destruction of the Jewish state by inundation with Palestinian Arabs, turning the Arab minority into a majority.

This is perhaps the most pressing issue in the dispute between Israel and the Palestinians, and there is no compromise solution to be found: even a partial return of refugees is regarded as impossible.

Today, forty-seven years after the establishment of the state of Israel, the Arabs are still not reconciled to this upheaval from majority to minority. The traits of a majority run in their blood, as a result of which they view themselves as both a minority in Israel, and simultaneously as part of a large majority in the Middle East – Arabs who are Palestinians. Within the Jewish state's borders, Israeli Arabs have developed as a unique society, different from the populations of neighboring Arab states and fundamentally distinct from them, although they share nationality, language and religion, and distinct also in their more sober attitude toward the state of Israel.

From the outset, the perspective of the Arab states and the PLO toward Israeli Arabs was a significant factor in forming their self-awareness. The attitudes of the Arab states and their peoples toward Israeli Arabs have always been ambivalent, mixed with reservations, suspicion and distrust. The result was a sense of alienation on the Israeli Arab side. These attitudes have hurt even young extremist Arabs, such as the nationalist poet Rashed Hussein from the village Musmus, who left Israel and died in a fire several years later in New York, where he held a senior post in the PLO propaganda machine. Hussein's poems were filled with venomous rage against the Israeli government, but to his great disappointment he never seemed to win the sympathy of his colleagues in the Arab states. Hussein was deeply hurt by the cool reception he received from Arab representatives at an international conference in Yugoslavia in 1959. Upon his return to Israel, desolate and shamed, he moaned: "Who are we, the Israeli Arabs? In Israel we are treated like a fifth column, outside we are treated like traitors. We live in two worlds and belong to neither."[5]

The turning point came after the Six Day War, with the growing centrality of the PLO in the Israeli-Arab conflict and the integration of some Israeli Arab leaders among its ranks. These Israeli Arabs helped raise the PLO's awareness of the resources within the Arab minority which could be used for the campaign against Israel, in light of their day-to-day interaction with the realities of "the Zionist State," and their significance in the Israeli political fabric as holders of the right to vote and to be elected to the Israeli legislature, and to other institutions in the ruling establishment such as local municipalities, the Histadrut,[6] workers' councils, and trade unions.

Individuals such as Sabri Jiryis, Habib Qahwaji, and Mahmud Darwish, whose role we shall discuss later, were able to clarify to the PLO leadership the need for a change in approach to Israeli Arabs, with a view toward integrating them within the Palestinian people. Since the Six Day War, the Arab population of Israel has been under constant pressure to collaborate in the struggle against Israel, both in terrorist activity and on the political level. The terrorist organizations did not adopt the lukewarm attitude of the Arab states; they "discovered" the Israeli Arabs. The failure of the Arab states to resist the Israeli army on the cease-fire lines increased the expectations for assistance from the Arab citizens of Israel who are involved in the life of the state.

These organizations appealed to the young Israeli Arabs who sought to regain their lost honor. They played on the fact that, for the young especially, feelings of anger can overwhelm basic rationality, and frustration can turn into a desire for revenge. Hostility to Israel was not difficult to foment. Since the war, approximately 3,000 Israeli Arabs have been captured on charges of terrorist activity. Proportionately this is a small number, but it is a warning signal:

1. Those drawn to the terrorist networks are mostly young (aged 13–17); products of Israeli schools, most have an elementary school education and their parents are rather well-off financially.
2. The motivation of these young people can generally be described as ideological; in any event, financial motivation was not the decisive factor. In the past decade, virtually all of them have belonged to extremist Islamic groups.
3. The reasons for joining hostile organizations are rooted in the atmosphere created around these young people by nationalist elements, who spread endless claims about being deprived, discriminated against, dispossessed, and robbed. No direct incitement to sedition is necessary; sometimes the constant dark description of Israeli reality is sufficient.
4. The absolute number of terrorists is not so comforting in light of the fact that the phenomenon continues, despite the success of the security services in exposing terrorist networks.

The attitude of the Arab public to this phenomenon is negative, undoubtedly as a result of fear of repercussions. Condemnations after an act of terrorism are not just lip-service, but they are nevertheless insufficient. The climate of public opinion in the Arab sector is still not strong enough to halt completely either terrorism or the various forms of collaboration that accompany it, including the keeping of a sympathetic silence. From time to time efforts are made to prevent deterioration of the situation, to promote peaceful debate with the Jewish majority, but these Israeli Arab voices are isolated, weak, scattered. Protest against terrorism is raised by individuals with limited influence and their declarations are swallowed up in the surrounding agitation. Groups of individuals who take upon themselves this mission are comprised mostly of intellectuals. They are unable to sway others or to bring about change.

It is not always possible to define precisely the forces that operate against the Israeli state. The boundaries are blurred. On March 30, 1976, "Land Day"[7] was a slap in the face of the moderates and revealed the power of the extremist forces. Ever since there has been an offensive against those who hold office in Arab municipal-ities, the satellites of power. Those individuals are contemptuously referred to as *adhnab al-hukumah* – the tails of the government.

In 1976 they were often surrounded by angry demonstrators during stormy rallies. Meetings were held in the local councils in order to topple the moderates. In Tayyibeh the former mayor, 'Abd er-Rahim Hajj Yahya, lost to the oppositionist Rakah[8] nominee, 'Abd el-Hamid Abu 'Isa. In the Arab village of Tira, siege was laid to the home of mayor Tareq 'Abd el-Hayy, who was considered a collaborator with the Israeli authorities. The pressure seems to have worked. Since 1976 – and until his sudden death in 1994 – he was prominent at nationalist events and toed the extremist line after joining Rakah, against which he had stood prior to 1976.

In the period of misleading calm after abatement of the storm of "Land Day," those with a realpolitik approach were consist-ently pushed aside. The Arab Lands Defense Committee, founded by Rakah, became a national association which brought together local committees in many Arab villages. Since 1976, the process of crystallizing a national leadership has clearly strengthened, with a decisive role given to volatile nationalist elements, especially since the Islamic Movement began to gain strength politically.

Israeli reality has gradually taken root within Israeli Arab culture, and the Arabs have become involved with it, absorbing the freedom of democratic rule and struggling to obtain equality, which is the cornerstone of Israel's legislative philosophy since its inception, although it has not always found it easy to put this into practice. Israeli Arabs learn Hebrew and speak it fluently. They read the Hebrew daily newspapers (as much as their Jewish counterparts), regularly watch the daily news programs and analyses, and enjoy the entertainment programs of the Hebrew television channels. They know well the corridors of the government offices, the law courts and the town squares, where they gather for protest demon-strations. They are familiar with the institutional and Histadrut by-laws. Arab companies are registered on the Israeli stock exchange, where their shares are transacted daily. The concepts of democracy are not foreign to them, and they follow closely the decisions of the Supreme Court when it convenes as the High Court of Justice.[9] They study the political map and they hone their organizational skills for deepening equality and preventing discrimination, which often lies in ambush for a minority group, national or religious, anywhere in the world.

The political map of the Arab community has witnessed the penetration of new nationalist currents saturated with hostile outside influences and with a zeal that Rakah finds difficult to rival. Groups of young people draw inspiration from the slogans of Colonel Qadhafi in Libya, or Khomeini's whirlwind revolution in Iran. The winds of unrest are blowing in every direction in the villages and the urban centers, in the universities, and even among the Bedouin tribes of the Negev and the Galilee, pulling toward new, vibrant movements, disdainful of any compromise solution. Clearly a showdown in the Arab sector is approaching. Rakah allures voters away from the government parties, and loses ground, in its turn, to the radical nationalists, who push it into more extreme positions. On the other side, the Islamic movement is rising, fiery and fanatic, carrying a burning faith to a public hungry for it. Its power grows daily; it will not compromise with the enemy – the Communist Party – which lost its outside patron with the collapse of the Soviet Union.

The escalation toward uncompromising violence among the younger generation was made vividly clear to me one evening in April 1980 in a lecture hall at the University of Haifa. A symposium was held about development trends among Israeli Arabs. Former Knesset Member Shemuel Toledano and I were "the Jews" there. Opposite us were "the Arabs": Attorney Ahmad Masarweh, an intellectual in his late thirties who had been mayor of Kafr Kara', a village in the Little Triangle, representing the relatively moderate view, which included implicit recognition of Israel as a state in its 1967 borders. Even his words, however, showed a tendency to identify with the radical slogans then being disseminated by the PLO.

Also speaking was the late Saliba Khamis, then a member of the Central Committee of Rakah. Khamis, from the founding generation of the Communist Party, was considered a radical nationalist among them, and was their strong man in Nazareth. Despite his hostile and aggressive tone toward Israel, his words sounded convoluted, overly cautious, inappropriate to the fury of young Arabs who demanded the passion of action and confrontation. On the benches in the hall were passionate university students, who listened to him with unconcealed derision. They scorned the expressions that seemed to them restrained, watered-down, disconnected to current reality. He tried to avoid polarizing the differences, taking an apologetic tone toward their radicalism, which he considered harbored a danger to the Palestinian nation; when he made do with a Palestinian state "only" in Judea, Samaria and the Gaza Strip, they cut him short with cat-calls.[10]

Khamis vainly raised his voice in a futile defamation of the state of Israel. To the young listeners, his arrows seemed dull, mere toys. They sat and laughed in his face, and he seemed to close his eyes to their ridicule. They showed no respect for his white hair. The spokesman of these young people was Ibrahim Nassar, with a black mustache, energetic, uninhibited, a leader of the Progressive National Movement which aspired to a secular Palestinian state throughout the land, from the sea to the Jordan River, and which opposed limiting it to Judea, Samaria and the Gaza Strip, as a sell-out to Israel. He spoke clearly, unambiguously, denying Israel the right to exist, sure of himself, unafraid of expressing his opinions, while denying that Israeli Arabs enjoy freedom of expression.

"The PLO will represent me so long as I live," he confidently thundered to the cheers of the Arab students in the hall. In contrast with Rakah, the Progressive National Movement is not willing to participate in the political life of Israel. The very act of participating would be tantamount to recognizing the state. Their political struggle is not conducted inside the Knesset. Its leader left no doubt about the character of the struggle for the desired goal, though here he was more evasive, general, vague. Perhaps he was also concerned about loosing all restraints, which would inevitably bring forth a strong reaction from the government. He accused Rakah of severing the connection between Israeli Arabs and the Palestinian people, of which it is an inalienable part. He paid perfunctory respect to the "glorious past" of the Communist Party, but made clear that the future belongs to *his* movement.

The applause that followed him off stage left the clear feeling that in the eyes of the nationalist Arab public, composed primarily of young people, Rakah had become too establishment, constrained, heavy, and was not meeting their needs. Against this background, Rakah lost 26 percent of its seats in the elections to the tenth Knesset in June 1981, in comparison with the 1977 elections. In parallel, the number of abstentions increased, at the orders of the extremist nationalist organizations – Sons of the Village, the Progressive National Movement, and the Muslim Brothers – which viewed the very participation in the elections as recognition of the State of Israel, and called for their boycott. For the first time, in the elections to the tenth Knesset, the proportion of Arab voters fell below the national average, despite the significant increase in the percentage of Arabs who had the right to vote in Israel.

From then on, new political forces emerged that are ardent supporters of Palestinian nationalism: first the Progressive List for Peace, then the Arab Democratic Party, and overshadowing them both with the genius of its religious-nationalist mission, the Islamic Movement. Religious fervor among Israeli Arabs is a surprising innovation, as it emerges during a process of disintegrating traditional values in Arab society, during the ostensible waning of belief and the waxing of an era of rationalism, sophistication and cynicism. There is no longer any doubt, however, that the radical religious movement is gaining power, spreading, widening, enlarging its ranks. It does not oppose the nationalist camp, but intervenes in it, enhances it, augments its passion, seeks to magnify it, to unite it, to remove the Marxist, secular elements with which Rakah had "corrupted" it.

The Islamic movement's striving for original, pure, undistorted Islamic faith as revealed by Heaven to Muhammad, "the Seal of the Prophets," is indefatigable. Its leaders and sages explicate the tenets of the faith in gatherings in villages and cities, among Bedouin tribes, in mass rallies, election meetings, mosques, and the living rooms of small apartments in housing developments of mixed Arab-Jewish cities. A veil of holiness envelops the religious faithful. The listening around them is rapt and resonant.

The rise in importance of religion among the younger generation forces Rakah to avoid confronting it; instead it tries to integrate this factor into its ranks – despite the fact that it is inconsistent with its philosophy. In Haifa, a body was founded called the General Muslim Committee, whose members included Rakah activists. They direct their anger at the government, demanding the release of property owned by the *waqf*.[11] The Communist Party, in response to the rise of the Islamic movement, has tried to create an artificial bridge to the religious public in order to limit the damage it has suffered as a result of the sudden wave of Islam in the Arab sector.

Despite the storm of transition, many Israeli Arabs are taking a sober path, paving roads of political influence, studying the errors of the past, and learning from them. They are not swept along by futile dreams. Rather they search for new forms of organization, and indeed a national leadership has already been formed – the Committee of Arab Local Council Heads. Despite the modest definition of its role as the sphere of local government, the Committee is clearly a national political body that serves as a mouthpiece for moods, trends, and aspirations that are well beyond municipal matters. The Monitoring Committee which grew out of this is a kind of supreme leadership for Israeli Arabs. It includes all Arab elected officials – in the Knesset, the local councils, the Histadrut, the teachers' unions and organizations of university and high-school students. It encompasses a wide range of camps and points of view – differences of opinion abound – but it has also managed to achieve national consensus among Israeli Arabs as a group.

This leadership makes decisions and often functions as "operational headquarters," calling for a general strike of the Arab population in solidarity with the residents of the territories or as a general sign of protest. All Israeli Arabs are called upon to walk off their jobs for one day, which is then designated a name, and these events are strung together in the calendar year as "Land Day", "Peace Day",[12] "Home Day" or "Equality Day" – each a name that befits the subject at issue.

The strike is accompanied by a demonstration, a mass rally in Nazareth or Shefar'am, or a protest in one of the larger villages in the Little Triangle or the Galilee. It is then that the ability of the organizers to control events is put to the test: can they ensure that the angry shouts do not turn into bloody riots, that the agitated demonstrators do not storm the highways, throwing stones or Molotov cocktails? For such things have happened, even on "Peace Day" in 1988, proving that the name is not an absolute guarantee of the real content of the historic day. Although in the main the Arab population of Israel has always shown sobriety, balance and restraint, when demonstrations and protests get out of hand, subversive elements within can easily draw the protesters to overstep the mark and destroy the rationale of the protest itself.

The senior leadership of the Monitoring Committee had no desire whatsoever for the young hot-heads to block the Wadi 'Ara highway. Similarly they were shocked by the outburst of hooliganism on the streets of Jaffa, which evoked grave feelings among the Jews, seeming to threaten a return of the "incidents" that characterized the pre-state era. In the wake of "Peace Day," feverish discussions were held among Israeli Arab leaders. With a sense of foreboding, committee members gathered to examine the significance of the expressions of revolt that they could not keep in check, understanding that the responsibility fell squarely on their shoulders, and that the outcome was liable to be very serious. Thus, national committee members called up all their resources to prevent a recurrence of this phenomenon on the following days. They indeed proved their ability to keep control of their public on "Land Day," March 30, and on "Home Day" on November 15, 1988, a day intended to express solidarity with the declaration of Palestinian independence in Algeria. Although publicly denying that this was their aim, the Israeli Arab leadership sought complex ways to bridge the abyss between legitimate protest and containing the Arab extreme fringe.

On "Land Day" in March 1990, which fell on a Friday, the leadership managed to navigate the demonstrations through stormy waters, but young hot-heads from Tayyibeh upset the order when, faces masked, they attacked police officers, stoning, stabbing and rioting in rage in front of the television cameras, as if trying to prove that the "Green Line" no longer existed, and that Shock Troops[13] also operated within Israel.

Between March 1990 and March 1991 a turbulent year passed which witnessed Saddam Hussein's occupation of Kuwait and the eruption of the Gulf War. This period demanded restraint of radical outside influences that threatened to draw Israeli Arabs into a storm of animosity toward their country coming from Baghdad, Amman, Tripoli and other Arab capitals. And primarily they felt the fury of nearby winds – from Nablus and Tulkarm, Qalqilya and Gaza. Under these circumstances, the sense of solidarity with Saddam Hussein did not pass over Israeli Arabs. At first, the reaction was rational – that one cannot support the Iraqi conquest of Kuwait and simultaneously demand that Israel leave the territories occupied in the Six Day War. However, the great fervor that gripped the masses in the Arab countries, the West Bank, and the Gaza Strip also doused the sparks of logic and rationality in the Arab population of Israel.

Brazen voices of agreement with the enemy could be heard from within the Arab sector, an enemy which threatened to torch half the country with the fire of a secret weapon, rejecting the thought that national brethren might also be caught in the firestorm. Even Saddam Hussein's statement that he did not have time "to sort lentils" did not prevent expressions of solidarity from the "lentils" themselves – his potential victims. But the reaction of Israeli Arabs was different here, too, and those who view it as identical with Palestinians across the "Green Line" are in error. The Israeli Arabs did not "dance on the roofs" as the missiles passed over the West Bank into Israel, and some leaders attempted to distinguish between support of the occupation of Kuwait and opposition to the attack on Israel.

When the war itself erupted, when the SCUDs themselves were launched, the patent contradiction became evident. It was now quite clear that a missile cannot distinguish between Tayyibeh and Netanya, and that everyone was in danger, both Jews and Arabs. The Israeli Arabs had no desire to commit suicide. When the sirens sounded, Israeli Arabs, like other citizens of Israel, ran to their sealed rooms, donned their gas masks and coaxed their babies into the gas-proof tents. They also obeyed the instructions of the army spokesman and used protective devices supplied by the Israel Defense Forces.

This was the first time in the history of Israel that Israeli Arabs participated in the war together with their Jewish compatriots – a war waged entirely in the rear, with no front lines. There is no doubt that the Gulf War deepened the process of reconciliation and made tangible the significance of living in one state. It even made evident the futility of nationalist boasting, which has tragic results, as proven during the 1948 war in which the leaders of the Palestinian Arabs led them on to the "Catastrophe of Palestine," in their vain attempt to annihilate the Jewish state. The PLO's bitter mistake of supporting Saddam Hussein also seems to have had an impact on the Israeli Arab population. Perhaps the shock had an effect on "Land Day" in the spring of 1991, which was marked by great restraint, no demonstrations and almost no violence, calmer than any previous "Land Day."

Clearly the image of the Iraqi despot in army uniform, chest covered with medals, spouting sparks through his mustache, for a while captured the hearts of young Arabs, hungry for a powerful leader, and again raised the longing for a ruler, like those distant days in the 1960s when Nasser would appear on television on the anniversaries of the July 23rd revolution, and the masses gathered to cheer him in the coffee houses of Nazareth and the villages. But when the television was clicked off they would return to their everyday reality, open-eyed, focused, listening to the voice of reason, suppressing seething feelings, adjusting to the very same Israeli reality that they had declared they would fight to the finish.

After the Yom Kippur War in 1973, I produced a film about Israeli Arabs called *Two Worlds*, in which I interviewed a young Arab who was known as a radical nationalist. "Tell me frankly what you felt, what you thought," I asked. "What did you want when the Yom Kippur War began?" "I wanted the Syrian army to cross the bridges over the Jordan, to strike the Israeli army, to conquer Israeli territories, but . . . " Here he stopped. "What's the 'but'?" I questioned. "Don't stop, you said you would speak openly." He hesitated for a moment, then continued, "But I didn't want them to come into my town, to enter Nazareth." In other words, the Syrian army, perceived as the army of liberation at the beginning of his utterance, is suddenly not wanted. Even this young Israel-hating radical finds it hard to exchange Israel for an Arab government.

This individual's doubts make perceptible the disparity between feelings and rational thought, known to anyone familiar with statements made by young Arabs. But one should not always take their statements at face value. Israeli Arabs are integrated in the life of the country, but they simultaneously view themselves as Palestinians and identify with their brethren in the territories. They did not hesitate to support the Intifadah, but they were fearful of it penetrating into their own neighborhoods. I was once told by a veteran mayor, one of the prominent leaders of the Monitoring Committee, the supreme leadership of the Israeli Arabs, "People who live in glass houses should not throw stones." And if stones are still thrown in Wadi 'Ara or on the road to Jerusalem, this is because emotions have gotten the better of reason, and a small group of hot-heads is endangering the general Israeli Arab public, which is not caught up in this dangerous tide.

Israeli Arabs are searching for the winding road between contradictions, and sometimes they walk on the brink of an abyss. They should not be judged harshly because the fundamental test is a practical one. From the outset, Israel was satisfied with this minimal test, namely, that Israeli Arabs would not act against the state, that they obey the law and meet their civic responsibilities. Israel has so far ignored the expressions of hatred in Arab poetry, the speeches of radical leaders, and statements by the passionate young. The repercussions of a changed attitude on both sides, if indeed a change is in the offing, remain for the future.

Since the 1967 Six Day War, more and more barriers have fallen between Israeli Arabs and the Palestinians in the occupied territories. Channels of mutual recognition with Arab states have also been opened. Every year, thousands of Israeli Arabs leave the country to participate in the Hajj pilgrimage to Mecca and Medina. The Arab press in east Jerusalem serves as an intellectual forum for Palestinian Arabs on both sides of the "Green Line" – a "mirror" for events and circumstances among Israeli Arabs, a stage for expressing solidarity and sympathy with residents of the territories. This is also true of colleges, universities, and religious institutes in the West Bank, which Israeli Arab intellectuals attend as both students and teachers. These institutions have served as a meeting place, which has had many ramifications. Since the first "Land Day" in 1976, various dates set by the leadership in the territories or in the Arab sector in Israel have become foci for identifying with each other through demonstrations, strikes and rallies, commemorated on the same day on both sides of the "Green Line".

Here, then, are two societies – Israeli Arab (living within the border of Israel proper) and Palestinian Arab (living in the West Bank and Gaza): unclosed, tangential, and sometimes integrated and interwoven. Observation of their behavior indicates the growing bridges between them, though not their complete overlap, through hostility toward Israel. Israeli Arabs do not conceal their unqualified support for the establishment of an independent Palestinian state. Indeed, this is emphasized again and again, boldly, defiantly and continuously. Most Israeli Arab leaders generally add "alongside Israel," i.e., Israel exists, is recognized, and has the right to remain a separate state. In their view, Palestine will be established beside it, bordering it, in the territories of the West Bank and Gaza.

Although the Intifadah was the means to achieve that goal, and evoked feelings of solidarity, it was assigned a border identical to that of Israel. In other words, uprising in the territories – yes, Israeli Arabs would proffer assistance, but they would not let themselves be caught up in this violent whirlwind. That the Intifadah must not spread into Israel – this view appeared in various formulations in the Israeli Arab sector; at its core lay the tenet that there would be no Intifadah among Israeli Arabs. This was the official position of the Committee of Arab Local Council Heads in its various manifestos, and of the Monitoring Committee. Arab Knesset members expressed the same view. But on the streets, it was harder to contain. Thus from time to time stones were thrown from outside the village of Jisr ez-Zarqa onto cars speeding along the highway to Haifa, and similarly from Abu Ghosh onto cars making their way to and from the capital. And from time to time, in other localities as well, painted slogans hostile to Israel appeared, and assaults on "collaborators" increased. The flames – in both senses – even reached Israeli forests near Arab settlements. Tires were burned in Tayyibeh and stones rained down on security forces during the demolition of illegal constructions several days before "Home Day" was declared. Israeli flags were burned in several Arab towns (even on Independence Day in 1991), following the Gulf War.

The Israeli Arab leadership initiated wide-ranging protest activities, emphasizing that they were all quite legal. But at the same time it approved illegal activities, if only against laws that the public finds intolerable, such as the Law for Planning and Construction 1964/65, whose violation led to the demolition of homes built on agricultural land in Tayyibeh, and which resulted in the declaration of the "Home Day" strike.

The Intifadah was not just a catalyst of solidarity, but also an arena for struggle among various political entities that wished to demonstrate fervid nationalist activity *vis-à-vis* each other. This kind of struggle could deteriorate into illegal activities by initiating expressions of latent and even overt incitement, intimations or open declarations justifying violent acts, and by creating an atmosphere in which young people approached "boiling point."

Following the summer of 1989, the Intifadah also became an educational tool, with the spread of "Intifadah camps" in forests near Arab settlements, sponsored by the Sons of the Village and the Rakah youth movement. Posters in admiration of the Intifadah "children of the stones" appeared, victory over the conqueror was promised, the works of Palestinian protest writers were solemnly intoned, and hate-filled drawings were posted among the red flags. In one, an Israeli soldier was seen injuring the arm of a child, from whose blood the Palestinian flag emerged. A picture of Israel's enemy at that time, PLO leader Yasser 'Arafat, gazed out beside portraits of Lenin and Nasser.

Parallel with this rising turbulence, the Israeli Arab leadership weighed its steps carefully, sensitive to the feelings of the Jewish population. During the coalition negotiations after the election of the twelfth Knesset (1988), Arab Knesset members searched for channels of influence, even from the outside. Activists of both Rakah and the Progressive List for Peace in the Galilee went so far as to call upon their parties to eliminate the condition of recognizing the PLO in their negotiations with the Labor Alignment, emphasizing that the main goal was to ensure equal rights to Israeli Arabs, and that a political party that sought this had to be unconditionally supported.

This trend increased after the collapse of the national unity government in 1990, when Shimon Peres struggled for support in the Knesset. It was crystal clear that the decision would be determined by a single vote. The so-called Arab parties – Hadash,[14] the Progressive List for Peace and Darawshah's Democratic Arab Party – did not try to squeeze exorbitant concessions in exchange for their support, without which there would be no hope of forming a coalition under Labor. They took the line of the parties on the left, which could be summed up as, "To prevent formation of a Likud government, we will support Peres," as decided by Hadash on April 10, 1990.

The Labor Alignment prepared a document undertaking a commitment to practical measures to ensure equality for the Arab population, with special regard to budgetary allocations. Attorney 'Abd er-Rauf Mawasi, among the leaders of the Democratic Arab Party, revealed that it too had a similar agreement. In practice, these agreements were never put to the test, as the Alignment failed to form a government for political reasons that were entirely unrelated. But these agreements were of special significance, as they were the first clear and unambiguous expression of the willingness of both sides to cooperate on behalf of a vital goal common to both, despite the primary political gap between them.

After the elections to the thirteenth Knesset in 1992, this willingness became a decisive factor in the formation of a left-wing government headed by Yitzhak Rabin. For the first time in the history of the State of Israel, it was the Israeli Arabs who decided who would head the government, both by voting directly for Zionist parties and by supporting the "blocking majority" through the Arab parties, Hadash and the Democratic Arab Party, which still support the coalition without actually being a part of the government. The Arab sector thereby proved its political power, which can at times tip the scales between the right and the left.

The subject of equality clearly has the highest priority among wide segments of the population which do not always make themselves heard, lest they be considered traitors. On the one hand are declarations, speeches, poems and leaflets demanding a Palestinian state; on the other, the practical daily life of the Arab citizen and the work of his representatives generally focus on attainment of practical rights – development of villages, raising the standard of living, and establishing a political force.

The hazy, fragile "Green Line" still constitutes an essential divide;

if eroded, the dam will burst. Both sides are aware of this complex reality. The Israeli Arab leaders request a license for demonstrations; the State of Israel does not refuse. The condition is: maintain order, prevent riots. The concept of "incitement" is broad, and the government does not wish to give it a narrow, pedantic definition.

There is no doubt about the growing sophistication of political behavior in the Israeli Arab sector. The connection with the PLO was not concealed, but was manifested by strongly recommending (akin to a demand) that the PLO be included in peace negotiations, rather than on the basis of organizational affiliation. Violent terrorist activity was ruled out. The peace accords freed the Israeli Arabs from their fence-sitting, but forced them to deal with the complex question of what attitude to take toward Hamas and the Islamic Jihad, two organizations that have declared all-out war on Israel and carry out deadly attacks against the Jewish population.

The source of funding for various Israeli Arab associations is known, although not openly discussed. It is patently clear that a certain library in Umm el-Fahm and a kindergarten in Acre were established with funding from "the Organization" through a certain body that resides in Geneva. A delegation of the Islamic movement returned from a trip abroad in late 1989, and it was no secret that elements hostile to Israel participated in the fundraising, although this activity is not illegal at the time this book is written.

These monies are used for activities that are wholly positive: education, culture, aid to the needy. The associations in charge of these matters in the Arab sector respond to their critics: What difference does it make what the source is? How the money is used is what matters! In a democracy, it is not easy to grapple with this argument. Legislation intended to undermine this system is bound for a rocky road. Israeli Arabs even conveyed monies through various channels to support the Intifadah. According to initial estimates, the aid in the first two years reached five million Israeli Shekels (about $2.5 million), and assistance was given by certain elements in other spheres as well: printing the leaflets of the United National Command,[15] allowing use of personal telephones for international phone calls of Intifadah activists, and opening bank accounts for the transfer of forbidden funding.

We are in the midst of a new chapter in the life of Arabs in Israel, one that is a complex integration of trends that are contradictory, interconnected, sometimes parallel – but never meet. Integration together with struggle, development alongside confrontation. The roads are narrowing, the tension is rising, and internal and external pressures mean that, inevitably, the political relationship between the Jewish state and Israeli Arabs will need to be redefined in the context of the Israeli-Palestinian peace process.

The Intifadah further escalated the process in which radical elements from both sides of the barrier merged in an effort to halt the integration of Israeli Arabs within the state, in order to heighten the division. Although the general Arab public has clearly not been drawn into hostile terrorist activity, the range of animosity has broadened through partial adoption of the techniques of the uprising in Judea, Samaria and the Gaza Strip or through declarations of solidarity with Saddam Hussein following the invasion of Kuwait.

The tendency of merging with the revolt in the territories was reflected not only by waving the PLO flag or writing hate-filled slogans on walls, but also in actual violence such as blocking roads, throwing stones and Molotov cocktails, and burning down forests. At the height of the Intifadah, more and more Arab localities became involved in these events. The question arises as to the restraint of the silent majority, which has proven its power to revolt against inequality through demonstrations, strikes and the use of the media ~~████████████████████████████~~ in a consistent attempt to amplify the Arab voice in the Israeli political system.

Meanwhile the Intifadah has ebbed, and the image of Saddam Hussein has paled. Simultaneously, the longing for a political settlement has grown, and the Israeli Arabs clearly want a peace settlement with all their might, with the exception of marginal extremist elements, or isolated groups in Rakah, whose spokesman, Samih el-Qassem, returned from Iran as an admirer of Khoumeini and called the Palestinians who support the peace initiative the "Arab moles of America."

Support for the Madrid peace conference in October 1991 was definitive, and expressed in newspapers, periodicals, debates, private discussions, and also in a direct appeal in late September 1991 to the Palestinian National Council to take a stand on the issue.

Since the Knesset elections in May 1992, the relative weight of Israeli Arabs has steadily grown, both politically and diplomatically. For the first time in the history of Israel, it is the Arab vote that tips the scales in the deadlock between two evenly balanced sides. The Arab parties made possible an obstructionist bloc against the right, enabling Yitzhak Rabin to form a government. What is more, votes from Israeli Arabs account for four seats to left-wing parties, a decisive boost in the complex struggle of the 1990s. In other words, it is Israeli Arabs who decided who will head the government of the Jewish state in which they constitute a minority. Israeli Arab support for the left stems from a clear desire to advance the peace platform, and indeed the Rabin government could not have reached agreement with the PLO without this support. Thus, Israeli Arabs have realized their old dream to serve as a bridge for peace.

Israeli Arabs even participate in the process itself, albeit indirectly. Dr Ahmad Tibi, an Israeli gynecologist born in Jaffa who now lives in Tayyibeh, was appointed advisor to Yasser 'Arafat and has facilitated many contacts between Israel and the PLO. Other Arabs have also attached themselves to the Palestine Liberation Organization to help it "read the Israeli map" for purposes of negotiation. A young educated Druze from the village of Daliyat el-Karmel, Attorney Usama Halabi, was appointed to the Palestinian delegation for multilateral talks regarding refugees in the Tunis meeting of February 1992, but the Israeli delegation refused to face an Israeli Arab as part of the Palestinian delegation.[16] This strange situation well reflects the dichotomy of the Israeli Arab, who stresses his Palestinian identity while an Israeli citizen, who strives for equality of rights in Israel, and fully stands on his right to be a Palestinian, including the right to conduct negotiations against his own country. This contradiction contains the seeds of a process antithetical to peace after agreements are reached between Israel and the Palestinians and other Arab countries.

Under discussion in the next stage will be the status of the Israeli Arab minority, and there is no doubt that what can be expected are vehement demands that Israel permit the return of Palestinian refugees to Acre, Jaffa, Haifa and many Arab towns in the Galilee, the Triangle and the Negev. The demand for self-government will also escalate. Calls are already being heard for cultural autonomy, which is not confined to literature, art, and theatre. The political influence of Israeli Arabs will increase; today they constitute more than 18 percent of the population, and their birthrate is almost double that of the Jewish population.

As long as sobriety and restraint characterize the struggle of Israeli Arabs to define their status in Israel, the delicate balance is maintained. It could become fragile, however, if Israeli Arabs consolidate into a powerful political force and attempt to establish a Palestinian entity *within* the State of Israel.

Such activity will be perceived by the Jewish majority to be diametrically opposed to the character of the state, and subversive of the very foundations of its existence. A strong reaction can be expected that will itself heighten the tension between the two nations. There is no doubt that under such circumstances, Israeli Arabs would gain the general support of their Palestinian neighbors and the Arab states. Israel would then have to grapple with demands that might turn into an ultimatum with its borders shrunk following the peace arrangements, and a sizable minority immersed within its lifeblood that is familiar with its weaknesses, and can attack it from within. Under those conditions, the fires of war could ignite, something which neither side wants and which is a product of the inability to square a circle at a time that Israel feels threatened by what might be a Trojan horse within.

This scenario is not inevitable, but it cannot be dismissed as impossible. At this early stage of the peace process, such an eventuality should be anticipated, and hence the status of Israeli Arabs should be defined within the context of the arrangements to resolve the Israeli-Arab conflict in general, and as part of each of its components. The fundamental positions are far from resolved. Under certain circumstances, they are conspicuously glaring. Until now, a general conflagration has been avoided. But the pendulum swings on, back and forth, up and down, and there is always the fear that the rocking may cause a sudden loss of equilibrium.

Government Policy toward the Arab Minority

In 1948 the fighting had not yet died down when an Arab minority – its world devastated, its dreams shattered – found itself facing the provisional government of a new Israeli state. Israel's call, made in the midst of ongoing hostilities, for the Arabs of Palestine to stay where they were went unheeded – silenced, as it were, by the successive waves of flight. The majority gave no credence to the Israeli promises and Arab propaganda kept alive the fearful image of Deir Yassin which was depicted in terms out of all proportion to the real event.[17]

When the fighting ended the Israeli government kept its promise to protect the Arab minority that remained. Despite their evident weakness, the remaining Arabs were considered a security risk, a hostile population, prone to be incited to take action against the young state, the existence of which neighboring countries resisted. Despite the Rhodes armistice agreements, the Arabs openly called for a "second round." Meanwhile, Arab infiltrators crossed the armistice lines, killing civilians. These infiltrators called themselves *fidaiyyun* (originally a religious term denoting those seeking death in a holy war, but now used rather in the sense of "liberator"). The proximity of many Israeli Arab villages to the borders gave rise to the suspicion that the villagers would cooperate with the infiltrators (some possibly their kinsmen) by sheltering and feeding them, and passing on information to them, or might even take part in their operations.

It was against this background that the main concentrations of the Arab population, in Galilee, in the Triangle and in the Negev, were placed under military government. Their residents now needed permits to leave their area; there was a night curfew; other clauses of emergency regulations (taken over from the British) could be and were applied to them, including administrative detention.

Since dealing with the Arab population was considered complex and different, Prime Minister David Ben-Gurion appointed Yehoshua Palmon, an orientalist and expert on local Arab matters, as Advisor on Arab Affairs, to serve in his office. Separate Arab departments were set up in the various ministries, making it necessary for Arabs to turn to them rather than to the official normally dealing with the matter in hand. The trade union federation, the Histadrut, likewise set up a separate Arab department. The task of the Prime Minister's Advisor was to coordinate the activities of the Arab departments in the various ministries, but he had no express legal authority over these activities.

The Advisor had a staff of trained orientalists, fluent in Arabic. They soon became the address for Arab citizens to turn to with whatever problems they had. The staff endeavored to create the widest possible network of ties with the Arab population, to follow developments in the Arab sector, initiate action and lay down policy guidelines. Despite the lack of a formal legal basis, the Advisor and his office quickly became a recognized institution. Every Prime Minister came to appoint his own Advisor (or successive advisors), and each of them left his mark on the office, according to his personality and also according to how much the Prime Minister felt the services of this individual served the interests of the government.

Often, particularly during the days of the military government, this was a sensitive and thankless task. The Advisor had to deal with security problems as the representative of the state, yet conduct himself and his business so as to keep bitterness among the Arabs at a minimum. Uri Lubrani, a gifted official who had the Prime Minister's ear, defined the job as that of a "fireman." "If we could 'measure' the heat of the Arab population in Israel," he said, "we would no doubt find that, against the background of their special situation, the temperature is high. We must do everything we can to keep the thermometer below the boiling point."

It is not easy to generalize about the attitude of successive Israeli prime ministers toward the Arab minority. Although there was a general recognition on their part of the importance of the issue, this recognition often became theoretical, seeking to avoid the difficulties of dealing with the issue directly. Memoirs or diaries of the various Israeli premiers refer to the Israeli Arab issue infrequently – no doubt because other issues were more pressing and higher up on the scale of priorities. Yet from time to time, Arab affairs claimed sudden attention when conflagrations erupted without warning.

During the first ten years of Israel's existence, it was the military government that dominated the daily lives of Israeli Arabs. But its many restrictions gradually relaxed and their contravention was condoned. At the same time, it turned into a problem of internal politics, preoccupying the parties, the Knesset and the press.

The country's first Premier, Ben-Gurion, was alien to the problems preoccupying the minds of the Arab population. During the first years, he found it difficult to dissociate himself from the attitudes of the past which saw the Arabs in Israel as an enemy force. His visits to Arab localities were few and far between. His Advisors on Arab Affairs tried to sharpen his awareness of the issue, but he reportedly refused to receive an Israeli identity card because its entries were written in Arabic as well as in Hebrew.[18] He refused to consider the abolition of the military government, which he considered a vital means to suppress possible uprisings, to keep down acts of terrorism, and prevent Israeli Arabs from joining the likely war effort of one of Israel's many outside Arab enemies. When the right-wing Herut party opposed him over the question of prolonging the military government, he regarded their attitude as a cynical use of a security issue for the sake of partisan gain and as a stick to beat the government with. In doing so, he charged that they were ignoring a vital national problem, thereby acting in contradiction to their own tenets. In the crucial Knesset debate, decided on the strength of a single vote, he needed, ironically, the vote of an Arab notable in the Knesset in order to avert the abolition of the military government. It was the Advisor's office which had mobilized his vote. The Arab population came to regard him as a traitor.[19] The Arabs who frequented the Advisor's office were notables of the traditional type: concerned with the welfare of their family, their *hamulah* (clan), their village, or their tribe. Nationalist quarters called them *adhnab al-hukumah* ("tails of the government"), but in more traditional circles, their conduct was considered natural and more suited to the unwritten rules governing their society.

The opponents of military government denied its being a security necessity and accused the ruling party, Mapai,[20] of having turned it into a partisan instrument intended to garner Arab votes for Mapai or its affiliated Arab lists. Travel permits, they asserted, were a form of political bribe – a benefit handed out in return for a promise to put the "right" party chit into the ballot box. The security reasons cited officially were, in their view, sheer hypocrisy.

But Ben-Gurion did not budge and rejected these charges emphatically. He genuinely believed that the military government was a security necessity vital to the state. More than that: he was convinced that obtaining Arab votes for Mapai was a national requirement, for otherwise they would go to the Communists, who had made themselves champions of Arab nationalism. Dealing with minority problems included, in his view, "guiding" them how to vote. Failing to do so would open the door to the electoral success of his rivals, or of the Communists, or would encourage hostile organizations to spring up. On these points, he seems to have listened to his Advisors on Arab Affairs and was ready to break his customary silence on Arab affairs and speak out – whether on the security aspect or on the internal political side, which, he held, was also a national one.[21]

Ben-Gurion's political rivals could, of course, cast doubt on the genuineness of these convictions – with or without inverted commas, according to whose views we may be thinking of – and claim that he, veteran tactician that he was, was using the "name of security in vain," while really intending to strengthen his personal power base and the standing of his party. But nobody could argue that his policy toward the Arab population was necessary for his survival in power; in those early years, the opposition was far from able to threaten the ruling party with an electoral overturn. The left–right balance, characteristic of the present day, had not yet come into being and, under the circumstances then prevailing, the Arab vote could not possibly tip the scales. Ben-Gurion was right in assuming that massive Arab electoral support for Mapai was an effective barrier to the rise of Communism. When the reins were relaxed, the Arab vote did indeed begin to go in the direction of the Arab-nationalist groupings, including the Communist party which had made that coloration its own. By that time, Ben-Gurion was in retirement.

It may be argued that the lengthy existence of the military government itself (introduced, defended and prolonged by Mapai) had caused the "desertion" of Arab voters, once they had greater elbow room to follow their electoral inclinations; similarly, it may be asserted that it had not been expedient in the first place to institute the "voting market" with its complex implications and its shadier sides; that it was a mistake, right from the start, to equate state and party in a manner bound to do damage to the very idea of statehood; and that the end result was a crisis of confidence on the part of the Arab residents which beclouded their future electoral decisions.

Against such critics it could be argued that the methods applied in the early years had indeed blocked, or at least slowed down, the emergence of radical nationalist trends and that it was not primarily the existence of the military government which created the bitterness that later prevailed; rather, ineluctable historical processes were at work.

In a democratic society, such poignant discussions cannot, however, be evaded, certainly not in a situation in which minority voters had equal voting rights and formed a sizeable constituency. No wonder, then, that the office of the Prime Minister's Advisor on Arab Affairs preoccupied itself with these issues, directly or indirectly. This is still true today when, in a greatly changed overall situation, the Arab vote may become decisive in determining who the next premier is going to be. Quite another question is how effective the means were which the Prime Minister and his Advisors had at their disposal for reaching their goals in such sensitive and complex matters. The answer is not cut and dried. Not all the evidence is publicly available; success was relative, and often a matter of preventing a deterioration rather than achieving positive results. Such nuances are difficult to prove, involving, as they must, hypothetical considerations incapable of a firm answer. No doubt, one aspect of the matter is the scope of the effort invested. We have already seen that Israel's first Prime Minister, though possessing greater authority than any of his successors, kept aloof from the discussion as much as was possible and occupied himself with minority affairs only under the influence of pressing events or when his Advisors succeeded in impressing him with the urgency of dealing with them, an urgency they themselves felt keenly. There developed, so to speak, an "inverse ratio" between the priority Ben-Gurion gave the issue as compared with the weight the Advisor ascribed to it. This is as true of Palmon as of his successors, Ziama Divon and Uri Lubrani, and also of Yitzhak Navon, the Premier's political secretary, himself a noted Arabist with a marked interest in the affairs of the minority. The same might be said of later Advisors under Ben-Gurion's various successors. Advice was forthcoming in abundance, but the government took it as sparingly as a bitter pill.

Yet it would appear that Ben-Gurion's successors were more open to learn about, and give of their time to, minority affairs than he was, whether for reasons of their different personality or for reasons connected with the Arab population itself. By their time, the Arab sector had come alive, its political weight was on the increase, its voice was being heard loud and clear. But even when the premier was prevailed upon to deal personally with some outstanding issue, there was usually no treatment in depth, no follow-up, no consistent policy initiation. Such one-time, often merely verbal, interventions, were not able to change the situation, promote solutions or even prevent undesirable developments.

An instance of Ben-Gurion's personal intervention was connected with the threatening collapse of a Jewish-Arab enterprise – a food-canning plant – in which, at the urging of the Advisor, a notable from the village of Baqa el-Gharbiyya by the name of Fares Hamdan had invested heavily. The firm was facing bankruptcy and a major government injection of financial aid was called for. The Prime Minister was asked to intervene and to address a personal letter to the Minister of Commerce and Industry, then Pinhas Sapir. Because it seems so typical of Ben-Gurion's approach, it is reproduced in full:[22]

Dear Sapir,
You are to do everything possible to help the factory at Baqa el-Gharbiyya – this is the major (and perhaps the only) joint [Jewish-Arab] plant and Fares Hamdan is about to lose a quarter of a million Israeli Pounds. I do not care (even though I do care) if a Jew goes bankrupt – but we have to prevent by every means at our disposal the bankruptcy of this first major attempt at Jewish-Arab cooperation.

This is of prime internal political value. I do not know what you can do, but *you* will know, and do it.

Yours
Ben-Gurion

On the face of it, this was a clear-cut instruction to put funds at the disposal of the firm and prevent its collapse; but even then, under an authoritarian Premier and a Minister of Commerce and Industry known as a "financial wizard," the laws of economics prevailed, as attested to by the following letter from Hamdan:[23]

The Prime Minister
David Ben-Gurion
Jerusalem

Today my house was foreclosed, as well as my furniture, my land and all I possess. Once or twice you promised to rescue me from the disaster that various government departments have brought upon me, including the Prime Minister's Office under your authority. Nevertheless, nothing has been done so far.
My situation is intolerable. I flee from my house and from the people of my village; shame and abasement prevent me from looking them in the face. If action is not taken immediately, even you will not be able to rescue me from the total destruction of what is left of my good name and my standing. Is an act of despair all I have left? If I despair of you as well – all is lost. Please act at once.
With all respect,

Fares Hamdan

But not even this *cri de coeur* sufficed. The plant was closed down, its "prime political value" notwithstanding. The conditions for rural industrialization in the Arab sector had not yet matured. The plant had had difficulties in finding suitable managerial staff, skilled labor and sufficient marketing outlets. The social structure of the Arab village, such as it then was, made its failure inevitable.

No similar letters signed by Ben-Gurion, written in such an intensely personal style, have been found. Levi Eshkol, and Golda Meir after him, intervened much more frequently in Arab minority affairs, but official letters on such topics were usually drafted by bureaucrats and signed by them, possibly after being revised by the Premier. The Advisors on Arab Affairs would, typically, turn to the Prime Minister with a request for his or her intervention, with the result of being asked: "What do you suggest?" They may then have suggested a visit to an Arab village or a more extended tour of an Arab area, or a meeting with some Arab notable, such as Seif ed-Din Zu'bi in his heyday, or a delegation of Bedouin sheikhs. Often enough, the Prime Minister, always under a heavy work load, would reply: "Draft a letter; I'll sign." Their speeches to Arab audiences were also ghost-written for them and at times they read them haltingly, in front of people who had pinned their hopes on them.[24]

Those who dealt with day-to-day Arab problems were always keenly aware that what was needed was a clearly-defined overall policy, binding on all ministries, outlining development plans, and touching on school curricula, military service on the part of Arabs, employment outside their places of residence, mixed housing, zoning laws, illegal building, urbanization, Bedouin settlement, communal religious courts, the status of women, political associations, the Arabic-language press, literature, university admission policy and a host of related subjects. The "lack of a firm policy" was a never-ending subject of severe criticism, in particular when things went wrong. It came to the fore over the increase in unlicensed building in the Galilee, the Triangle and the Negev; and the growth of radical nationalism; the "desertion" of former "moderates" (meaning: people collaborating with the government or with Mapai) to the radical camp for lack of support on the part of those they had aided. The government had exposed them to the charge of being traitors to their own people and had laid them open to attack by the radicals. Then, the government did nothing to protect them. On the contrary: it appeased the radicals, and neglected its old supporters. However, this was not the main point of weakness: a policy did gradually emerge, touching on virtually all the key issues of interest to the Arab minority.

The first principle of policy was equal legal rights, complemented by the right to be different. Thus Israeli Arabs went on having Arabic as the language of instruction in their schools; no measures were taken, or attempts made, to assimilate them or throw them into the "Israeli melting pot"; they were to preserve their own national uniqueness, and have their own religious courts adjudicate matters of personal status. Muslim and Christian Arabs, as distinct from Druze Arabs and Muslim Circassians, were to be exempt from compulsory military service, but might volunteer, as has actually taken place by some Christian Arabs and by (Muslim Arab) Bedouin. The need for an extended new infrastructure was recognized, as well as the need for employment, education at all levels, changes in the curricula, Jewish-Arab cooperation, free expression (except for incitement), and political freedom, though efforts were made to prevent the emergence of a purely Arab nationalist grouping.[25]

Eshkol's first Advisor on Arab Affairs was Rehav'am Amir, formerly head of the Foreign Ministry's public-relations department. He, too, soon discovered that he needed close working relations with the Prime Minister to do his own job properly. The most pressing task in his time was to deal with the Al-Ard movement. There was not much spare time to deal with overall policies, though their elaboration had already begun.

Three years later, Shemuel Toledano succeeded Amir. During his twelve-year tenure, he worked hard to lay down not only overall policies, but detailed guidelines, and these were indeed confirmed by Golda Meir's cabinet. Occasional further discussion during Rabin's first premiership did not change their basic clauses. Toledano was an opponent of the military government, and in 1966 he convinced Eshkol to abolish it. This period saw the removal of restrictions, greater openness, and less land confiscations. A new wind was blowing from the Jerusalem government quarter in the direction of the Arab sector.

But formulating policy was one thing; implementing it was another. The faltering attitude, on the part of the cabinet, with regard to minority questions prevented the creation of effective administrative tools and the elaboration of practical working schedules. The Advisor was not given the necessary legal authority to carry out his plans; as his staff was wont to say – he had "no teeth." He remained an advisor, at best a coordinator, but had to try and curry favor with the various ministers, each of whom felt free to accept or reject his advice. What was lacking was a single hand steering government action in the Arab sector. The Advisor was not actually in charge of the people "on the spot" in the Arab areas, many of whom dissociated themselves from the policies he had laid down. They thought of them as either "too liberal" or else impracticable. Some senior officials followed their own convictions and inclinations regardless of official policy. The so-called "Koenig Paper" was the most salient example of this trend.[26]

Yet the Advisor was not powerless. He exercised personal influence and was able, from time to time, to "harness" the Prime Minister for some mission or gesture toward the minority. Unfortunately, the Prime Minister's door was not always open to him, and when it was not, the matter leaked out and was taken as further evidence of the "toothless" nature of his job. Toledano knew many difficult periods during the tenures of the three premiers under whom he served. Golda Meir was severely critical of him for supporting the return to Iqrit and Bir'am of the evacuees who had left their villages during the fighting in 1948, and had been promised that they would be allowed back later. A period of coolness ensued between the Premier and the Advisor. Similar "barren" periods occurred under Eshkol and Rabin.

All these difficulties notwithstanding, the Advisor succeeded in establishing certain patterns of action to promote his policies. Inter-ministerial committees were formed to deal with Arab affairs, the most important of which dealt with urgent security matters. Whenever the Advisor managed to persuade the committee of the correctness of his approach, he was able to move forward. But even if committee members agreed with him, this sometimes remained rather theoretical, and practical measures were often in stark contrast to the supposed agreement.

At the time of the 1977 landslide which brought Likud to power, Toledano was no longer in office; he had resigned some time earlier in order to run for the Knesset. His deputy, Benny Gur-Aryeh, had succeeded him. But when Menahem Begin became Prime Minister, he appointed Professor Moshe Sharon of the Hebrew University in Jerusalem to take over from him. The latter was known for his right-wing views. Policy discussions took place during his tenure as well, based on a working paper he had prepared, but the basic guidelines remained unchanged. Sharon in turn was followed by Gur-Aryeh. During the period of the National Unity Government beginning in 1984, the latter was replaced by Professor Yossi Ginat. Ginat brought to his post 35 years of experience in the Arab sector, in a variety of positions, all the while combining practical field work with academic research. His personal connections with Arabs from many parts of the minority population were a major asset in themselves. He had been Toledano's deputy for many years and shared the latter's preferences for lowering barriers, relaxing restrictions, and displaying greater openness. Another advantage – almost unprecedented – was his close relationship with Prime Minister Shimon Peres. He was probably the Advisor who had the premier's ear more often than any of his predecessors or successors. At his instance, Peres thoroughly covered the ground in the Arab villages, often until late at night. In this period, certain areas sequestered for the purpose of live-ammunition army exercises were returned to their owners; no land confiscation was carried out; some pressing local problems were solved; and the large village of Umm el-Fahm was proclaimed a town. Efforts were made to improve Jewish-Arab relations. All this was done in cooperation with Ezer Weizman, who was then minister in charge of minority affairs, yet without severing the Advisor's personal links with the Prime Minister. But this period was too short to produce broad results; moreover, it proved how hard it was for the government to at all influence basic processes at work among the Arab population.[27] When the Likud government followed the Government of National Unity, it did not attempt to press for the assimilation of Israel's Arabs, and the overall policy lines remained much as before, even though from time to time a tendency toward strong-arm tactics could be discerned. One such sign was the refusal to recognize the Committee of Arab Local Council Heads. By contrast, the Likud government showed particular interest in fostering relations with the Druze, the Christian communities, and the Bedouin, assuming that the settled Muslim population was in any case unlikely to vote for it.

When Yitzhak Shamir became Prime Minister within the Government of National Unity in 1986, he followed – by and large – the precedents set earlier on. A reserve brigadier-general, Amos Gilboa, became Shamir's first Advisor on Arab Affairs. After some time, he was replaced by Eliezer Tsafrir, who had gathered experience when he was on the staff of Rehav'am Amir. He and Shamir had come to know each other when both served in the Mossad (the Israeli intelligence service). Tsafrir concentrated on work in the field. One of his chief preoccupations was to prevent the Intifadah from spreading into Israel within its pre-1967 borders. He was eventually replaced by Dr Alex Blay, of the Hebrew University, who had also vital previous experience on the staff of the Advisor's office and was called upon to apply his academic knowledge to the resolution of practical problems. He faced a situation greatly different from that of his predecessors: a situation in which the government was proving unable to ensure full peace and quiet in the Arab sector. When the left-wing government came to power in 1992, Yitzhak Rabin decided to eliminate the position of the Prime Minister's Advisor on Arab Affairs, due to the sharp criticism of the existence of such a position as a manifestation of a patronizing attitude toward Israeli Arabs. Benny Shiloh, a kibbutz member, was appointed to head the Minorities Section in the Prime Minister's

Office, in a sense the successor to the previous position; there have also been charges that the Minorities Section is merely the same office in different garb.

A fair assessment would be to say that no Israeli government – whatever its party coloration – went out of its way or took notable initiatives with regard to the Arab population. They remained "firemen," putting out fires when and where they occurred. Their main concern was to keep Israeli Arabs apart from the Arabs of the territories and, once the Intifadah had erupted, to prevent it from spreading to the Arab minority in Israel. Summing up the main trends in retrospect:

1. Successive governments became more keenly aware of the weightiness of the minority issue, yet failed to allocate the resources necessary to deal with it.
2. Israeli Arabs distanced themselves from government offices when the reservoir of benefits available to them became meager; they matured, became more self-confident and less inclined to engage in the old game of give-and-take; hence the decline of the Advisor's influence, at least at the level of personal or family ties.
3. During the period of British mandatory rule, Arab crowds had at times shouted: *"Al-hukumah ma'ana"* ("The government is with us," i.e., on our side). Today, the feeling is that the government is against the Arab population. That does not necessarily mean that Arabs will go all out against it; but the traditional desire to set up independent, all-Arab institutions can be noted. These institutions are liable, eventually, to form a country-wide Arab leadership which would no longer be a client of the authorities, but would be pragmatic enough to avoid a head-on confrontation.
4. At the same time, the government is probing for conduits of dialogue with groupings that have attained political influence among the Arab population, groupings of strong self-confidence, who have set themselves goals often seen as dangerous to the state. Despite harsh criticism, Foreign Minister Shimon Peres met with the head of the Islamic Movement, 'Abdallah Nimr Darwish in March 1995. At the time of this writing, the danger of confrontation is increasing because of the problems attendant on the Jewish mass immigration from the former Soviet Union. Arabs fear that they will have to pay

the price in terms of land confiscations or dismissal from work places in favor of immigrants, as well as by the shrinkage of their share in the country's electoral make-up and the concomitant loss of political leverage.

This is therefore a time when new politics should be considered, decided upon and implemented. The present relative calm may not last. Conflagrations like the 1976 "Land Day" or the 1988 "Peace Day" demonstrations may erupt again. Most likely, there will be no early warning.

2

Arab Society in Israel

Demographic Changes

Demographic data are not "dry numbers" in the Middle East, where the quantitative ratio between ethnic, religious, and national groups is a sensitive factor replete with political implications. Censuses are a cause of constant internal friction, and several countries refrain from conducting them in order to avoid the commotion that they provoke and, at times, to overlook the results. In Lebanon, it is an unchallenged fact that a population census is more dangerous than elections. The most recent census there was taken in 1932, when the Christians still held a small majority, which was soon overtaken by the Muslims' high birth rate. Since then, the Lebanese regimes have made do with inconsistent estimates.[1]

Other Arab countries, too, allow a long time to pass between censuses; even regular measurements of current birth and death rates are lacking. Various population groups still withhold their cooperation as the census is conducted, and in the subsequent reporting and updating. This boycotting of censuses is especially evident among Bedouin tribes.

The widespread illiteracy in many countries leads to errors in census results, because the respondents do not understand the canvassers' questions or the canvassers do not understand the respondents' answers. Respondents also tend to conceal certain facts or provide the answers they think the canvassers want. A sense of mistrust, especially among the Bedouin, peasants, and members of the lower classes, often stifles truthful answers. Suspicious that the government's undisclosed intention is to use the information to pressure them or increase their taxes, they distort their answers.

Consequently, there is a tendency to under-report family size for fear of conscription or taxation, and the contrary tendency to overstate family size at times of food rationing or as a way to acquire social prestige. During World War II, when Palestine was placed under a rationing regime, people withheld information on the death of family members in order to keep the deceased's rations.

Dread of the "evil eye," as well, induces people to conceal the birth of a son or to report the birth of a son as the birth of a daughter in order to ward off misfortune. The number of women is, of course, a very sensitive issue. Even the fact of remaining single after marriageable age is something that many women are ashamed of and attempt to hide.[2] Occasionally the regimes themselves attempt to suppress inconvenient findings or distort them for economic, social, or political reasons. The Hashemite Kingdom of Jordan has conducted several demographic surveys and censuses since the 1960s but suppresses the data on the number of residents of Palestinian origin – their share is estimated at some 60 percent – in order to avoid having to recognize officially that they have become a majority.[3]

The government of Saudi Arabia regularly falsifies its census data. The first census was apparently conducted in 1962 and 1963, but its results have not been published to this day. Another census was taken in 1974 and a population of 4.3 million was announced. A short while after that, however, a "minor" revision was made, causing the population of the Saudi kingdom to rocket upward to 7 million. Since then, the demographic map of Saudi Arabia has periodically been sprinkled with "amended" data. An official estimate of 10.4 million residents in 1983 dwindled to only 8.5 million four years later.[4]

In other words, demographic data in Middle Eastern countries are subordinate to economic, social, and political considerations; they are flexible statistics that adapt themselves to the circumstances.

Researchers identify five stages in the demographic development of Europe; these stages will be helpful in putting the Arab situation into perspective:[5]

Phase 1 There is no family planning, and birth rates are high and unrestrained by artificial means. However, the results are more or less balanced because of high mortality, which also fluctuates and is strongly affected by epidemics, famine, and war.

Phase 2 Mortality diminishes because of preventive medicine and control of epidemics. The birth rate remains as high as before, so the rate of natural increase rises slightly, as happened in the nineteenth century.

Phase 3 Mortality continues to decrease, but so does the birth rate as family planning and contraceptives make inroads; consequently, a rough equilibrium is once again attained.

Phase 4 Both the birth rate and the mortality rate decrease, with emphasis on the former, and the population declines gently.

Phase 5 The birth rate takes an upturn; because mortality continues to fall, the rate of natural increase also rises. The fertility rate increases but intentional family planning is invoked, as it had not been in the previous two phases.

The demographic developments in the Arab countries are not all uniform or identical, but their unquestionable "common denominator" is a high birth rate resulting from the high rate of fertility among women in Arab society – itself a corollary of hallowed tradition and economic need. When mortality begins to decline, countries such as Egypt face the menace of a population explosion – the second phase described above, which our region is experiencing today.

Most changes of trend in the Middle Eastern countries have been slow and gradual, but the demographic development of the Israeli Arab community is different, unique, volatile, and affected by powerful exogenous factors. At the beginning of the period under review, after the 1949 armistice agreements finalized the map of Israel within the Green Line, the minority population was 156,000.[6] By early 1995, it had soared to an estimated 1,035,000, 18.5 percent of the total population of the country.[7] This prodigious growth, with its profound socioeconomic implications, is the result of the following factors:

1. In the last stages of the 1948 War of Independence and immediately afterwards, 35,550 Arab refugees entered the country, either under the arrangement of family reunification or as illegal infiltrators who were allowed to stay *post facto*. This was a goodwill gesture, meant to help take the edge off the Arab-Israeli conflict, but it was unrewarded as the enmity of the Arab countries continued.

2. The reunification of Jerusalem in June 1967 boosted the Israeli Arab population by the 65,857 residents of the eastern sector of the city. In 1995 the Arabs of Jerusalem numbered 172,000.

3. From 1951 until the Six Day War, natural increase was the only cause of the swift growth of the Israeli Arab population.

Between 1950 and 1967 their annual birth rate was 4 percent on average. The migration balance affected the total increase by about 0.5 percent, and most of this is evidently attributable to the return of the refugees when the hostilities ended. The Arab community in Israel has one of the world's highest rates of natural increase – as high as 4.5 percent in the 1960s, exceeding natural increase in Arab countries.[8]

This rapid population growth unquestionably marked the demographic development of the Arab community in Israel as unique; it is the result of two related factors:

1. A high birth rate, typical of the structure of societies in the Arab world and the East in general. It is a consequence of the child's status as a vital human resource in the peasant family, the social prestige that large clans earn, women's interest in having as many children as possible as protection against divorce, marriage at an early age, and the stigma applied to single women.[9] All these factors impede the use of contraception even where ignorance is not a factor, let alone where couples are ignorant of family planning methods.

    A definite turnabout took place in 1977; since then, birth rates have fallen steadily, with an immediate and significant decline in natural increase. Live births among Muslims in Israel totalled 51,700 in the period 1960–64 but only 37,500 in 1984.[10]

2. A sharp decrease in the mortality rate. This factor, unparalleled in neighboring Arab countries, is the result of actions by the Israeli health authorities that transformed the structure of Israeli Arab demographics. Progress in this sphere is palpable: during the British Mandate period there were 28,700 live births among Arabs in Palestine in 1923 and 21,400 in 1941.[11] Under Israeli statehood, the Arab mortality rate fell swiftly while the birth rate did not decrease commensurately. The death rate among Muslims, 8 per thousand in the period 1955–59, has declined to only 4.3 per thousand today.[12]

The development of medical services and rising standards of living in Israeli Arab localities have raised average life expectancy to 74 years, surpassing the low life expectancy of Arabs in Mandate-era Palestine and in Arab countries today.[13] These two processes combined to bring about an unparalleled rate of natural increase, a

Table 2.1 Non-Jewish Population of Israel (End of Each Year, Thousands)[14]

Year	Total	Muslims	Christians	Druze & others	Percentage
8.11.48	(156.0)				
1949	160.0	111.5	34.0	14.5	13.6
1950	167.1	116.1	36.0	15.0	12.1
1951	173.4	118.9	39.0	15.5	10.9
1952	179.3	122.8	40.4	16.1	11.0
1953	185.8	127.6	41.4	16.8	11.1
1954	191.8	131.8	42.0	18.0	11.1
1955	198.6	136.3	43.3	19.0	11.1
1956	204.9	141.4	43.7	19.8	10.9
1957	213.2	146.9	45.8	20.5	10.7
1958	226.5	157.8	47.3	21.4	11.1
1959	229.9	159.3	48.3	22.3	11.0
1960	239.2	166.3	49.6	23.3	11.1
22.5.61	247.1	170.8	50.5	25.8	11.0
1962	262.9	183.0	52.6	27.3	11.2
1963	274.6	192.2	53.9	28.5	11.3
1964	286.4	202.3	55.5	28.6	11.3
1965	299.3	212.4	57.1	29.8	11.5
1966	312.5	223.0	58.5	31.0	11.7
1967	392.3	289.6	70.6	32.1	14.1
1968	406.3	300.8	72.2	33.3	14.3
1969	422.7	314.5	73.5	34.7	14.4
1970	440.0	328.6	75.5	35.9	14.5
1971	457.0	342.7	76.9	37.4	14.6
1972	472.3	360.7	73.8	37.8	14.6
1973	493.2	377.2	76.7	39.3	14.7
1974	518.7	392.5	84.5	41.6	15.1
1975	540.0	409.0	88.0	43.0	15.4
1985	749.0	577.6	99.4	72.0	17.5
1986	769.9	595.0	100.9	74.0	17.7
1987	793.6	614.5	103.0	76.1	18.0
1988	817.7	634.6	105.0	78.1	18.2
1989	842.5	655.2	107.0	80.3	18.4
1990	868.0	676.0	109.0	83.0	18.5
1991	894.0	698.0	111.0	85.0	18.5
1993	992.5	751.4	151.8	89.3	18.6
1994	1,034.9	776.2	157.3	101.4	18.6

unique demographic phenomenon by international standards.

The birth rate dipped perceptibly after the Six Day War, causing natural increase, too, to slow gradually. It was initially unclear whether this marked a trend toward family planning that would coalesce in the future. Although the birth rate had declined slowly and gradually in the three years before the war, the demographic picture from 1967 on was affected by natural movement of the urban Arab population of Jerusalem, which had not been counted among Israel's minorities.

Until this watershed, traditional forces had prevailed over the emergence of family planning, even when mortality dropped and the young had opportunities of which their parents had never dreamed. During the transitional phase, the tendency to use children and youngsters as farm labor had an effect, as did the wish to utilize wages that they earned outside the village. At that time, family size had much to do with social status among rural population groups; boys magnified the family's power and girls were a future economic asset because of the dowry they could command upon marriage.

The rise in living standards affected the falling birth rate more slowly than it did the declining mortality rate, but as time passed the following factors combined to create a virtual "demographic revolution":

1. Education in the Arab sector developed steadily; growing numbers of rural and urban youngsters, including girls and Bedouin, were enrolled, first at the primary level but subsequently at the secondary level. Thus an integrated infrastructure for higher education took shape, displacing the "large family" at the top of the social status pyramid.

   The desire for an academic degree reversed the order of priorities. The investment was worth whatever resources were required to pay for studies at a university, the Technion, a regional college, or a teachers' college. In order to afford legal and medical studies it was even sometimes necessary to sell land, the formerly inviolate patrimony.

2. A large upturn in average expenditure per child, meant to bring the youngsters up to a higher standard of living, entailed investments in education, health, nutrition, and clothing.

3. As the importance of agriculture as a factor in the rural economy receded, so did the utility of child labor.

4. Broader education for women broadened women's horizons, mitigated their dependence, and enhanced their awareness of the use of contraceptives and the importance of family planning as means to achieve family goals amid changing values.

This trend, however, did not eliminate the disparity in natural increase between Jews and Arabs. From the Six Day War until the mass Jewish immigration from the former Soviet Union, the share of minorities in the population of Israel rose steadily. Only since 1990 has the beginning of a reversal come into view. There is no certainty that the new trend will continue unless further immigration at the current rate is assured.

The Communal Structure

The communal structure of Arab residents of Israel is the result of long-term historical developments that left their imprint on all Middle East countries in two basic senses that are evident to this day:

1. Denominational fragmentation, caused by schisms within Islam and Christianity over the centuries and by miscellaneous factors that, as such, have diminished in importance over the generations but created consequences that survive in the regional denominational mosaic.
2. The coalescence of denominations with special autonomous contours, as reflected in the Ottoman Empire through the *millet* system, in which the Muslim authority granted jurisdictional autonomy to certain groups in matters of personal status, administration of charitable trusts, and organization of religious and judicial institutions.

The *millet* system was based on the Muslim recognition of the special status of "protected groups" and the resulting willingness to let these groups live in accordance with their faith.[15] This led to a mushrooming of independent religious institutions and a tradition of denominational organizational structure. The intergroup differences in Israel today arise, to some extent, from the different effects of these two historical processes on shaping the groups, because, importantly, not all denominations were given autonomy to any marked degree, nor were the Muslims organized on the basis of a denominational group, Islam being the state religion of the Ottoman Empire.

In the present century, Middle Eastern countries have witnessed government attempts to circumscribe the jurisdictional competence of religious courts. In Egypt, such tribunals were abolished on

January 1, 1956, and their competence transferred to the civil courts, which adjudicated questions of personal status in accordance with religious law.[16] In Turkey, the religious courts of law were abolished after the revolution of Kemal Atatürk, and Swiss civil law was introduced in 1926. In Lebanon and Syria between the two world wars, factional leaders thwarted recurrent attempts to curtail the authority of the religious courts. A Lebanese law of April 2, 1951, reaffirmed these courts' exclusive jurisdiction in all matters of personal status – betrothal, marriage, divorce, dowry, adoption, custody, succession, legacies, wills, endowments, and other aspects of this vast domain. Lawyers attacked it in vain, demanding the introduction of uniform civil law for all denominations.[17] The juridical competence of religious courts still prevails in Saudi Arabia, Iraq, Jordan, Yemen, Sudan, and the Gulf Emirates.

Israel, too, chose to preserve the religious judicature, at times extending it to denominations that had been subject to other courts and had demanded their own separate framework; now they were empowered to adjudicate matters of personal status within their own instance, outside the civil system.

The various denominations' substantive law in these matters continues to apply to their members, unless it clashes with restrictions that the state saw fit to apply to all citizens in matters of basic personal rights, i.e. prohibition on polygamy, divorcing a woman without her consent, and marriage between minors.

Israel also ascribes much importance to religious affiliation as a *social* framework that embraces various organizations, committees active in a wide variety of causes, charitable institutions, youth movements, business enterprises, publishers, journals, and other entities. The religious groups are given broad prerogatives to conduct their internal affairs in accordance with their needs and traditions, without outside intervention, and their demands for financial assistance or exemption from taxes and duties are treated sympathetically. On the sociopolitical level, the denominational group serves its leaders as a power base.

The sense of belonging that unites the group is based on religious faith rather than the blood ties that unify the clan, but faith itself is not sufficient to create political power, which requires a solid structural base. The internal organization is vital for preserving the group's power, and a cornerstone of this edifice is economic clout. The group's institutions depend on this, and without these institutions its life loses its anchor. Juridical autonomy is the second type

of cement that binds the individuals to their denominational group.
Another crucial element is the group's external relationship with its
religious centers outside the country, such as the Vatican for the
Catholic community. In terms of socioeconomic development, there
are differences between Muslims, Druze, and Christians, which are
rooted in historical factors.

Numerical Ratios

Muslims accounted for a sizable majority of the population of Palestine during the Mandate period. The first census under British rule,
conducted in 1922, found 668,258 Arabs in the country, of whom
88 percent were Muslims, 11 percent Christian, and only 1 percent
Druze and other.[18]

This ratio held firm until the 1948 War of Independence. In the
meantime, Jewish immigration reduced the share of Arabs from 89
percent in 1922 to 68 percent in 1947.[19] A few months before the war
erupted, following the UN partition resolution, the Arab population
of Palestine was estimated at 1,320,000, of whom 1,157,000 were
Muslims (still 88 percent), 146,000 Christians (11 percent), and
16,000 Druze or other.[20]

The war upset the numerical ratio. The mass flight of Arabs
affected the Muslims far more than the Christians and Druze,
who may have been less fearful of the Jewish community than
the Muslims were because they were less supportive of the Arab
gangs and Qawuqji's "Army of Salvation." It may also be that the
percentage of Muslims was higher among residents of the West
Bank and the Gaza Strip than among the 800,000 Arab inhabitants
of Israel's current borders.[21]

Israel's first population and housing census, conducted on
November 8, 1948, found that 70 percent of the members of minority
groups were Muslim, 21 percent Christian, and 9 percent Druze.[22]
These ratios recurred in the second census (May, 1951), when the
Muslims slipped slightly to 69.3 percent, the Christians held firm at
20.6 percent, and the Druze inched upward to 10 percent.

The reunification of Jerusalem after the Six Day War increased
the proportion of Muslims overnight, for they had accounted for
83 percent of the population of the eastern sector.[23] For this reason,
and because of their higher rate of natural increase, the proportion
of Muslims has been rising steadily, to 76.4 percent in the census of
May 1972, and to 77.9 percent by late 1990. Since 1977, their share of

the minority population has risen only slightly because the fertility level of Muslim women has fallen, from a record high of 9.9 children per Muslim woman on average in the mid-1960s to slightly over four children in late 1993.[24]

Relative to the Mandate period, the Muslim majority among minority groups in Israel has eroded to 75 percent; the Christians account for a slightly higher share at 15.2 percent. The difference has been made up by the Druze, who now account for 9 percent.

There is no doubt that the minorities in Israel are conscious of their religious affiliation. Muslims tend to identify Islam with Arab nationalism, in the manner expressed to Michel 'Aflaq, the ideologue of the Ba'ath movement in Syria: "What are you, Christian, doing in our midst?"[25] The Westernization of the minorities in Israel is weakening the religious frameworks, albeit slowly, gradually, and erratically. The denominational groups still cling to their distinctness, and it seems unlikely that their defining characteristics will blur easily. Table 2.2 presents an ethno-religious breakdown of minorities in Israel:[26]

Table 2.2   Ethno-religious breakdown of minorities in Israel

Muslims – approx. 776,000

1. Sunni Muslim Arabs: approx. 771,000 country-wide, chiefly in the Galilee, the Triangle, and Jerusalem, and among the Bedouin tribes.
2. Sunni Muslim Circassians: approx. 4,000, mostly in the villages of Kafr Kama and Reihaniya in Galilee.
3. Ahmadis: approx. 1,000, in Kababir (Mt. Carmel) and in Haifa.

Christians – approx. 157,000[27]

1. Greek Catholic: approx. 24.6 percent.
2. Greek Orthodox: approx. 33 percent.
3. Latin rites: approx. 18.4 percent.
4. Maronite: approx. 4 percent.
5. Others (Protestant denominations, Armenians, Ethiopian Copts, etc.): approx. 20 percent.

These data include Christian communities in Jerusalem. Druze – approx. 101,000.

The Changing Face of the Arab Village

At the last decade of the twentieth century, Israeli Arabs are being tested in the crucible of social shock. The community rushes into a new era, one characterized by upheaval of social systems with numerous implications, manifested principally in the shift of the economic epicenter from the village to the city, the emergence of a ramified stratum of intellectuals that has broken through to the top of the social spectrum, and, in contrast, the coalescence of a working class with its own internal stratification. Waves of criminal behavior unknown in the past have erupted. Drug abuse, hitherto unknown, is spreading.

Rural Arab society no longer stays within its closed circles as age-old tradition prescribes. Its limits have been breached in the complex process of shrinking distances and changing ways of life. The city is encroaching with ever-growing speed and relentless pressure. The source of livelihood in the Arab village has moved quickly to outside localities as villagers now derive their sustenance and livelihood from jobs elsewhere. Land seems to have lost some of its previous aura. It is no longer the symbol of village life; its importance has declined considerably and, with it, the status of landowners on the social scale.[28]

The Arab village today is inextricably linked to the Israeli economy. It thrives and grows when the Israeli economy does and responds to its fluctuations and crises. The economic connection is more than just that. It is a multifaceted conduit to exogenous social influences that cannot but clash with the traditional rural ways of life. The result is a westernization process that inevitably collides with rural realities. Consequently, daily customs are changed, ancient concepts disrupted, and the truths of an old world rent asunder. In this fashion, the boundaries between city and village are blurred. A real geographical rapprochement is taking place between these two types of localities because of more sophisticated transport, more vigorous road-building, and the proliferation of motor vehicles.

Traditional rural agriculture has been transformed. Since the 1960s, Arab farmers have been interrelating more extensively with exogenous economic players and have become more independent. Gradually they have freed themselves from the yoke of debt and adopted new methods of cultivation. The advent of basic services in Arab villages has energized the development of agriculture as a business and expedited the transition to market crops. Israel's own rapid development has caused this process to accelerate.

As the farm economy has developed, an additional process – corresponding to it, influenced by it, and complementary to it – has emerged to help raise the standard of living in Arab villages. The structure of employment has been transformed by the increasing acceptance of jobs outside the village and the relative contraction of agriculture as a livelihood. In this process, the breach of the traditional framework of the Arab village by closer relations with the city manifests itself strongly.

The very factors that helped streamline and diversify agriculture to meet market requirements have also diminished the human resources available to agriculture. In the past, nearly all villagers worked on the farm or in petty crafts related to agriculture. The backwardness of agriculture entailed much manual labor. However, this labor force was not fully utilized throughout the year because of idleness during "off seasons." This helps explain the low income of farm laborers. A factor of even greater importance was the customary laws of succession in the village, under which fields were partitioned into small, scattered plots from one generation to the next, causing farming efficiency to diminish each time. Thus a string of factors combined to depress the standard of living of the rural family. With the introduction of farm machinery and innovative methods of cultivation, however, it became necessary to adapt the labor force to the changing structure of agriculture and an impetus to diversify consumption was provided.

This process was aided by the concurrent growing demand for manpower outside the village. Thus, many young men leave the village for work in towns, Jewish rural localities, and kibbutzim. The factor of geographical distance is less important than before because of the development of transportation, and even residents of remote villages can commute to the large cities. In most cases, they spend the week near their place of work under provisional conditions and return to their villages and families for weekends only. They are attracted by the wages they earn, and even though their consumption habits are changing more slowly than the purchasing power of their wages, their standard of living is rising steadily.

Consequently, the village is undergoing steady renewal, as reflected in large-scale construction which has transformed its appearance. By 1981, an estimated 90–95 percent of village buildings were almost completely new.[29] Today, only a few houses of former times survive, mainly in small villages.

These changes have occurred because most disposable income in the Arab sector has been diverted to construction, and the momentum of building therefore reflects the vast increase in income flowing into the village. However, planning on the outline level is still lacking. Although most buildings are low-rise, flat-roofed dwellings resting on piles, in the past few years there has been a trend toward multi-story building and an inclination to use the ostentatious appearance of one's residence as an avenue to social prestige. Many grand villas perch on hills or mounds, surrounded by spacious yards.

Awareness of banking has grown vastly and effected radical change in saving habits. A survey by the Israeli-Arab Bank in the early 1980s found that most Arab citizens no longer sought to conceal their money "under the floor-tiles" and considered the bank the safest place to keep it. Galloping inflation in the first half of the 1980s undoubtedly helped this process along by prompting individuals to safeguard their income against erosion. In 1981, 105,000 Arabs participated in long-term savings schemes at the Israel-Arab Bank totaling IL 5.6 billion, 60 percent of the balance sheet of this bank, which provided approximately 50 percent of the Arab sector's banking services in the north of the country.[30]

Consumption patterns are also changing swiftly. Although there is still mistrust of purchase on installments and payment through checks and credit cards, significant and substantial change has occurred even here. A stratum of "elite consumers" has come into being; it makes frequent purchases of quality products and is clearly predisposed to ostentatious display of prestigious items as an expression of social status.

The esteem of home-made products has dropped. Fewer and fewer women are eager to knead their own pita-bread, and the traditional oven has been abandoned in most households. The standard loaf of bread has taken their place, and cheeses and yogurt made by firms like Tnuva and Strauss have replaced homemade cheese and *labaneh*.

The old-style house layout has become a rarity that deserves to be preserved as a historical artifact; the long row of windowless rooms entered through a small, creaking, hinged door with the living room adjacent to the animals' pen and the haystack has simply gone out of existence. The poultry run (*khumm*) that once appeared regularly in the back of the room, the cattle trough (*midhwad*), the storehouse (*khabiya*), and the granary have become almost completely obsolete.

However, even the modern houses all have a spacious reception room, the *diwan*, copiously equipped with comfortable sofas for reclining and walls lined with pictures and documents. The tradition of hospitality is preserved in the *diwan*: sitting at ease and recounting endless stories, legends, and current news. It is a place where coffee is still served in *finjan* cups.

Nevertheless, the significance of these changes should not be exaggerated, because the fundamentals of the social structure have remained intact. The transition has not been drastic, and the extent of the change is not easy to define. It is often erroneously regarded as being almost total because of *external* indications that do not always reflect the internal order, which has indeed changed but is still subject to the gravitational laws of an ancient social code.

The changes that transformed the village have turned it into what it once was – a nostalgic symbol of the past, an object of personal yearning, and, perhaps, an element in the national heritage. The following poem by Na'im 'Areidi, which describes how the peasants have become "workers with smoke in their throats," demonstrates the last-mentioned point:

> I returned to the village
> where I first learned to cry . . .
> I returned to my house, built of stone,
> that my fathers had hewn from rock.
> I returned to myself –
> and that was my intention.
>
> I returned to my village,
> where I had been in my former incarnation,
> one tendril in the myriads of vines,
> until this wind came
> and flung me afar . . .
>
> Here are the paths that are no more,
> and houses that soared like the Tower of Babel.
> Where is my village that was,
> where the lanes that have now become
> asphalt roads had names?
>
> I returned to my village,
> where the barking of dogs is extinct
> and the dovecote has become a floodlit turret.
> All the peasants with whom I wished to sing
> the song of the meadows with the melody of the nightingale
> have become workers with smoke in their throats.
> Where are all those who were and are no longer?
> Oh, this heavy dream of mine . . .

> I returned to my village
> as one who flees civilization,
> and I came to my village,
> as one crossing from exile into exile.[31]

The strength of the traditional social frameworks manifests itself more intensely during election campaigns or when clans engage in blood disputes. Quite often, a "volcano" between two rival clans erupts after having long seemed dormant, its lava sweeping the village from end to end as if the remote past has returned with a vengeance. Disputes usually claim many victims on all sides; in some cases, one of the participants is killed.[32] Sometimes a conflict between villagers ignites on denominational grounds, as when inhabitants of the Druze village Julis attacked the Christian inhabitants of Kafr Yassif in early 1981.[33]

The Waning Influence of the Village Elders

The Arab village has always been based on kinship ties. Households with such relations constitute a social unit known as a *hamulah*. In many villages, members of a clan tend to live in one neighborhood, where they form a closely-knit unit with mutual responsibility. Marriages between members of families within one clan are quite common. This arrangement reduces the dowry and reinforces the clan's power at the same time.

At times, the insularity of a clan has been caused by traditional enmity between it and a rival clan in the same village. In the past, clan leaders were selected from among the elders according to the size of their families, their property, and their personal talent. Those chosen, who became the village's dignitaries, frequently struggled with each other for supremacy. These dignitaries were known as *mukhtars*. Only on rare occasions did rival clans agree to appoint one *mukhtar*; each would rather choose the person it considered best qualified for the position, who would then be appointed by the government. The clans' demarcation lines dissected villages in criss-cross fashion. Residential neighborhoods were separate; each clan sometimes had its own grocery store. A village with a population of 3,000 might have twelve stores.[34]

The *mukhtars* were representatives of the government, a kind of village leadership. Their roles were varied and sometimes quite important, because they issued permits for land transactions, had the authority to register natural movement in the village, confirmed the identity of village residents, and dealt with everything else that required official endorsement of an individual fully immersed in local affairs.

The development of the *local council* institution had an adverse effect on the *mukhtars'* status. The council relegated the *mukhtars* to the sidelines and eliminated their political positions.[35] The *mukhtars* initially managed to integrate into the new set-up but as the process continued, they were forced out, unable to adapt to the western form of local government. Only at the transitional stage did the *mukhtars* chair the councils; little by little, the reins were taken from their hands by talented, college-educated young adults who found the village elders incapable of meeting the needs of village development.[36]

At first, the new appointees, too, generally climbed the ladder by virtue of their clan affiliation. Gradually, however, the job entailed other personal qualities; the erstwhile skills and clan backing proved to be insufficient. In the fierce battle for "votes," it was no longer possible to rely on only one clan, however strong. It was essential to mobilize smaller clans, sometimes those at the bottom of the social hierarchy, whose votes the candidate would need to get into the council. The village elders did not know how to attract votes.

Thus young intellectuals entered into confrontation with village elders, at the time when education became a powerful social indicator that threatened to smash a tradition that had held sway for generations. It was in the late 1960s that the first generation of intellectuals made its breakthrough into the higher echelons of Arab local councils. A case in point is the election of Ahmad Masarweh as chairman of the local council in Tayyibeh; this young attorney, a graduate of the Hebrew University of Jerusalem, was elected to the council and immediately began rallying supporters on the council who would vote for him as chairman. His gambit succeeded. In Baqa el-Gharbiyya, a young student named Jalal Abu To'meh, a graduate of the Arab teachers' college in Haifa and a student at Bar-Ilan University, was elected to the position of council chairman. To'meh campaigned at the head of an electoral list of young adults under the slogan: "For the development of Baqa el-Gharbiyya."

To'meh did not have the support of a strong clan. His own family did not belong to the village elite. Disregarding the traditional clan structure, he urged the young villagers to elect him as their representative. Rumor has it that his electoral success was largely

due to the support of young women in the village, who were
influenced by his promise to take action against the custom of
dowry, which restricted their marriage possibilities.

These two young Arabs began vigorously to discharge their
duties as council chairmen in their localities, two of the largest
villages in the Little Triangle. Their success evidently triggered
a larger "youth revolution" in other villages. Some asserted that
the rule of village elders had reached its end. Before the two
young intellectuals completed their first year in office, however, it
transpired that the traditional forces were still strong in the villages.
The attorney Ahmad Masarweh consequently reached an agreement
with his rival, a relative and the village elder, Abu 'Afif, to "take
turns" in the council chairmanship. This kind of compromise was
typical of the transitional period. No agreement was reached in
Baqa el-Gharbiyya. Jalal Abu To'meh, the young student, neglected
his university studies and worked frenetically to implement his
ideas. He fired unqualified schoolteachers and began to organize
an efficient tax-collection system. He considered himself entitled to
prove that the clan era was over. Notwithstanding his intentions,
however, he misread the situation.

The forces of tradition in his village arrayed against him. One
of his supporters defected to the rival camp, thereby tipping the
scales against him, and the eager and dynamic council chairman
soon had to attend a council meeting with one item on its agenda:
his dismissal. He tried to prevent the denouement by petitioning the
Supreme Court in its capacity as the High Court of Justice, but only
succeeded in postponing the judgment for some time. Eventually he
had to acknowledge his loss of power in the council. The highest
instance of justice in the country did not consider itself empowered
to intervene, without legal cause, in the inter-generational struggle
that raged in Baqa el-Gharbiyya.

Thus the court's interim injunction against the council meeting
was revoked. When the council met, the psychology student was
unable to marshall enough votes to retain the chairmanship. Even
after being forced to yield his position, however, To'meh did not
cease his public activity. He even continued fighting within the
council by waging a running internal contest for the chairmanship,
supported by a group of young adults in the village that evolved
into an interesting "debating society." Personalities from all over
the country were invited to the group's meetings, usually held on
Friday evenings: directors-general of government ministries, party

leaders from all ends of the political spectrum, industrialists, and army generals.[37]

The group discussed the full range of issues that preoccupied young Arabs in those days, from the problems of the state and ways to effect their integration into it, to day-to-day concerns. No holds were barred. The meetings began with lecture, followed by a general discussion that sometimes turned into sharp verbal sparring. Thus the young village intellectuals began to build their power, their ascent gradual rather than meteoric, as dictated by realities.

Attorney Ahmad Masarweh was re-appointed chairman of the local council in Tayyibeh, the most developed village – now town – in the Triangle. He managed to reach an agreement with the elder of his clan, Abu 'Afif, who honored its terms and allowed him to take over. This young intellectual understood that he could not disregard traditional forces and that he must take them into his political consideration. He also owed much of his electoral success to votes cast by the young adults of his clan. Consequently, his prospects at this stage of social development were superior to those of a young "revolutionary" leader who wished to upend the entire system.

Masarweh's colleague, Jalal Abu To'meh, in contrast, had to devote more attention to his studies as his prospects of regaining the chairmanship diminished. Perhaps his unsuccessful experience with the method he had chosen showed him the cost of misreading the situation. He may not have taken into account sufficiently the strength of the traditional social frameworks that defeated him after he had challenged them frontally. Since then, these council chairmanships have changed hands again; the incumbents today are two young intellectuals, both "alumni" of the Arabic-language service of Israel Television, where they acquired self-confidence, valuable experience, important contacts, and reputation.

The struggle of the attorney Masarweh and of Jalal Abu To'meh to reach the pinnacle of local government seems distant in retrospect, but they were the pioneers who exemplified, in unequivocal terms, a general process that recurred in many Israeli Arab villages. This process was neither as marked nor as direct in all villages as in Tayyibeh and Baqa el-Gharbiyya, but in essence it reflected the same natural competition for governance, amid the internal tensions that accompanied it so intensely.

Today, the Tayyibeh municipal council is chaired by a dynamic young man, Rafiq Hajj Yahya, a member of a powerful village clan from which his predecessors had also vaulted to the top. Hajj

Yahya has not repudiated his origins. The chairman of the Baqa al-Gharbiyya council is Samir Darwish, another former journalist with broad horizons, who is well-versed in the social realities of Israeli Arabs. He sees no need to trample on the previous generation; deftly he derives influence from the village clans without forgoing the effort to adjust to the demands of modern times. This is because, even though the traditional social structures retain sociopolitical power as they adjust to changing circumstances, they no longer demand pride of place for the elders.

Indeed, there is no doubt that the penetration of exogenous influences into the village, as a consequence of closer relations with the city, has mitigated the authority of the village elders, the heads of the dignitary clans, in Israel as in other Middle Eastern countries. The Israeli reality has narrowed economic disparities between social groups in the village and, at times, has inverted the social pyramid. Prestigious families that had sometimes derived their power from their land and property could no longer compete with families of inferior status whose cumulative income was substantial. This process caused a reshuffling in which elders of esteemed lineage lost influence for lack of an adequate economic basis and because of new social concepts spawned by developments in education.

Rapid Urban Change

The Arab city of yesteryear has been eroded in the stream of upheavals since 1948, when its social elite abandoned it at the head of the mass flight. The leadership vacuum is much more perceptible and substantial in the city than in the villages. Practically speaking, only members of the lower classes remained there, those who could not afford to relocate at the right time.

Some urban population groups virtually disintegrated. Jaffa, the "press capital" in the Mandate period, totally collapsed. Acre and Safed in the north, Beersheba in the south, and Ramle and Lydda in the center lost their Arab coloration. The elite neighborhoods in western Jerusalem were emptied. Beit She'an lost its entire Arab population and became an Israeli "development town." The Arabs of Safed also fled. In Acre and Haifa, nuclei of Arab communities were preserved that could prosper anew within Jewish towns. Shafa'amr (Shefar'am) held its own but was still a semi-rural village despite its official designation as a town.

Only Nazareth survived virtually unscathed. Its inhabitants did not flee during the war, even though it had been the headquarters of Fawzi el-Qawuqji's "Army of Salvation," the Ajnadayn battalion, and miscellaneous gangs that circulated about; and even though the entire area was in turmoil.[38]

In other towns, the lower strata of society struggled to survive in the narrow streets, jammed with buildings on the verge of collapse, seeking their livelihood at the bottom of the occupational pyramid. Masses of Jewish immigrants took over Arab houses in Jaffa, Haifa, and Lydda; while in other cities the proximity of the Jews became immediate, acute, and sometimes oppressive.

Slowly the urban population emerged from the initial crisis, even spawning talented entrepreneurs who joined in the economic development boom in Israel. The "municipal capital" moved to Nazareth, where until the late 1970s the Zu'bi and Fahum families continued to fan the embers of traditional leadership despite the seismic changes taking place around them.

Even in Israel the Arab city maintained its ancient walled core, but new streets, unlike the tortuous alleyways of the old city, developed outside it, without the cul-de-sacs that served the innermost houses. The large mosque and ancient citadel still punctuate the skyline of the old cities of Nazareth, Acre, and Jerusalem. Life in the covered market still continues – open stalls along the street, without windows or doors, with shutters that close at sunset. Here traditional wares are still sold and the factories that make them are located. Each industry has its own special alley in the bazaar: *Suq al-'Attarin*, the perfume market; *al-Lahhamin*, the butchers' market; *an-Nahhasin*, the coppersmiths' market; *an-Najjarin*, the carpenters' market, and so on.

Nevertheless, the ambience of the traditional market has changed completely. In Nazareth it has turned into a virtually commercial street, although remnants of the former market still exist. *Suq al-Khawajat*, the gentlemen's market, where fabric and clothing stalls were once located, is at the top, followed by the cobblers' market, the blacksmiths' and knifemakers' market (where saddle and harness workshops are also situated), and also *Suq al-Khan*, near the *Khan el-Basha* caravanserai, with its abundance of tourist souvenirs alongside blacksmiths' workshops and accessories for horse-drawn carts. The central bus terminal of Nazareth is near the site of the old wagon station. Next is the seed market, where to this day one can spot the odd *tarbush*, the red headgear of the former notables, and the *Suq ash-Shum* which has its assortment of watchmakers, storekeepers, tinsmiths, and barbers. In the adjoining Farah family market, shoemakers and cloth vendors nestle in their alcoves; then there is the Protestant market, where most of the shops belong to the Protestant charitable trust, and of course the popular vegetable market and the cafés.[39]

In the urban neighborhoods that have developed in Israel, mosques and synagogues of a different style have been built, alongside impressive public buildings, cultural centers, cinemas, and office buildings that house bank branches, insurance companies, commercial enterprises, and other centers of dynamic economic activity typical of the increasingly westernized city. The offices are spacious, contemporary in style, and furnished with state-of-the-art equipment: computers, facsimile and telex machines, and sophisticated telephone systems have become the prevailing fashion.

At first the café replaced the bathhouse, the *hamam*, as a men's club where one could mull over daily affairs. Although most functions of the café have been curtailed in the television era, this institution is still holding its own, watching over the city, well attended, congested, teeming with life.

In the past, the city was divided into distinct quarters, *harat*, each inhabited by members of one clan or one denomination.[40] In the period of Israeli statehood, the boundaries between the neighborhoods have become blurred. Members of different denominations and clans have intermingled, vitiating the traditional social structure.

This process took place much more rapidly in the city than in the village, although the influence of family lineage has not abated altogether. A member of the Zu'biya family in Nazareth still commands respect, but increasingly it is a vestige of the past. The venerable elite families no longer reign supreme. The sociopolitical power centers have changed radically, and the focal points of economic power are totally different today. Members of the lower classes have risen to key positions in the city. The relative importance of kinship in local elections, not to mention parliamentary elections, has decreased more precipitously in the cities than in the villages.

Every now and then, however, hostilities erupt in the cities between large, powerful clans that have been given a *casus belli*. Sometimes a protracted blood feud develops, leading to a string of reprisals. In the early 1990s, the Arab community in Jaffa was convulsed by a clash between two well-known families, 'Ashur and

Hamad, which originated in a marriage relationship between them that ended in a severe schism when the wife, from the 'Ashur family, was forced to leave her Hamadi husband and return to her parents' home, as is customary in traditional Arab society, after a dispute between the spouses.

Tension soared, reaching its climax with the murder of Sayyid Yussuf 'Ashur, the *imam* of the great mosque in Jaffa, and his brother Khamis 'Ashur. A third son, Kamal 'Ashur, aged 25, was murdered several months later. The identity of the perpetrators was not in doubt, and in late July 1991 it was the Hamad family's turn to pay a price for the clan war, when two masked men assailed young Anwar Hamad; the boy was shot in the street with intent to murder. The town dignitaries attempted to extinguish the flames of revenge, but all attempts to arrange a *sulha* (peace agreement between the warring parties) were in vain. It was as if the Arab population of Jaffa had retreated to its distant past, when such scenes were common.[41]

On the religious-communal plane, the lines of demarcation persist because of the Church's ramified activities and growing observance of Islam. However, one can no longer speak of a Muslim quarter *vis-à-vis* a Christian one; instead, in today's urban structure, these population groups have blended into a complex mass of class contradictions and growing national consciousness.

Even today, no one doubts the existence of large pockets of poverty, especially in the mixed towns, where some married couples cannot afford to leave the parental home or are forced to rent terribly run-down old dwellings. Socioeconomic friction fuels the national conflicts that divide the Jewish and Arab inhabitants of these cities.

In the Arab neighborhoods of these towns, crime – robbery, burglary, pickpocketing – is making inroads among the youth. At night-time, under the extinguished lamps, teenagers smoke hard drugs. The stench of garbage dumps in these disadvantaged neighborhoods permeates the air as rats, mice, flies, mosquitoes, and other vermin abound.[42]

Change in the status of women initially occurred more quickly in the towns than in the villages. It was especially evident in the mixed towns, where assimilation took root first in clothing, then in affectations, and finally in the general lifestyle, including interaction patterns among family members. Urban Arab women began to work outside the home before their rural counterparts did. They achieved higher levels of education, married later, and had a lower fertility rate, with each generation having fewer children on average than its predecessor. However, the gap has narrowed in the last decade. The 1983 census found only slight differences between towns and villages in respect of cumulative fertility according to women's age.[43]

After the establishment of the State, the Arab urban population was the first to develop, followed by that of the villages. This is why Nazareth became the "political capital," Haifa "the Arab media capital," and both cities the cradles of cultural activity in general.

In the few purely Arab cities, the municipality coalesced as a major power center. This was particularly evident in Nazareth, where there was an undeclared presumption to turn the town council into a national body with country-wide influence, a "government in the making" in miniature. As a holy city, Nazareth hosted a set of institutions of diverse denominational affiliations. The Municipality of Shefar'am rose in status when its head was elected to head the "Monitoring Committee," the supreme leadership of Israeli Arabs. It also served as the host for stormy political conferences.

Bedouin Settlement in the Negev

Throughout the northern Negev and the Ashqelon subdistrict, and beyond the Negev in the Judean Desert, are Bedouin tribes that had a population of 100,000 persons in early 1995. These Bedouin account for approximately 12 percent of all the minorities.[44] They are scattered over a 250,000–acre swath of land, a crescent-shaped area east of the Shoval–Beersheba–Mis'af Hanegev axis. A lengthy stretch used to abut the political border with the Jordanian West Bank.

The array of Bedouin encampments is of necessity determined by geographic conditions:

1. Most of the tribes are concentrated in the Beersheba–Arad Valley, the main catchment basin of the surrounding mountainous area. Near it lies the climatic boundary between the Mediterranean zone in the north and the desert in the south.
2. The other area of Bedouin presence is the Shoval region, north of Beersheba.

The political frontiers set forth after the 1948 War of Independence bifurcated the Bedouin tribes' area of migration and, consequently, drove a geographic wedge between them. They continued to practice a nomadic way of life on both sides of the border until 1950; since then, these movements and border crossings have not resumed.

Many of the 50,000 Bedouin who were displaced from the Negev during the battles settled in the Gaza Strip; some Bedouin used this area as a base for attacks on Israeli border settlements during the first decade of statehood.[45]

Eighteen tribes remained within Israel's 1948 frontiers, most of them fragmented, and their other parts roam through the Sinai Peninsula, the Gaza Strip, and the Hebron hills.[46] In 1953, the government decided to gather the Bedouin tribes into an area east of the Beersheba–Hebron highway, thus forming the "enclosure area" (*ezor ha-siyyag*). This displacement from the areas where they had traditionally paused in their migrations scarred these Bedouin and induced 12,000 of them to cross the border into Jordan's West Bank, where the authorities subsequently forced many of them to return. Slowly the rifts mended, and the Bedouin began adapting to the harsh new reality that had ruptured the structures of their past.

Bedouin society is based on kinship, from the smallest cell to the largest tribe.[47] The structure of this society is based on several elements:

1. The basic unit, the extended patriarchal family (*ahl* or *'ailah*).
2. The *hamulah* – clan, i.e., a group of families descended from a common patriarch who lived five to seven generations previously. The clan is a unified entity that possesses its own wells or land, and it migrates or encamps as a group. Its members usually practice collective responsibility to the fifth degree, thus giving the clan an alternative name, *khums* ("fifth"). This term, however, generally refers to the accountability group only, i.e., to the *men* of the clan who descend from the common patriarch.[48]
3. The tribal subgroup, known as *rub'*, a unit positioned between the clan and the tribe. This unit also includes non-members who join the tribal framework, i.e. persecuted or non-affiliated Bedouin, who are termed *dakhil* or *tanib*.
4. The tribe, *'ashirah*, a political unit that includes "migrant"

refugees from other tribes and protected individuals. It unites for purposes of war, and sometimes all of its members encamp together in the summer at the wells from which they draw their water. The tribe imposes its authority over settlements, which pay it the *khuwwa* tax.

The tribe is headed by a *sheikh*, who is subordinate to the *sheikh al-mashayikh*, the elder of the *sheikhs*. The latter, the head of an aggregate of tribes, is historically the supreme leader.

The Bedouin sheikh is "first among equals," endowed with special privileges in the apportioning of spoils and other material affairs. His office is bequeathed within his family by succession, but not necessarily from father to son, for personality is also an important factor. The sheikh must have leadership skills, because he must command the tribe in war, guide it in its migrations, find pasture, settle disputes, and attend to other matters of paramount importance to the tribe. The leader of the strongest *rub'* is often chosen as the sheikh, and this appointment is confirmed by the district representative of the Interior Ministry.

The sheikh fulfils two roles concurrently: representative and administrative. The government applies to him with respect to members of the tribe, and he represents them *vis-à-vis* the government when they apply for assistance. The door of his tent is open; every tribesman is free to enter and share his thoughts as the coffee simmers. In the evening, the sheikh and the tribal elders gather in the tent to discuss topical matters. Sometimes a tribe has two sheikhs: one to represent its members and another to lead the tribe in battle and migration.[49]

Several interrelated factors have rapidly transformed the socio-economic lives of the Bedouin in Israel:

1. Contraction of the nomadic territory following armistice agreements with the Arab countries and the demarcation of political boundaries.
2. The imposition of stable government in the Bedouin's semi-sedentary areas, as reflected in all fields of life: education system, health services, taxation, justice, assistance for the chronically ill or disabled, and financial aid for the needy or assistance in the purchase of seeds.[50] It was this that transformed Bedouin life; the characteristic contours of the nomadic tribe became blurred and new patterns emerged. The Bedouin

sometimes found the new format hard to assimilate, but gradually they accustomed themselves to it. Nevertheless, one can still find ancient traditions that have been preserved; the erstwhile customs are as influential as ever.

3. The economic and agricultural development of the Negev. An extremely important factor in strengthening relations between the Bedouin and the Jewish community was the building of roads in the Negev. Today the Bedouin themselves make extensive use of motor vehicles. A luxury car is a sure sign of the sheikh's status. This, of course, has diminished the value of horses and camels. The swift development of Beersheba and the establishment of two new cities, Dimona and Arad, created focal points of attraction for the Bedouin and furthered their rapprochement with the values of modern culture and society. The formation and expansion of development works in the Negev created new jobs for Bedouin.

4. The periodic droughts that afflict the Negev, to the detriment of flocks and herds, were another factor in the transformation of the Bedouin socioeconomic structure.

5. Today, the Bedouin earn their livelihood by accepting salaried jobs outside their encampments. As far back as January 1962, the Arab Department of the Histadrut opened a Negev branch in association with the Beersheba Labor Council. Bedouin workers have integrated into this structure since then, benefiting from union protection and the medical services of the Histadrut health fund.

6. As a result of these socioeconomic changes, permanent buildings began to rise alongside the encampments. These buildings, scattered throughout the area with no planning, indicate that the time has come to finish planning the Bedouin settlements in accordance with changes that have occurred there and measures taken in neighboring Arab countries.

For the Negev Bedouin, however, the transitional period has not yet ended. It will probably continue longer than it did with the Galilee Bedouin, but clear indications of the next stages in the tribes' permanent sedentarization are already evident:

1. Demarcation of boundaries for settlement clusters. Seven Bedouin towns have been built in the Negev thus far. Tel Sheva was the first link in the chain (founded in 1965 without

proper planning) which would take Bedouin needs into account. Other permanent settlements followed: Rahat, Kseifa, Laqiyya, 'Aro'er, Segev and Hura.[51] The Bedouin inhabitants of these towns receive services which, while convenient and near their homes, are not yet completely consolidated. In the town center are public buildings – clinic, cultural center, baby-care center, social club, restaurant, parking lot. Houses are connected to the electricity grid. The planning work for these towns was carried out incrementally, and special efforts to persuade Bedouin to settle in them are still being made.

Today, only 48.3 percent of Bedouin are considered to dwell outside the settlements,[52] but their personal indicators are difficult to trace, and the editor of the *Statistical Abstract* defines such data as "incomplete." These Bedouin report the name of their tribe, not their settlement, as their address. This implies that many more have become sedentarized; they no longer dwell in encampments or temporary structures. The problem illuminated here is that the dividing line that distinguishes sedentarized Bedouin from their non-sedentarized counterparts is sometimes vague.

2.   Help with vocational training for young Bedouin who wish to practice an urban trade for their livelihood. Here, too, much progress has been made; one can already find experienced Bedouin craftsmen, qualified technicians, and skilled workers.

There is no doubt, however, that the transition to sedentary life entails considerable adjustment difficulties, and the sedentarization process must be gradual. As the Bedouin become more aware of the importance of education, they are more strongly predisposed to dwell in an orderly settlement with a full range of services. The young generation will certainly determine the nature of this process.

The Status of Arab Women

It is difficult to measure the extent, depth, and currents of change in Arab society. There is no doubt that the "bottleneck" is situated within the family, in the interrelations of its members, and, particularly, in the nuclear family, the small cell that constitutes the basic social core, within which the status of the woman resides.

The Arab woman is no longer sequestered at home or confined to her courtyard, field, or orchard. She no longer wears the *thawb*, a long, dark blue cotton dress embroidered with multicolored silk threads, with an opening for the head, tied around the neck with two laces. A headscarf, neck scarf, or sash serves as a belt (*hizam*) in which she conceals her personal effects and from which the wooden key to her house dangles. No longer does she tuck her hair under the headcover known as the *shika*, a headdress of sorts fastened with two lengths of chain in which Turkish or Egyptian coins no longer in circulation, such as the *majidi*, are embedded. No longer does the peasant woman pierce her nose for the insertion of a clove known as *karful* or *qurunful*. Only older women bear a burn mark (*kayya*) on their forehead that emphasizes the part in their hair, which is combed to either side.[53]

Although the Arab woman will frequently circulate in jeans, even in the village, she does not yet dare to wear shorts and a sleeveless shirt. While she may walk along the beach in a bathing suit, she would not do so alone. She often wears a watch and a fashionable handbag; and in the street, at the university, at the market, or in the office, one could hardly recognize her nationality – she is a young, "modern" Arab woman.

She also speaks with men – co-workers, customers, the occasional stranger who visits. She laughs aloud and understands sophisticated allusions. However, flirting does not go very far with her; she usually nips it in the bud. She is no longer quite as shy as before, but she is still different from most of her Jewish contemporaries. She has already learned many western "secrets," with contraception at the top of the list. The decrease in the birth rate over the past generation has been sufficiently dramatic to indicate that this vital family-planning tool has been fully assimilated. She now has four or five children on average, and in certain social groups only two or three, a 50 percent decrease in the last fifteen years.[54]

Nevertheless, on their wedding night the mother of the groom would still wait outside the newlywed couple's room until her son shows her proof of her daughter-in-law's virginity. The mother then ventures forth with the traditional ululating cry of joy, the *zagharit*.[55] Proof of fertility is of the utmost importance in both rural and urban Arab society. Therefore, however they may wish to plan their family, the couple will rush to bring their first child into the world so that the evil tongues will have no opportunity to wag. As one young husband put it, "People may think that something's wrong."[56]

Young women's education levels have soared at all layers of society. Illiteracy has nearly vanished; one no longer finds young women who cannot read and write or who failed to complete primary school. It is true that many girls do not attend high school, that the gender disparity in the higher grades is still acute, and that the matriculation exams seem to be less important to girls than to boys.

As the age of marriage rises, however, so does the girls' wish to earn a matriculation certificate, a prerequisite for higher education and, today, a prestigious social symbol. At the very same period of time, young women are murdered time and again by their fathers or brothers for having "defiled the family honor." Ibrahim Nimr Hussein, chairman of the highest agency of leadership among Israeli Arabs, testified in this matter, after being duly cautioned, in the following way:

> This tradition is binding on the entire Muslim Arab population, both urban and rural, but it is emphasized much more strongly in the insular rural society. It is difficult for such a person to continue living, as I explained earlier, and he cannot cleanse the stain or shame in any way other than bloodshed. Traditional Arab society regards the defendant with respect because this is the tradition.[57]

Thus, indeed, did the village accept this act, with sympathy, empathy, and painful understanding. The defendant's family rallied around him and are now fighting to free him on medical grounds.[58] He was a popular man in his village, known for his generosity, common sense, and friendliness. In this crisis on the sensitive issue of family honor, he followed the dictates of an age-old tradition.

Woman's sexuality is perceived as *dangerous*. She needs protection but must also be kept under guard to ensure that she is not enticed into a forbidden relationship.[59] Her behavior may impugn the honor of the man responsible for her, i.e., her nearest relative – father, brother, or husband – unless it is redeemed through the shedding of her blood. *'Ard* is the concept of honor that focuses totally on woman's purity, which she cannot enhance but can surely impugn. It is a different honor concept from *sharaf*, which depends solely on a man's actions.[60]

The very existence of two separate, distinct concepts of honor in the Arabic language indicates how sensitive Arab society is to the preservation of woman's innocence, which, once sullied, may be atoned for only by her death. The murder is committed not when the adultery becomes known but at the moment the man, his honor at stake, faces the accusing finger of his social environment. He must not be perceived as weak, miserable, lacking in *'ard*, for then his entire world would shatter and he would not be able to look others in the eye. This is an ancient, powerful, deeply-rooted code that, even in the last decade of the twentieth century, has lost none of its potency, although the government authorities adamantly and relentlessly pursue and punish its adherents who take the lives of their daughters or sisters.

In this respect, Arab society evidently finds it hard to shake off the shackles of the past. Young intellectual circles oppose this violence, but their sphere of influence is limited. Only seven women and one man attended a demonstration in Tayyibeh, held in 1992, against the murder of women in Arab society. An organization known as *Al-Fanar* (The Lighthouse) was established but has not yet swept away the benightedness of customs that it defines as "a backward tradition that has wrought violence in the lives of Arab women, especially in the murder of women for defilement of family honor." The vanguard of women in this new movement is exceedingly small in number. "Everybody ignores us; they're afraid to hear the truth. It can't be that elected public figures would remain neutral between executioners and their victims," implored Manar Hassan, a woman aged 25, one of the organization's founders. The demonstrators held a protest vigil that failed to attract public participation. The public seemed to scorn them; a handful of children gathered to wave banners, and a young woman from Tayyibeh joined the sparse ranks with her baby.[61] The absence of reverberations from a demonstration of this kind in a progressive town such as Tayyibeh, coupled with Nimr Hussein's testimony, reflects the present stage of the campaign to liberate the Arab woman in this respect.

Westernization has not yet made strong inroads in the predisposition of women, especially Muslim women, to work outside the home. Their labor force participation is still minimal, or so it appears from the statistical findings, because some of those who accept work outside the home are reluctant to "admit their guilt." It transpires that taking a job is still a sensitive issue, and a woman who works in an office or factory, particularly outside the village, may be considered a deviant from the desired norms. Such behavior is no longer totally rejected and is certainly not a pretext for condemnation or ostracism, but it carries a heavy load of preconceptions, anxieties, and fears, the feeling of being exposed to dangers or temptations that lurk "out there," far from the safe confines of the village, where protectors are always within eyeshot.

Only 15 percent of Muslim women aged 25–34 belong to the labor force, as against 42 percent of Christian Arab women and 65 percent of Jewish women in the same "sensitive" age group. Only ten percent of Muslim women aged 15 and over belong to the official labor force.[62] At times, it is because of an extension of study that reduces the number of young women who work outside the home; as they grow older, their labor force participation rate rises. Muslim Arab women with higher education (more than thirteen years' schooling) show hardly any difference from their Christian counterparts.

Much progress has undoubtedly been made in the living standards, education, and social integration of Israeli Arab women. Nevertheless, there is still something peculiar about their status. This peculiarity almost defies definition because of the diverse elements of which it is composed. The external "shell" of the process of change protrudes, but the more one approaches the core, the slower the change is, although any movement on the surface has profound implications.

It is precisely at this time of transition, as the dividing line between permissible and forbidden behaviors is obfuscated amid general confusion, that Arab women come under even stronger protection against exposure. Therefore, it is not always possible to discover what real actions Arab women have taken to liberate themselves from the chains of the past.

The Arab woman often finds herself in two worlds, which, although ostensibly lacking any common border, are not entirely divorced from each other. Under the law, she enjoys the same rights as her Jewish counterpart. The Equalization of Women's Rights Law, 5711–1951, states unequivocally that "men and women shall have equal rights in any legal proceeding; and any legal provision that discriminates against women *qua* women in respect of any legal proceeding is to be disregarded."[63] Realities in Arab society are still different, and the law has targeted these realities for change.

The following account illustrates the lives of Arab women in rural localities at the end of the British Mandate period:

> All their lives they work in the fields, at home, and in the yard. They marry very young, while they are still girls, and are rarely

consulted in the choice of mate. A husband may easily divorce his wife, and polygamy is permitted although not very common. Women usually bear one child each year and are already old by the age of 30–35 . . . [64]

For centuries, the Arab woman was inferior in traditional Middle Eastern society, including that of Palestine.[65] This basic fact seems to accompany her throughout her life to this day. The birth of a daughter is not celebrated at all. As a child she is consigned to housework, and the load becomes heavier from year to year. She is married off at a young age. In the past, her father was the sole arbiter in the selection of her husband. Her own choice is far more important today than before, but she is not allowed absolute discretion; her father still wields the ultimate authority in rural society and among Bedouin tribes, although his power in this regard is unquestionably slackening, especially regarding educated women. The size of the dowry did much to determine the choice of mate, since this criterion reflected the social status of the prospective husband.

Although the importance of this factor has declined considerably in the last decade, related families are still wont to exchange brides within one wedding contract (*badl*), i.e., "exchange marriage," in which a son of each family marries his counterpart's sister. This custom was created in an attempt to keep women within the clan or, at least, within the village. It seems, however, that both the groom and his father often frown on this practice, and it is only one of the marriage patterns in Arab society. The studies show that the rate of such transactions falls in the range of 14.6–27.3 percent.[66]

Aharon Layish regards the exchange of brides as a clear manifestation of the clash between social custom and religious values, and proffers serious arguments against it.[67] A young man who wishes to avoid marrying his cousin may protest: "I grew up with Jamila; we've known each other since birth. I want to marry a woman from outside the village, not someone who's like my sister. Our fathers are brothers, our mothers are sisters, and our fathers and mothers are cousins."[68]

The considerations that determine a marriage are numerous and diverse; they vary with social class, local customs, and type of locality. However, they still depend largely on material motives, and it is no easy matter for a girl to withstand them. She frequently expresses her consent under duress, knowing from the outset that her will is not the decisive factor. In the past, a father could apply extreme power to enforce his choice; he could, for example, promise his daughter to a widower at his wife's funeral, as a kind of "gift of the grave" (*'utiyat al-qabr*).[69]

After her marriage, the woman still remains bound to her parental home, which provides her with its protection. She visits her parental family from time to time, either for social purposes or with specific requests. Her father and brothers always remain her patrons, and whenever she and her husband quarrel, she returns home until they mediate the dispute. If she is divorced, she returns to her parental home until she remarries.

A woman who abandons her husband's home is called *hardanah*, i.e., "offended," or even "angry." Among the Bedouin, she is known as *za'lanah*.[70] This is a privilege of sorts that a woman may invoke if she despises her husband or is angry with him; she can effect a temporary "separation" from him, at the risk of divorce. In past times, when the couple lived amid the extended family, this departure was not a drastic act because other women in the extended family would take care of the "rebel's" children. Today, as each nuclear family has its own house, the threat of a woman's leaving during a marital dispute gives her far more power.[71]

The young couple still tends to establish its household near the parental home, sometimes because the wife's father owns the land, sometimes because the husband has not yet received his inheritance from his father and prefers to remain close to him. Each house has its own *diwan*. Landless, low-income couples purchase an apartment in a tenement for lack of choice, even if it is far from the parental home.

Upon marriage, a woman "renounces" her part in the inheritance, although according to the Quran she is entitled to half as much as men of the same degree of kinship. Practically speaking, this explicit religious ruling is almost always disregarded; women are denied their share in order to keep property within the family. Instead of the inheritance, the sons compensate their sisters with various gifts. It is possible that women actually prefer this method, because were they to receive a share in their deceased fathers' estate, it would almost certainly vanish into their husband's property, whereas for their renunciation they are compensated with a kind of "credit" that is held for them by their brothers. This gives them a sense of backing and confidence in terms of having a "right" to return to the family home, if needs be.

The renunciation of inheritance does not enjoin women from accruing property of their own. It transpires that exceptional women have managed to establish "private funds" and even to purchase land and livestock. Women are increasingly adamant about registering their houses in their name.[72]

In her husband's home, however, the Arab woman has no independent life. Her burden of labor has lightened considerably but still lasts from dawn to dusk. In the past, her status was determined by the number of her children, because a large family wielded considerable influence in traditional society and enjoyed the advantage of a large pool of readily available labor. But with the decrease in the relative importance of agriculture and the introduction of modern farm machinery, many women are excused from having to toil in the fields. Release from this arduous duty has become the symbol of a woman's status in recent years, as educated women prefer to marry landless men.[73]

The Arab woman has greater freedom of movement than before, because her husband, a wage-earning employee far from his village, no longer escorts her to the doctor or on visits to relatives. Public transport – taxis and buses – has replaced the donkey and is considered much safer, since the woman is no longer alone and vulnerable to attack or seduction.[74]

Because Arab women have fewer children today, they have more leisure time. They use it to run the household as their husbands work in towns or settlements distant enough to prevent their carrying out the functions by which they were defined in the past. Thus the Arab woman's way of life has changed and her status is very much enhanced.

Today, an Arab woman's kitchen is equipped with modern electrical appliances. These function as social status symbols as much as they lighten the housewife's workload. Women are also becoming more influential behind the scenes, even in matters that fall within the purview of the male. They are more involved in relationships within the family or with the village, and sometimes they succeed in resolving difficulties with which husbands cannot cope. They forward vital information and intervene in political affairs; in one celebrated instance, a woman persuaded enough villagers to vote for Rakah that the party paid for her son's medical studies.

Now that political progress is no longer determined by social origin, women are learning to apply their intelligence to help their husbands climb the steep ladder to high ranking positions.

They know how speak their minds and guard their tongues when necessary, so that no one will know who really "pulled the strings." They invoke the "strength of the weak woman" in order to attain goals beyond their own personal needs or those of their families.[75]

Summing up, the inferiority of the Muslim women in Middle Eastern society manifests itself in three respects that have unequal and varying effects in different regions, but which are gradually disappearing in Israel of the 1990s:

1. Polygamy is limited by the Quran to four concurrent wives in addition to concubines. The tradition of polygamy was most prevalent among the affluent and rare among the less well-off. In Israel, polygamy has been declining and hardly exists today, chiefly because of the legal proscription and the threat of prosecution embedded in Paragraph 8(a) of the Equalization of Women's Rights Law, which abolished the protection that polygamists had previously enjoyed. However, the law does not annul bigamous or polygamous marriages that were contracted before it went into effect; the criminal sanction is meant to deter similar marriages in the future.[76] Interestingly, the first large-family allowances awarded by the Israel National Insurance Institute were given in the Arab sector. The very first allowance was granted to a Muslim, Mahmud Diab Taha of Nazareth, aged 39, who had 17 children by his two wives. An Arab resident of the Triangle village of Tira demanded that the tax assessor recognize his entitlement to an exemption for both of his wives, whom he had married in the Mandate Period. When his application was turned down, he did not hesitate to appeal to the Tel Aviv District Court.

2. The second manifestation of the Arab woman's inferiority, more widespread than polygamy, is marriage under duress, where she is not consulted. Writer Su'ad Qaraman speaks of girls who committed suicide in the 1960s in order to avoid marriages arranged by their parents. Increasing numbers of young women complain to the *shari'a* court of parental pressure to marry elderly relatives. Layish himself once attended a tumultuous legal debate of this kind, held before the *qadi* of Tayyibeh.[77]

3. The third manifestation of the Arab woman's inferiority is the manner of her divorce. To divorce her, irrespective of her wishes, her husband need merely utter the word *talaq* three times in succession. Divorce is rather common, although here

again vast changes have occurred. The threat of divorce stalks
the Muslim woman at all times; it may cause her to depend on
her husband and submit to his demands. Husbands have been
known to divorce their wives without the wife's knowledge in
order to marry other women.

Accordingly, the turnabout created by the Israeli legislature,
when it made divorce without consent an offense punishable by
up to five years' imprisonment, was revolutionary.[78]

It seems that Arab society did not adjust easily to this new,
exogenous legislation that contradicted its basic philosophy and
ways of life in matters of personal status. A trial of the Jaffa
qadi Sheikh Tahir Hamad, which lasted a full year, illuminated
the difficulty of the transition imposed by the law. It transpired
that the law did not enjoin the *qadi* himself from collaborating with
a man who had sought to divorce his wife; he authorized the divorce
without her consent and disregarded the forging of her signature.

The impact of the Israeli reality is not confined to legislation. The
increasing prevalence of contact with Western culture is gradually
opening new horizons for Arab women, as manifested on several
planes:[79]

1. Women are working outside the home. This is undoubtedly
   influenced by the Israeli way of life, although its extent is still
   rather limited.
2. The general tendency to work outside the village and the
   undermining of the traditional social structure have disrupted
   family life and led to much controversy concerning women,
   as the "spirit of progress" clashes with the rigid traditional
   perceptions of woman's place and sensitivity to family honor.
3. Arab women are increasingly preoccupied with *discovering* their
   rights, after which they will insist on *invoking* them.
4. Women's education has become broader and deeper. It is still
   not comprehensive, but the Compulsory Education Law is
   being implemented to a growing extent. Women's high-school
   enrollment, municipal and vocational, is increasing steadily,
   and Arab women have begun to enroll in various departments
   of universities.
5. Arabs are marrying later in life. At the end of the Mandate
   period, most girls married before age 18 and nearly 30 percent
   before age 15. This is a very rare occurrence in Israel today.[80]

6.   Traditional shackles are slowly being loosened. The first mixed-sex public assembly took place in Nazareth in 1962. Today, such events are quite common. In 1963, a Jewish-Arab youth camp in Acre, organized by the author of this book, set a precedent by inviting Arab girls to participate with the boys. After this breakthrough, the number of female participants grew from year to year.

7.   Young Arabs have struggled against the dowry for many years, aiming to marry as the result of ordinary, natural contacts. In a seminar held in Tel Aviv in April 1963, Arab women challenged the dowry custom as a humiliation of women. Indeed, the dowry is losing its significance and is no longer the debilitating factor that it was until the late 1970s.[81]

8.   The National Insurance Law, which has awarded women a social-security allotment for their children since 1977, is important because it gives Arab women an economic power base within the family, even if they do not work outside the home. To a certain degree it raises their self-confidence.[82]

9.   In the political arena, the voice of the Arab woman has yet to be heard. The right to vote, coupled with women's inferior status, actually reinforces the traditional framework by doubling the clan's political strength.

The movement to augment women's independence and assure their political standing is expanding, and it is men who articulate these ambitions, as is typical at this stage of social development. Thus Abu Iman admonishes his fellow men of the Druze community in his newsletter:

> Do not quarrel with your wives in order to force them to vote for a certain list. Let her find her way in society. Do not limit her freedom. The period of toil and domination has vanished, never to return.

Women themselves have become more active in the cause of truly equal rights. Arab women are organized in their own section of Na'amat, the Histadrut women's organization, which has branches in various localities and has taken the initiative to sponsor vocational courses and Hebrew study groups for Arab women. The Arab women intellectual class has given rise to the pioneers of the Arab women's liberation movement – secretaries of cultural clubs, labor council activists, nurses, teachers, and school principals. Their overarching goal is to urge Arab women to aspire to progress in the course of struggle for the acknowledgment of equality of rights in Arab society. Nellie Karkabi, a Labour Party candidate for the twelfth Knesset, was a product of this group. Although her place on the list was not electable, it was the first time an Arab woman had appeared on such a slate.

All these changes, however, are still in their infancy. Even among young Arabs who wish to change the values of their society, conservatism in attitudes toward the status of the Arab woman is still very strong. Her insularity is sometimes perceived as a "national" asset. A young Arab once said: "If I went to the beach with my wife, it would be like betraying my nationality and becoming a Jew." When asked about the public baths in Egypt, he replied, "True, but they are in an Arab country."[83] Reluctance to touch this sensitive subject is diminishing today, but manifestations of conservatism are still strong.

Relations between young women and men in Arab villages have not yet fully overstepped the erstwhile conventions that banned social contact between the sexes. In the 1960s, it was common to hear a young Arab admit that when he wished to see his girlfriend, each of them would travel separately to the nearest Jewish town, and only there did they dare to meet.[84] Today, although the restrictions have loosened somewhat, relations between men and women are the field in which the influence of the West is weakest. There is no doubt that the attitude toward women is an extremely sensitive issue and, despite the changes, the Arab woman in Israel is still on the sidelines.

In 1965, Rustum Bastuni wrote bitterly about Arab society in Israel:

> Two hundred fifty thousands Israeli Arabs today are deprived of half of their human potential – the women.[85]

This is gradually changing. The basis for change has gradually been laid, particularly in women's education and measures that promote women's public activity.

In the past few years, Arab women intellectuals have begun to stand out in political circles. In this respect, they are following in the footsteps of their counterparts in eastern Jerusalem and the towns of Judea and Samaria, such as Dr Hanan 'Ashrawi, Zahira Kamal, and Fadwa Tuqan, who preceded them and have participated in the top echelons of the leadership for many years. The Association of Arab Women, founded in Jerusalem in 1965, swiftly showed itself to be a dynamic and highly influential organization.

During the intifadah, women were conspicuously involved in tumultuous demonstrations in which they confronted Israeli soldiers, and neighborhood committees were formed under women's leadership. In the same breath, however, wife-beating continued to persist, as did forced marriage and divorce. As the female director of the Palestine Advisory Center puts it, "The veil has not yet been lifted."[86]

The Intelligentsia

No one can doubt the swift spread of higher education among the minorities in Israel; it has wrought far-reaching socioeconomic changes and has become a crucial factor in determining the nature of labor supply among Israeli Arabs and in fashioning their employment structure in terms of industrial sectors and occupations.[87]

Taking a comparative view, statistical indicators illuminate the following traits in the development of education among Israeli Arabs:

1. The gap between males and females is highly evident in high schools, where girls account for 27 percent of total enrollment as against 49 percent at the primary level, where sweeping change has occurred.[88]
2. The gender gap narrows in higher education.
3. This contraction reflects greater inequality in the "apportionment of education" among Arab women, i.e., in the higher levels of education, the proportion of women is larger.
4. Among males, there is a negative correlation between the level of education and age, i.e., the older one is, the fewer years of schooling one has.
5. The illiteracy rate is lower among Israeli Arabs than in most Arab countries.

The level of education among minorities is lower on average than among nearly all Jewish population groups. However, the formation of an Israeli Arab intelligentsia marks an unmistakable and unequivocal change, a *qualitative* revolution. In a Government meeting on October 27, 1991, Minister David Magen described a study at the University of Haifa showing that Christian and Muslim Arab students were outperforming students from the Oriental Jewish communities.

At first the Arab students were few and far between, but their numbers have increased each year, and their presence at universities throughout the country is increasingly evident. Their confidence has risen, they have formed separate committees, and their social and scholastic activities have expanded, including confrontations with their Jewish counterparts on various issues.

The national issue has erupted at the forefront of controversy. The Arab students, regarding themselves as spokesmen for all Israeli Arabs, demonstrate and lead fierce struggles on problems affecting them or issues of importance to the Arab sector at any given time. Clashing factions have emerged within the student aggregate – communists against nationalists. Control of the committees has changed hands, sometimes amid serious clashes.

Students from Jish, Majd el-Kurum, 'Arrabeh, Baqa el-Gharbiyya, Rahat, and other Arab localities around the country feel free to express themselves frequently and outspokenly. They regard the campus as a stronghold, impervious to the authorities. Sometimes Arab students branched into blatant illegalities, including terrorist attacks.

The Arab students are unwilling to renounce their committees and merge into the general students' union. They have maintained their separate frameworks and even refused to participate with Jewish students in guarding the dormitories. They argued that it was their "national duty" to evade this duty and predicated their participation on the establishment of a Palestinian state. Needless to say, this rationale, no less than the attitude itself, set off a furor, but the Committee of Arab students in Jerusalem has not budged. On November 29, 1975, the committee issued a pamphlet making it clear beyond all doubt that the guard duty requirement was part of Israel's security system and that the Arab students could not meet the university authorities' demands as long as the Palestinians' right to self-determination had not been fulfilled.

Clashes among university students on national issues have erupted repeatedly, the camps lining up on opposite sides of whatever issue had arisen. Jewish students staged counter-demonstrations during protests organized by the Committee of Arab students in Jerusalem against President Sadat's peace initiative, on

"Land Day," during the war in Lebanon, at the outbreak of the Intifadah, after the massacre of seven Arab workers in Rishon Letzion in 1990, after the Iraqi invasion of Kuwait, and whenever a "burning issue" caused tension between the two peoples in Israel to flare.

The campus proved to be an extremely sensitive seismograph that was set off by the slightest tremor, responding immediately, caustically, and audaciously, without excessive concern for the niceties of scholasticism. The Arab students neither succeeded in integrating into campus life nor wished to assimilate. The extremists among them kept the fires burning by shouting, "We are here, proud Arabs, sons of the Palestinian people! You shall not oppress us! You shall not succeed in silencing the thunder of revolt that pulsates within us! You'll get nowhere with the traditional dignitaries, whose time has passed; we are a new generation, Arab intellectuals, vanguard of a people struggling for its independence, bold and free, and the PLO is our legitimate representative, like it or not!"

"We shall keep on demonstrating, more and more! We will not slow down," asserted Jaber 'Asaqlah, chairman of the committee of Arab students at the Hebrew University at a demonstration on Mount Scopus shortly before the outbreak of the Intifadah.

The Arab students' conferences, assemblies, declarations, and passion antagonized the Jewish students, who warned them on several occasions that they would not accept an Arab nationalist stronghold on any campus, be it in Jerusalem, Tel Aviv or Haifa. "This is an Israeli university, not a Fatah training camp," they would proclaim in a coarse tone not particularly imbued with student fraternity.[89] The Hebrew University students always opposed the separate activities of the Committee of Arab Students until the outbreak of the Intifadah, when a decision to recognize the committee was made. It was at this very time that the friction between Hadash and PNM supporters flared.[90]

Off campus, too, Arab students were frequently pushed to the side and treated as aliens. They often had problems finding housing when landlords "discovered" their nationality and brazenly shredded signed leases. In view of this difficulty, the universities had to make special efforts to accommodate Arab students in dormitories, which led to a relatively high concentration of Arabs there and, consequently, more nationalist activity and further friction with Jewish students.

The Arab students prefer to enroll in departments that pave their way to the liberal professions, particularly law and medicine.

This is borne out by the relatively high proportion of minorities among graduates of medical schools in the academic year 1988/89 – 9.1 percent as against a general average of 6 percent. The share of minority graduates in law is lower at 4.4 percent, apparently because the entrance requirements are toughened each year. In 1990 they accounted for 8.2 percent of degree holders in the humanities, 4 percent in the social sciences, 6.4 percent in the natural sciences, 6.1 percent in agriculture, and 4.2 percent in engineering and architecture.[91] This ratio remains more or less intact in 1995, although at the present writing the official statistics are not up-to-date.

In this respect, a more sober and careful choice of majors seems to be emerging: a perceptible decrease of enrollment in Arabic language and literature and Middle East history, coupled with a gradual transition to the exact sciences, although deliberate counseling for this is still lacking.[92]

Moreover, Arab students are younger than their Jewish counterparts when they begin their studies at the university or the Technion, because they are not liable to the draft. They are eager to earn academic degrees and do not always keep in mind the prospects of finding work after completing their studies in the distant future. They are attracted to prestigious subjects and rarely gravitate to majors with which they may fill a vacuum in Arab society, which badly needs college graduates in the social sciences, teaching, and agriculture. These are last choices, defaults invoked by students who failed to gain admission to schools of law, medicine, or engineering.[93]

Having completed their studies, Arabs accept their degrees and flaunt them proudly. From that time on, however, they are on their own, no longer able to rely on the student collective from which they derived confidence on campus. The family can support them financially until they find a suitable job or a way to earn a living independently. The hunt for a suitable job, however, is usually frustrating.

The Arab sector itself can absorb only a limited number of the thousands of Arab graduates, while many options on the "outside" are blocked for reasons of security. Some jobs do not lend themselves to Arab candidates because they are offered by the Ministry of Immigrant Absorption, the Jewish Agency for Israel, and similar institutions. On the whole, Jewish society is not yet ready to give appropriate consideration to an Arab candidate for a specific position, either in the private sector or in government offices. The government has made special efforts in this field, but even it has not succeeded in assuring large-scale hiring of Arab intellectuals in its own bureaus.

Most of the university graduates find themselves with no choice but to accept teaching jobs, often against their will, at a time when the status of teachers in Arab society has been seriously declining. This has caused a high incidence of unemployment among intellectuals, and the rate increased with economic recessions in Israel. The situation worsened in the past as waves of Jewish immigrants arrived, thus intensifying competition over jobs and relegating university-trained Arabs to the bottom of Jewish employers' priorities.

A broader infrastructure, which may ameliorate this urgent problem to some extent, is slowly taking shape in Arab localities. However, its impact is increasingly felt in the political sphere, where young Arab intellectuals have succeeded in recent years in taking over top leadership positions at all levels – the "Monitoring Committee," local agencies, political parties, and the Histadrut.

These academically-trained Arabs are the bearers of the "mission of the intellectuals" in Arab society, and there is no doubt that their personal frustration affects their political views, the intensity of their responses, and their attitude toward Israel. This is an expanding class that exudes ferment by its very nature. When it fails to attain its goals, whether these be the general goals of the sociopolitical community or the personal goals of its members, it is akin to a dangerous volcano that may erupt suddenly with great force.[94]

It is a class that has no doubts about its identity. The Arab intellectuals view themselves first and foremost as Palestinian Arabs. In every survey conducted since the Six Day War, they ranked their Israeli identity at the lowest level of priority.[95] This is a generation of proud Arab intellectuals, Israeli-born, educated at the Hebrew University, the Technion, and teachers' colleges, extremist in nationalist outlook but prepared to interrelate more intimately with the Jewish majority, even as it proclaims vociferously its national and socioeconomic grievances.

These rebels realized very quickly that they could not disregard the Jewish community, that they had to "explain themselves" to it in their own language and terms, and that they must reach its every secluded corner, break through to it, persuade it, gain its sympathy. They wrote on themes of vital importance to them *in Hebrew* and courted their targets, the Jewish readers, overtly. In their introductions, they explain the importance of making their acquaintance. The attorney Sabri Jiryis, who petitioned the High Court of Justice on behalf of the Al-Ard movement, wrote a book on Israeli Arabs from his own point of view. Fawzi el-Asmar chose the form of autobiography, *To Be an Arab in Israel*. El-Asmar writes:

> The person who helped me a lot while writing this book, and who encouraged me to continue, was my friend Sarit; this is not her real name, but this will be her name in the book because, for some reason, she did not want her real name to appear in it, nor even the name of the kibbutz where she lived for many years.[96]

Relationships between nationalist Arab intellectuals and Jewish women have become a common occurrence that has not been researched sufficiently. It sometimes seems that the minority intellectual, who sets out to fight for his people, needs the personal backing of a "daughter of the majority" in his confrontation with that majority. This may explain the fairly high rate of mixed marriages among members of the Israeli Arab political leadership.

Among Israeli Jews, a bipolar process is taking place. At one extreme is an upturn in nationalistic hostility toward Arabs as Arabs, based on abysmal ignorance; at the other extreme are expanding groups of intellectuals who are willing to recognize Israeli Arabs and identify with their struggle for equality. Eagerness to acquire first-hand knowledge about Israel's minority citizens is on the rise, and the Arab intellectuals respond avidly because they, too, are keen to make themselves known, to demand their rights, and to place Israeli society as they perceive it in the defendant's chair.

The outpouring of articles, monographs, and books by members of minority groups in Hebrew should be mandatory reading material for any Israeli Jew who does not wish to shut his eyes to reality and intends to cope with it without rose-tinted glasses. As the study of Arabic becomes more widespread, so the literature of the minorities, at all levels, will be read in the original – and understood in its vernacular context.

3

The Political Arena

The Traditional Leadership Fights for Survival

The political disposition of Israel's Arabs reflects their socioeconomic development from the time of the State's establishment. Its most salient feature seems to be the very process of change, along with the internal tension related to sharp turns and a constant clash between old and new.

By the time fighting broke out between Jews and Arabs in Mandatory Palestine following the UN partition resolution in November 1947, the traditional local leadership had already lost its dominance; the focus of decision-making had passed to the Arab states. Under the tutelage of the latter, the local leadership continued their rule, which progressively weakened and was accompanied by much internal friction, until its final disintegration with the declaration of Israeli independence.[1]

The leaders of the Palestinian Arab population were the first to flee in the mass exodus from the country in the winter of 1948. By the end of the war, the top political leadership had vanished without a trace. All organizational frameworks had completely disintegrated: associations, political parties, youth movements, and economic bodies. The web of Arab self-government in former Palestine had collapsed, including the Higher Muslim Council, the Higher Arab Committee, and the other institutions that were formed during the period of the Mandate.

At the end of the War of Independence, the first government of the infant State had to face the problems of an Arab minority in the Galilee, Negev, and Little Triangle areas struggling to find its way in the new reality, yet totally bereft of leadership in all spheres.[2] Gradually, prominent figures emerged, acquiring public influence, with the aim of capturing representative positions; however, due to the changed circumstances, the image of the emerging leadership was completely different in outlook compared to what had been in the past. This leadership grew up during the recovery of Israel's Arabs. It was aided with encouragement, direct and indirect, from the outside by the organs of the State which saw the need to foster it so as to ensure the regeneration of Arab life.

What, then, were the characteristics of this leadership, which was making its way from the crisis to a reality permeated with contradictions?

The Traditional Fabric and the Formation of Political Leadership

The various patterns of traditional society, which had taken form over many generations, created two basic, interlocking frameworks:[3] (1) The *hamulah* (clan), or the extended family; (2) The confessional community, which has served as a focus of the individual's loyalty beyond the *hamulah*.

At times there was an overlapping between these factors. Indeed, in communally mixed villages there was often an internal dividing line, although the communal framework was too broad to be preserved in its entirety, and there were often internal lines of division as well, by clan.[4]

The basic unit of the traditional political structure was the clan, and as long as its position was firm and unchallenged, it had control over its members. Internal conflicts between households or competition for clan leadership were, as a rule, kept internal, although over time, they could result in an internal schism. The size of a clan is always of critical importance in determining its political power. The broader its base, the stronger the position of its leader, although additional factors also determined his stature: his personality, his economic means and "outside" connections – with governmental authorities and other institutions – through which he would settle the affairs of his clan members. This intermediary power, called *wasta*, had tremendous impact on traditional Arab society, as it created the dependence of the clan upon its leader. It was he who came into contact with the authorities and other external bodies in the name of clan members. He had the sole prerogative to conduct negotiations, whether to obtain a tax exemption, credit for seeds, or a license for the breadwinner of one of the clan households. It was even he who contracted with a lawyer in the name of a clan member who needed one.

In the past, the *wasta* had taken root and was granted formal recognition, both by the Ottoman authorities and the British High Commissioner. The clan elder even held sway over members who held official positions, men who had the power to grant or withhold benefits. The authority to decide how to exploit the connections, positions, and stature of his people was concentrated in his hands. Hence, even when dozens of people in a village would take up various positions outside the village – in government offices, the police, and in large economic concerns – the traditional rule of the elders remained intact.[5] In its early stages this process enhanced the influence of the clan heads, although later on it was a stumbling block to them, opening fissures within the entire clan system.

The power held by the clan heads enabled them to amass considerable wealth, oft-times through coercion. Within every village, traditional rivalries between clans hardened, which helped preserve the influence of the elders. Inter-clan rivalry was one of the foundation stones of politics up to the end of the British Mandate. With education, a strengthening of ties to the cities, and the coming into their own of those who held outside positions, who were no longer willing to put their power unconditionally at the disposal of the clan elder, fissures could be found in the traditional structure by the end of the first decade of Israeli statehood. Changes in the traditional political structure began making themselves felt:

1. The relative importance of the size of the clan increased, because of the importance of elections in determining the composition of the institutions of the state, local government, and the trade unions.

A large clan, united around its leader, constituted solid backing for him in his political struggles. A leader was often measured by the number of votes assured him at the time of election.[6]

2. At the same time, the reality of Israel also hindered the power of the large clans. This was in part due to the essential contradiction between a democratic regime and the clan system, and more directly due to economic processes, which undermined the position of the dominant clan elders.

The place of the clan as the basic political unit was initially taken by the extended family, as its closer blood ties were a factor in preserving internal cohesion, and the ties of economic dependence within it were stronger, although a constant slackening process could be discerned within the extended family, as well.

3. In Israel, the power of *wasta* declined because of the direct contact of government offices and public institutions with the individual. Work at outside places of employment, and even more so the broadening of the class of educated young people, had an impact on this process. Nevertheless, this age-old institution continued. Its beneficiaries fought for its survival. They improved their methods and endeavored to adapt to the new needs. As recently as the 1970s, it was not unheard of for a dignitary of the old generation to go to the office of the dean of a university faculty and try to intervene on behalf of someone from his village or community who was not accepted. He would frequently be accompanied by the youngster involved. Ironically, the elder who so took pains for the education of his protégé would invariably be bereft of even elementary schooling.

The clan elders, the heads of extended families, the dignitaries of the confessional communities, and indeed the entire traditional leadership fought in vain for the soul of the younger generation. It was a struggle doomed from the start to failure.

4. The nature of internal village relations continued in Israel, despite the far-reaching ramifications of the war of 1948. The establishment of the State did not result in a cessation of inter-clan conflict. At times, it remained as it had been, although no longer interwoven in a nation-wide struggle, which, during the Mandate, constituted a central axis of the contentious sphere that was the political life of Arab Palestine. The forms of inter-clan rivalry also changed.

The contest between rival families was rendered local after the creation of the State. The lack of national leadership resulted in a severing of the threads that had once connected clans in different villages, on the basis of their affiliation in larger rivalries. In various villages rival clans grouped together as a means to bolster their position *vis-à-vis* their deeper adversaries, who themselves coalesced with rivals, each attempting to obtain dominance over the other, but each, in the end, in its own way, blocking the rise of forces that threatened the traditional order. However, isolated from a national framework, clan rivalries gave way to an alternative scale of values that struck, and progressively deepened, roots in the Arab village. The transition period accelerated in pace, although the tradition of generations braced itself to moderate it. In the beginning, that transition imposed adaptation on the existing frameworks, while a thorough change was taking hold of the clans and the balance of power between them. The transition period brought about the decline of once-dominant clans and the rise of rival clans, while maintaining the traditional framework. Such revolutionary change in the balance of power did not always reduce old animosities, but did occasionally variegate them.

In some villages, the traditional balance in strength between rival clans was upset because they were unequal in their abilities to withstand the new conditions. As they were locked in rivalry, the signs of disintegration were already discernible in one of them. The clan elder had lost his absolute authority, to be replaced by heads of households who in turn found preservation of the extended family difficult. Layer after layer was removed from the old structure. Other clans that had previously given their support withdrew, or qualified, it. Then the rival clan seemingly gained the upper hand, but it was a gain in relative strength, and only a temporary one, because the same phenomenon commenced against them, and so on.

The process varied from village to village, depending on a variety of factors: (a) its occupational structure; (b) the prevailing educational level; (c) its communal composition; (d) distance from a city; (e) village size, the amount of its agricultural land and that land's fertility; (f) whether it was located on a plain or in the mountains; (g) the nature of its surrounding area; (h) its distance from the border; (i) the quality of basic services, mainly water and electricity, schools, access roads and medical services.

These factors were interwoven, and all had an impact on the prevalence of outside employment, which in turn was an immensely important source of feedback.

Yet, there were still villages where it seemed that the traditional structure had been preserved, with political life continuing to flow in the same time-hewn channels. However, in such villages as well, profound change was taking shape.

Initially, traditional social frameworks made common cause against the forces of change. Old animosities were shunted aside, clan heads who had never exchanged greetings met and extended aid to one another. This was inevitably one of the critical stages in the transitional process that took hold of Israeli Arab politics. Yet here as well, a deep-rooted contradiction of traditional Arab society became manifest: internal fragmentation is an integral part of its essence.

5. Reality in Israel even changed the *character* of political life in Arab society. Furthermore, traditional forces came to operate in new patterns which had been unknown during the British Mandate. On the "outside," beyond the clan, confessional community or village, new institutional frameworks, born of the democratic regime – such as the Histadrut Labor Federation and political parties – were being created. They could not be ignored, as they spread their arms into the Arab villages and influenced life there, directly and indirectly.

The old leadership perforce integrated into the new frameworks, even if such frameworks were less comfortable than the arenas of old. By their very nature, they clashed with the traditional political structure, which nevertheless became dependent upon them. Hence, the traditional structure sought to adapt to them and adopted the new "rules of the game."

The last of the traditional leaders was, without doubt, Seif ed-Din Zu'bi, member of the Knesset and mayor of Nazareth until 1975, and who has since died. He derived his power from the Zu'bia clan, which was concentrated in Nazareth and seven surrounding villages. Yet internal contradictions developed in the fabric of this clan, compromising Seif ed-Din's political power. On the other hand, this traditional leader advanced his public standing by expanding the range of his ties beyond the clan and entrenching himself in the Israeli establishment as one of the country's outstanding Arab leaders. His political grip was compromised when he was unseated as mayor of Nazareth, in the face of new political currents. His cousin, 'Abd el-'Aziz Zu'bi, was appointed deputy minister of health in early 1975. His political development was different, as he had hitched his fortunes to Mapam.[7] Hence, he was an opponent to Seif ed-Din within the Zu'bia clan, although without any doubt, he benefited from his clan origins, if to a lesser degree.

None of the other large clans produced leaders of comparable stature. In Nazareth, the wide-flung Fahum clan declined; in Galilee villages and the Little Triangle, the focus of political power passed from the clan to the extended family.

Traditional Leadership: Almost Entirely Local or Communal

No national Arab leadership appeared in Israel until the establishment of the Committee of Council Heads. There were four main reasons for this:

1. Palestinian Arab leaders were left outside Israel, either because they fled or simply lived in cities left outside the borders of the State – east Jerusalem, the three "Big Triangle" cities of Nablus, Tulkarm and Jenin, in Ramallah and Hebron.
2. The prestige of the old leadership suffered as a result of the defeat, and its various ramifications.
3. The geographic fragmentation of Arab population concentrations. The distance between the Galilee and the Negev, or even the Little Triangle, engendered a segmented leadership. Contact between these areas even during the Mandate was weak.
4. The traditional leaders who came to power after establishment of the State faced complex challenges for which they had scant preparation, education, or experience. Hence, they found it difficult to extend their influence beyond the family, village, or vicinity upon which their power rested.

Seif ed-Din Zu'bi was perhaps the only one who succeeded in acquiring wide influence, beyond the Zu'bia clan, Nazareth, or even the Galilee, but even he never attained the stature of a truly national leader.

The attempts made by two veteran leaders to reach the pinnacle of Arab leadership in Israel are fascinating in this context: Nimr el-Hawari, a lawyer who represented Arab refugees at the Rhodes armistice talks at the end of the 1948 war, and Archbishop George Hakim, Primate of the Greek Catholic Church in Israel. They were both "refugees," since they left the country during the war. Both returned, with the consent of the Israeli authorities, clearly aiming to take up the reigns of *national* power. They were different in background, character, their circles of influence, and the political paths they took in Israel. However, both of them, in their aspiration to become leaders of Israeli Arabs, accentuated the void created in the Arab leadership. During the Mandate, Nimr el-Hawari commanded the Najadah, a paramilitary organization preparing to fight the Jews, but which was quickly routed. He became a public figure among the refugees and was allowed to return to Israel in 1951. He failed in his attempt to win a seat in the Knesset that year, and ever since has led a vocal group of Arab nationalists that also included the Christian lawyer Elias Kusa and the Druze figure 'Abdallah Kheir. After a while, their association broke up and el-Hawari, seeking a political prop, backed Mapam in the 1961 elections. In 1965, he ran in the

Nazareth municipal elections on an independent list he established, apparently in collaboration with Rafi.[8] He also drew public attention with his courtroom appearances, in which he frequently attacked the government; he did, however, apparently reconcile himself to Israel's existence. His repeated attempts to reach the pinnacle of leadership ended in successive failures.

His dream, upon returning to Israel, of exploiting the confusion and resulting void and filling it with the force of his own political personality, was shattered. His assessment of his chances, based solely on the halo of his past, proved unfounded. The defeat shattered the prop on which the strength of the Mandate period leadership rested, even though it fell short of removing that leadership altogether from the political stage, so long as its members could derive clan or communal support.

It is doubtful whether el-Hawari's former troops considered the authority he once had over them sufficient reason for supporting him after his return. Many of them no doubt had reservations about him *because* of that factor; many Israeli Arabs still saw the picture of their leaders' flight in their mind's eye in bold relief. It is no wonder that Nimr el-Hawari, a commander who deserted the field of battle, could not reach a position of leadership without a large clan or confessional community as the vehicle for such a comeback.

The case of George Hakim, who also made his appearance as a "returning refugee," stands out in stark contrast. He quickly climbed the ladder to leadership, deriving his political support from the Greek Catholic community, of which he was leader.[9] Immediately upon his return in 1949, Hakim threw himself into the task of forging the life of his community. He devoted his considerable energy to building himself up as a leader and to extending the scope of his influence. He adapted to the new reality. Relying on his solid backing from the Greek Catholic community, he dared speak out against the extreme views toward Israel of the Arab nationalist movement; at the same time, he criticized the Israeli government bitterly, positioning himself as spokesman for all Israeli Arabs.

Without doubt, he managed to extend his influence and establish it, mainly on the basis of the support of the Greek Catholic community. Here lies one of the critical differences between him and Nimr el-Hawari, who was not able to call upon a traditional social framework as a political prop.

Without the communal support he received, it is highly likely that

George Hakim, despite the force of his personality, would not have succeeded in attaining a position of prominence. During a trip to Rome in 1965, manifestos against him were issued, reflecting fermentation in certain circles within his community, thus damaging his prestige outside the Greek Catholic community, as well. Upon his return, he managed to restore his position, but despite all his efforts, he never succeeded in becoming the leader of all Israeli Arabs.

The leaders of other confessional communities lacked the type of solid support the Greek Catholic community was able to give, either because their communities lacked such solid organization or were too small. No Muslim leader of stature ever emerged. The last Muslim authority of consequence to remain in the country was Sheikh Taher et-Tabari, who in his last years served as *Qadi* of Nazareth and the Galilee. He was enveloped by the halo of religious authority, which was probably enhanced by his political pronouncements, as well. But his 1952 call for a population exchange between Israel and the Arab countries evoked no response. He never became a national leader and his political influence was nil.

The Druze leader Sheikh Amin Tarif attained prominence as spiritual leader of that community, although his stature was also marred by internal strife. Since no national Arab leadership emerged, the traditional leaders felt constrained to cooperate among themselves from time to time, making mutual compromises, in order to preserve their positions.

The Critical Test: Knesset and Local Elections

An election year is often connoted with irony in the Arab sector as *sanat al-marhaba*, or "the year of greetings." The contending candidates come to the villages with greetings, promises, and enticements for all.

It is in election years that the real contest, a bitter one, is waged for key positions in the Knesset and local councils. The results have decisive impact on the relation of forces between competing individuals and rival clans, and between traditional lists and the newer political trends.

Hence, constant tension accompanies election campaigns, during which old contradictions are either woken or consolidated, and latent loyalties come to life. Traditional forces compete among themselves, suspended between the public they appeal to and the Israeli parties that "adopt" them. A consistent ideological line there never was, although there are repeated calls for increased economic development and a raising of educational standards. Traditional lists generally pay little attention to broad political issues, preferring to concentrate on local issues while attacking their opponents. In Knesset elections, the traditional political forces have been arrayed against parties that have attacked them furiously, or at times joined them, by adopting clan-based lists of candidates. Unlike the past, the clan or family lists in local elections now tend increasingly to consist of young, educated leaders chosen for their charisma.

In Knesset elections, it is impossible to guarantee seats to even a fraction of clan or family candidates anxious to reach the national legislature. Hence, there has been a progressive weakening of the traditional political frameworks. Internal strife causes a split in the vote. There has been a complete waning of the authority of the traditional leaders who in the past dictated the way their clans or confessional communities voted, even if there was no clearly discernible connection between the vote and the special interests of the clan or community; it was impossible in any event to have complete representation for every strong clan, confessional community or village.

On the other hand, in elections for local councils, direct links to a clan help. Clan members vote so that one of their own gets to sit on the council. Many young clan members split their votes, voting one way for the Knesset and another for the local council, with resulting clear-cut differences in the vote tallies for the different levels of government. Such "split-voting" indicates that there is still significance to the clan, as opposed to a nationalistic focus of identification, which is broader in scope and hence less immediate. The new political currents do not always make themselves felt in inter-clan struggles for control of villages. There are educated young people who constantly reiterate their opposition to the traditional frameworks, yet find themselves tied to their families and want to see them overcome their rivals; the prime consideration is to build up personal political strength on the basis of family connections, and this overrides other aims. But there are signs of transition. Although the clan has not been destroyed, the range of its political strength is no longer what it was in the past. It is weaker, more fragmented, and much more exposed to the blows of new political currents born of Israel's complex political reality.

The Emergence of New Trends

Even during the British Mandate, Arab politics was not a unitary phenomenon, existing entirely along the lines of the traditional structure. The rise of the city and the appearance of a working class helped engender the formation of a Communist party, although it lacked real influence. Its sway in the villages was marginal, and even in the cities its ranks were thin.

New political currents detached from traditional frameworks, gradually began making their appearance in Israel, occupying the void engendered by the decline of traditional influence. There can be no doubt that with the decline of the clan or confessional community as the basic socio-political unit, there has been a concurrent rise in the relative importance of the individual. The ordinary Arab "man in the street" has become less dependent on the *wasta* of traditional leaders, less dependent on the clan to fall back upon and less willing to accept its authority.

The young Arab in Israel is fully conscious of the profound socio-political changes he is destined to bear in the society which produced him. He is not completely free of the traditional frameworks, and realizes the weakness of his socio-political position, which is at times painfully salient. The young Arab struggles to find his way in the complexity engendered by the transitional period, in which his loyalties, based on familial links, have weakened. He now struggles to define his perception of his identity; he feels himself different from his father, as well as from his Jewish peers, but has not yet been able to articulate within himself the essence of his own life.

This, then, is the background of the "crisis of the crossroads," at the center of which the Israeli-born Arab inquires about his identity and the thrust of his loyalties. He desperately needs to be able to commit himself body and soul to some framework based upon the individual, where he can satisfy his yearnings and find answers to such basic questions as: Who am I? What is the focal point of my life? What are the goals with which I seek to identify?

The elders of his family, village and community have been

removed from the political scene and are not likely to help guide his reflections. The young generation of Arabs is searching for leaders of stature who achieved positions of influence, not through clan connections, but on personal merit: higher education, astuteness, an ability to represent and an innovative view of the world, which includes clear road signs for the complex existence of the Arab minority in Israel.

The growth of such a leadership was not easy. Its fabric was spun slowly, with "substitute figures" making an occasional appearance. In the meantime, organizations based on the individual have been established. Among the suggestions for filling the void in identity are: the Arab nation, the PLO, and/or world-embracing ideologies. These, in whole or in part, direct the youthful enthusiasm of the young member of the Arab minority against his country and even against the elders of his clan. At first glance it seems that answers have been given to the vital questions. Yet it transpires that their "solution" is a black-and-white solution; the two colors contradict each other. Reality, of course, is composed of the entire spectrum of political and social shades. Despite all their criticism, young Arabs are not entirely willing to turn their backs on their clans, their elders, their traditional religious leaders.

Even the ideology offered them seems foreign, distant. Even manifestations of their natural inclination to identify with the PLO is not consonant with their need to find a place for themselves as citizens of Israel, in which they grew up and against which they are called to take action.

The new organizations include activists of all ages who are anxious to lead Israel's Arabs. While they are "liberated" from the traditional frameworks, they do not yet meet the expectations of the younger generation. Hence, at this stage of Israeli-Arab sociopolitical development, the questions remain unanswered. This being the case, the younger generation of Arabs shuttle between poles: between the clan and "the party" or "the movement," between the traditional structures and new currents. Their "party" tendencies are reflected more in Knesset elections, less in local or municipal elections. They do not, however, join as members of a party, which remains a kernel consisting of a small number of activists.

We shall illustrate these tendencies in the following pages, by describing the development of the main political organizations, which had been established in opposition to the traditional leadership, from which they were different both in form and content.

Communist Party Activity among Arabs in Israel

The Communist Party did not actually originate in the State of Israel; its basic structure and constituent groups gestated in the British Mandate period. Until 1943, the Palestinian Communist Party, known as the PCP, was active in Palestine under joint Jewish-Arab leadership. Most of its Arab functionaries also belonged to the Arab national movement and participated in attacks on Jewish settlements, especially at the height of the Arab uprising in 1936–37.

The internal contradictions intensified during World War II. The rising power of the Arab intelligentsia within the party, under new leaders such as Emil Habibi, Bulus Farah, Emil Toma and Fuad Nassar, undermined the status of the party's old leader, Redwan el-Hilu (alias Moussa) and friction with Jewish members became increasingly severe. The final schism occurred in 1943.

A new Arab Communist group appeared on the Arab scene at this time, the self-styled National Liberation League (*'Usbat at-Taharrur al-Watani*). Gradually it took over the Arab Communist leadership by superseding the old-time proletarian guard of the PCP, headed by "Moussa." Unlike the PCP, the NLL was composed almost exclusively of Arab intellectuals, among whom proletarian origins were not a prerequisite. In the very first stage of its development, the NLL dissociated itself from the Jewish Communist organizations. To emphasize its all-Arab nature, the NLL summarily rejected membership applications proffered by Jews. It sought to align itself completely with Arab nationalist aspirations. Its political platform adopted the major views of the supreme Palestinian leader of the time, the *Mufti*, Hajj Amin el-Husseini, although, unlike him, it was prepared to "recognize" Jewish inhabitants as citizens of the Palestinian Arab state. The *Mufti* reserved this "special privilege" for Jews who had reached the country before the Balfour Declaration of 1917.

The NLL leadership stayed in close touch with the *Mufti*. On June 23, 1946, the Communist journal *Al-Ittihad* expressed warm congratulations to the *Mufti* on his escape to Egypt from France, where he had been kept in prison following his cooperation with Nazi Germany during World War II. Delegations in his honor set out continuously until the war broke out in Palestine.[10]

After Soviet foreign minister Gromyko declared Soviet support for the UN partition plan of Palestine in 1947, the NLL split into two. One faction, headed by Fuad Nassar and Emil Habibi, accepted the Soviet decision-making prerogative; the other, the "rebel camp," subordinated itself to the *Mufti*'s Higher Arab Committee and opposed partition vehemently. This faction was headed by Emil Toma and Moussa Dajani. In the meantime, the fires of war became hotter, and the Arab Communist leaders of all factions were dispersed in every direction. Many fled; others were taken prisoner by the Egyptian army.[11]

When the fighting subsided, many key players in the Arab Communist organizations began to return to Israel. The senior leaders – Emil Habibi, Tawfiq Tubi, the attorney Hanna Naqara, and Emil Toma – returned from Lebanon, re-established their headquarters in Haifa and Nazareth, and reconstructed the cells of the NLL. Under the new circumstances, they saw no choice but to bury their former differences, at least for the time being. Therefore, they gladly accepted the initiative of the Jewish Communist leaders to reunite. The result was the establishment of the Israel Communist Party (Maki – by its Hebrew acronym), re-embracing the remnants of the PCP, the active members of the NLL's two factions, and the Jewish Communists who had masterminded the formation of the party. Ironically, the ranks of the resurrected party were bolstered by the Israeli Army, which, as it advanced into Sinai in late 1948, liberated Arab Communists whom the Egyptians had incarcerated at the Abu Aguila camp.[12]

Arab leaders now took over senior positions in the Israel Communist Party alongside the Jewish comrades against whom they had struggled so bitterly before Israel gained its independence. However, the conflict between the two factions had not been resolved, and the schism persisted throughout the history of the Israeli Communist Party, despite constant attempts to gloss it over. Finally, in 1965, the party split again, as an inevitable consequence of the internal contradiction of its composition.

This notwithstanding, Maki functioned in its early years with great momentum. It was the only Arab political framework in independent Israel that managed to rehabilitate itself with relative alacrity and shrug off the aftermath of the bloody hostilities, which had just ended and left a deep and destructive impression on the Arab population in general.

Maki was a whirlwind from its very inception – a vigorous

political force that aspired to supplant and succeed the traditional groupings. From its first steps in Israel, Maki exhibited its solidarity with the Arab national movement, viewing it as an effective path to support of the Arabs in Israel.

In October 1949, Maki leader Meir Wilner emphasized his party's support for "the autonomy of both peoples in the State of Israel." The phrasing of Maki's attitude toward recognition of Israel, however, always tended to be vague, camouflaged behind a general style that was sometimes ambivalent or allusive. This was the result of Maki's wish to find a common denominator between its Jewish and Arab constituencies. The final wording may also have been the outcome of protracted internal bargaining between two basic attitudes that were difficult to bridge. The Arab national stance usually won out.

In its first national convention, Maki adopted a resolution acknowledging the "just aspirations of the Arab people in Palestine for autonomy in political life and its natural and lawful right to determine its destiny." The resolution also went out of its way to stress: "We are struggling to establish an independent and democratic Arab state on the other side of Palestine."

The Arab Communists attempted time and again to assert that the State of Israel within its present boundaries must not be condoned, but this gambit evidently met with the opposition of Maki's Jewish leaders. They were afraid of such an explicit declaration, which was tantamount to advocating the amputation of bits of Israel as the first step toward its destruction. In 1952, the Maki convention adopted a platform that included the following key sentence on this basic issue: "The Arabs of Israel have the right to self-determination, to the extent of secession."

This compromise formula was the outcome of a pitched debate in which the Jewish Communists made most of the concessions without satisfying their Arab colleagues' demands. The platform also included a demand to revoke the territorial annexations and to recognize the right of the Arabs of Palestine to establish their own state and the Arab refugees' right to return. Maki's internal squabbles continued at each succeeding convention. The Arab leaders did not conceal their support of the Egyptian president, Jamal 'Abd en-Nasser, repeatedly stressing their ultranationalist attitude toward Israel. The Jewish Communists attacked Israeli government policy but refused to accede to their Arab counterparts' narrow-minded nationalism, which they regarded as the antithesis of Marxist worldview.

A general uproar broke out at the Maki conference in June 1956, where preparations for the thirteenth party convention were made. Arab leaders in the Central Committee sought to insert in the convention platform a clause explicitly favoring the contraction of Israel's territory to the confines stipulated in the November 1947 partition plan.

Most of the Jewish members of the committee protested, arguing that it was the wrong time to expound such a view so unequivocally. They sought a compromise formula and found it by stating once again that the members of both peoples had the "right to self-determination." This time they even managed to delete from their draft the loaded words "to the extent of secession." The Arab nationalists in the party, incensed by this "retreat," succeeded in restoring the key phrase in the final resolution of the convention itself (June 1957), which was hammered out in protracted bargaining:

> It is the duty of the State of Israel to recognize the right to self-determination, to the extent of secession, of the Palestinian Arab people, this right being the basis of the solution to the territorial problem, and to recognize the right of the Arab refugees to return to and rehabilitate themselves in their homeland. By the same token, the Arab countries must recognize the State of Israel and conclude a treaty of peace with it [and] acknowledge Israel's right to freedom of shipping in the Red Sea and the Suez Canal . . .

It seems that, in exchange for the right to secede, the party moderates had managed to work out a less extreme formula for Jewish consumption. The demand to "rescind the territorial annexations," included in the 1952 platform, was shelved, and the convention stipulated that "a solution to the issues at dispute between Israel and the Arab countries be sought solely through peaceful channels and negotiations between the sides."

These resolutions, generated after tumultuous debate, were not the last word for the Arab Communists. After the convention, they agitated to carry their ultranationalist policy to full expression. Their partnership with the Jewish comrades was an obstacle that they wished to overcome, and their attitudes were fueled by mounting tension in the Arab sector that reflected the upheavals sweeping the Arab countries.

Their plan began to take shape in late 1957. Within the highest Arab leadership of Maki, the nucleus of a national liberation movement was secretly formed. The purpose of the new movement was to undermine Israel with the help of an underground military arm that would operate alongside the political struggle as it reached its peak. The ideational platform of the breakaway movement lacked the labyrinthine rhetoric that characterized the platform of Maki, the multifaction parent party. This platform stated unequivocally that the State of Israel was "a manifestation of Imperialism," that Israel should be regarded as "occupied Arab territory," and that the Arabs living there were an oppressed people in occupied territory. The "National Liberation Movement" set out to unite all Arab groups that feared for their people's future. It would integrate with the national Arab movements that fought Israel and would maintain close relations with the Soviet Union, whose support was so vital to the struggle.

The movement's ultimate goal was indeed to destroy Israel, but to achieve this it had to adopt a phased strategy. Therefore, it refrained from broadcasting its goal at once. The objective of the first phase was to implement the 1947 partition plan, i.e., to constrict Israel's post-1948 boundaries, and to obtain the right to self-determination for Israeli Arabs and the right of return for Arab refugees. This would ready Israel for the *coup de grâce*, the country collapsing from within and masses of returning refugees embracing it in a deadly vice.

The new enterprise matured in early 1958, at which point the Jewish members of the Maki leadership discovered it, to its founders' dismay. The Jews realized immediately what was going on and began to pressure the Maki core to nip it in the bud.

In fact, the Jewish leaders had considerable influence in the party, and the extremist Arab factions were afraid of a frontal collision with them. They did not consider the time ripe for such a confrontation, because the first indications of the rift between Egypt and the Soviet Union had become visible just then. This conflict ruptured the united front that the Arab Communist leaders had envisioned, one that would include both the Soviet bloc and the Arab nationalist movement headed by Jamal 'Abd en-Nasser in the attempt to defeat Israel. Consequently, the Arab Communist leaders fell into sharp disagreements about the proper course of action under the new circumstances. The attempt to set up a clandestine movement had failed, but the motives for doing so had not disappeared. The pulse of Arab nationalism continued to throb within the Communist Party, seeking a breakthrough. An outburst that occurred during the May Day demonstrations in 1958 reflected the prevailing moods. Maki had always considered May Day the ideal occasion to flaunt its image as the patron of "the oppressed Arab minority in Israel" with giant banners denouncing "the expropriationist Israeli government" and advocating "the repatriation of Arab refugees," "the return of stolen land," and "a halt to national oppression."

This time, the Maki processions in Nazareth and Umm el-Fahm were accompanied by violent rioting and deliberate clashes with Israeli police. The security forces restored order by arresting the chief inciters.

The Arab Communists considered this development an opportunity to obtain compensation for their failure to establish an underground national liberation movement, and they quickly established an "Arab Public Committee for the Protection of Detainees and Deportees." Thus, the stated intention of this committee sounded very humble at first. To expand the base of the committee, nationalist Arab activists outside Maki were co-opted, including three aging notables: Yanni Qustandi Yanni, chairman of the Kafr Yassif local council; attorney Elias Kusa of Haifa; and Jabur Jabur, mayor of Shefar'am.[13] The new auspice swiftly metamorphosed into the Arab Front, founded on July 6, 1958, under Yanni Yanni, a venerable, seasoned operator known for his hatred of the State of Israel.

Some members of the Arab Communist leadership may have entertained the hope that the fledgling organization would rise to greatness and become the nucleus of the long-awaited resistance movement. However, the Jewish leaders of Maki were vigilant, although without losing sight of the utility that the new organization might bring to the party. Maki extended its patronage to the Arab Front and thrust its own goals upon the new grouping until the two were virtually indistinguishable. The only factor that separated them was the omission of several social and economic issues from the Front's platforms so as not to identify too closely with Marxist doctrine.

The Arab Front, renamed the Popular Front some time later, was headed by a thirteen-member executive composed mostly of Maki stalwarts. Branches were set up in several villages, but they were very small. The Arab community knew perfectly well that the Popular Front was simply an extension of Maki. Ultranationalist activists in the Popular Front, unable to accept this situation, resigned about a year after the Front was founded in order to establish the Al-Ard group.

The Popular Front was a virtual stillborn, its main activities focusing on unsuccessful attempts to instigate mass protest rallies, incite Arab villages against the government, and bombard international organizations with defamatory anti-Israel memoranda. From time to time it published "nonrecurrent" journals bearing various permutations of the title *Al-Jabhah* ("The Front").

The storm that swept Maki in 1958–59 was followed by a period of relative calm in relations between Jewish and Arab leaders among the party's top echelons. The disagreements, however, did not dissipate. The party attempted to burn the candle at both ends by presenting itself as the zealous champion of struggle for Israel's Arabs and trying to soft-pedal its solidarity with Arab nationalism for Jewish ears. Its statements were frequently ambiguous or deliberately vague and general. This two-facedness was the result of the conflicting currents that warred within the party and of an attempt to maximize support by invoking tactical camouflage.

It was on the grounds of this "tactical need" that the party moderates, before the fourteenth party convention in the spring of 1961, refrained from mentioning in their agenda the phrase attached to the formulation of the right to self-determination: "to the extent of secession." Again, however, the Arab members protested the omission, and once again election considerations were unable to placate them.

Over the next four years, the Arab leaders gained power in the central committee and the dispute within the Maki leadership intensified. Impatient young Arabs dropped out of its ranks from 1958 on, as the Arab leaders continued to bridge the differences with their Jewish counterparts in order to hold the party together. The Arab leaders, alarmed at this development, stepped up their pressure to voice the Arab nationalist message. The Jewish Communist leaders, who had not made significant inroads in Jewish public opinion, opposed them.

They sharply condemned the "compromise" line that their party had adopted, noting its proximity to the stance of the Arab nationalist movement. They could not shirk responsibility for the blatant statements printed in the Arabic-language Maki organ, *Al-Ittihad*, and in leaflets distributed in Arab villages. With dizzying speed their Arab colleagues backed them into a corner, for they no longer retained the degree of control in the Central Committee that they had had in 1958.

Shortly before the fifteenth convention in 1965, Maki hovered on the brink of rupture and attempted desperately to heal the inevitable schism. Its two camps were now diametrically opposed; its partition line was almost identical to the country and bore a surprising resemblance to the schism within the Palestinian Communist camp in 1943.

The elections to the convention would determine the balance of forces in the party leadership. The "Jewish" faction, headed by Shemeul Mikunis, Moshe Sneh, and Esther Wilenska, had a considerable likelihood of success under the Maki electoral system, because a majority of branches in Jewish localities supported them. In the Central Committee, however, the rival faction, headed by Tawfiq Tubi, Emil Habibi, and the Jewish leader Meir Wilner, held the advantage. The latter did not flinch from exploiting its position of power to push through a resolution changing the electoral system, thus assuring its victory *a priori* by technical means. To foil this scheme, the local branches of the Israel Communist Party embarked on a "revolt of the districts."

The discord spread; the chasm was too wide to bridge. It was described at length in the pages of the party's Hebrew-language paper, *Qol ha-'Am*, which made an attempt to keep its coverage "balanced." Party functionaries still asserted emphatically that "no matter how fierce the debate within the Communist Party is, it need not lead to a schism." However, the path to compromise was increasingly hard to find. An agreement was almost reached after arduous negotiations, but the Tubi–Wilner group backed out at the last minute. The "Arab" faction of the party evidently stepped up its pressure, expressing confidence in its power, and the schism became a fact after two separate conventions were held, each with its own platform, reflecting the ideational conflict that had broken the party in two.

Thus the New Communist List, known by its Hebrew acronym Rakah, came into being alongside Maki – two Israeli Communist parties, "sisters" but sworn rivals. Maki remained chiefly a "Jewish" Communist party, although its leaders were initially loath to admit the loss of their foothold in the Arab sector. Only a handful of Arabs remained in Maki. To sustain its declared image as a "mixed" party, it promoted Arabs who had not held key positions to the top. Notable among them were Muhammad el-Khatib and Muhammad Hassan Jabbarin. *Qol ha-'Am* became the organ of Maki. Its activities in Arab localities dwindled greatly, although its platform still stressed its allegiance to Israeli Arabs and concern for their problems. The party eventually disappeared from the political landscape, succeeded by other parties on the left.

Rakah, in contrast, focused its attention on the Arab population. An estimated one-third of its members were Jewish Communists, and it maintained a headquarters in the Jewish sector by renting a small private apartment in Tel Aviv. Its Hebrew-language newspaper, *Zo Haderekh*, was also based here, but the small circulation of the paper gave clear indication of its ineffectiveness in the Jewish sector.

Rakah was never independent, of course. It was always a Communist party that toed the Kremlin line, with which it identified unreservedly. Until Israel-Soviet relations were severed in 1967, Rakah leaders stayed in close touch with the Soviet ambassador in Israel. At the time of the Maki break-up, the ambassador apparently worked frenetically to prevent it, to the extent of visiting Nazareth at the height of the tension in June 1965. Even the might of the Soviet Union, however, was of no use at that critical time; once its authority over the party weakened, the schism began, as in 1943, as if according to some rigid, unchallengeable formula.[14]

After the schism, Rakah had to develop its own separate mechanism and wage uncompromising struggle with Maki for the party's assets, both human (members and sympathizers) and material (the organizational set-up, branches, and property). The new party found it easy to emphasize its Arabness. Although Jews continued to serve on its Central Committee and in other power centers, and although Meir Wilner and other Jewish personalities still remained at the top, the Arab leadership effectively seized the reins of power.

From the very start, the top rank of Arab leadership was occupied almost exclusively by key figures of Communist organizations that had existed in Palestine toward the end of British rule. The quadrumvirate of Emil Habibi, Bulus Farah, Hanna Naqara, and Emil Toma regrouped in Haifa immediately after the 1948 war.[15] They lost no time in pulling strings and rallying their faithful in order to re-establish their party cells.

The most prominent of the four at this time was Emil Habibi, a natural leader, rousing speaker, resourceful organizer, and prolific writer and journalist. A regular columnist in his party's newspaper, Habibi sometimes signed his articles with the pseudonym

"Juhaynah." He was the party's strongman, an aggressive fighter who always took his target by storm.[16]

At the top of the political pyramid of the Communist party in the Arab sector, almost no significant changeover in leadership occurred until the late 1970s. Its perennial deputies in the Knesset, Emil Habibi and Tawfiq Tubi, were unquestionably at the top of the hierarchy. Their personalities were utterly different. Tubi, a man of serious, almost stern mien, conservative in manner, was considered a staunch loyalist of Moscow, the most moderate of the "Old Guard," and an orthodox Marxist. It was rather easy for him to bridge the two factions within Maki, because he, more than his Arab colleagues, could find a common language with the Jewish Communist leaders.

Emil Habibi, in contrast, was known in the Arab street as a zealous nationalist leader. According to rumors, possibly spread by his rivals, he had asked Soviet leaders, in the course of one of his meetings with them in Moscow, to declare the Soviet support in 1947 of the establishment of Israel as a "Stalinist error."[17] He was quick with his tongue, a prolific writer, a superb political strategist, and a fiery orator. For several decades, until he was ousted by a young intellectual opponent, many regarded him as Rakah's true leader. Practically speaking, the first rank of the founding generation petered out in the 1980s with the resignations of Emil Toma and the attorney Hanna Naqara. At that time, too, Emil Habibi chose an independent line, thereby incensing Rakah leaders to the extent that a colleague, the late Tawfiq Zayyad, accused him of "heresy" and wrote a venomous lamentation portraying Habibi as

> weak of character and faith . . . not ashamed to avert his glance from the land he once trod, from the home that raised him, the wealth on which he drew . . . His face has turned to rubber and his eyes to glass . . . He dances to all tunes, is full of vain blabber, feeds off the collapse of ideology and principle, and prostrates himself and sleeps in any bed . . . [18]

Ahmad Sa'd, a member of the party's Political Bureau, also claimed that Habibi was bearing a "message of surrender" to the Palestinian people, asking them to abandon their methods of struggle, and advocating that they "put on any garment the Arab League sewed for them."[19]

Even his literary colleagues in Rakah, the Druze poet Samih el-Qassem, former *Al-Ittihad* editor Salem Jubran, and the writer

Muhammad 'Ali Taha, were among Emil Habibi's detractors. Together with As'ad el-As'ad of Ramallah, who defected from the Palestinian Communist Party because of Gorbachev's "pro-Zionist" positions, they demanded Habibi's ouster from the chairmanship of the Israel-Palestinian Authors' Committee after Habibi condemned Saddam Hussein and criticized the PLO. Indeed, Emil Habibi had expressed independent opinions since he was ejected from Rakah, first in his paper *Al-'Arabi* and, when the latter ceased publication, in the weekly *Kull al-'Arab*. He staunchly opposed Saddam Hussein's aggression in the occupation of Kuwait, and after the Gulf War he built support for a realistic political settlement of the Arab-Israeli conflict in the spirit of the folk saying, "Stretch your legs to the limits of your blanket." In his new capacity as an independent, albeit still oppositionist Arab political figure, Habibi even won the recognition of the Israeli establishment under the Labor government, which in 1994 granted him the prestigious Israel Prize for his literary achievements (in the Arabic language!). It was the first time in Israel's history that an Arab citizen was given that prize, which has had an important symbolic effect on state–minority relations. By that time, Rakah itself had undergone certain ideological transformations, which made it defend Habibi's decision to receive the prize in spite of the fierce opposition by Arabs in Israel and the Arab world.

The expulsion of Emil Habibi from Rakah, as if placing him on the other side of a barricade, undoubtedly reflected the depth of the changes in the Communist Party leadership. In 1990, Tawfiq Tubi's retirement from the Knesset marked the end of his political career, although he retained the position of party secretary-general.

Today, the party leadership is formed by its present, "new" members of the Knesset such as Hashem Mahamid. The Arab mayors and local council heads elected under the Hadash banner form another power group among the party's decision-makers. Another power-wielding group in the party is composed of leading Rakah activists in the trade unions and the various front organizations led by the party.

The slow changing of the guard that has characterized this party is fascinating. Until the 1980s, the decisive influence in the Rakah leadership was wielded by Christian Arab leaders, chiefly members of the Greek Orthodox community. They formed an absolute majority in the Arab Communist leadership, in contrast to their proportion in the Arab population as a whole. This "Old Guard" that lost its power included the experienced leaders of an aging generation.[20]

Surprisingly, the missing link throughout these years was the lack of a young cadre in the party's senior leadership that could appeal to the youth and portray itself as a revolutionary force. Another salient feature of the party leadership was its lack of Muslim representation. The election of the late Tawfiq Zayyad as mayor of Nazareth in 1975 marked a watershed in the history of Rakah:

1. The fact that a Muslim attained this key post indicates an unquestionable peak in the expansion of the party's influence, and points to the party's success in forming a political alliance with the organization of academics and other nationalist circles that were willing to yield control of "the front" thus established to Rakah.

2. However, Rakah now had to cope with the challenge of keeping the promises it made to its electorate. Administration of such a complex municipality proved to be a double-edged sword, as the challenge of daily performance took the edge off the party's uncompromising nationalism.

3. At approximately that time, the Committee of Arab Local Council Heads was formed and swiftly became the country-wide leadership of Arabs in Israel. Rakah made an enormous effort to place the committee under its control but managed to secure a tie at best; sometimes it represented only a minority of committee deputies. The first chairman of the committee, Hanna Muweis, was a Rakah activist, but after his death the party lost its hold on this position with the election of Ibrahim Nimr Hussein (Abu Hatem), mayor of Shefar'am.

4. On March 30, 1976, the newly-declared "Land Day" became "blood day." The sizzling tempers in the Arab sector called for extreme measures that Rakah was hesitant to invoke. However, the party also had to contend with other elements that were inciting Arab youth, i.e., the Sons of the Village and the Progressive Nationalist Movement. After the Al-Ard movement had vanished from the political map, the Communist Party again had to gird for competition with organizations of effervescent young adults who mocked its "conservatism" and branded it a degenerate "establishment." Rakah was caught in a double bind: inciting and restraining, agitating and cautioning

against loss of control. It fathered the general strike on "Land Day" but denied paternity of the bloodshed that the day's events claimed.[21]

Concurrently, Rakah was assailed by the Arab functionaries in the Zionist parties, such as Mapam Knesset member the late Muhammad Watd, who probed its soft underbelly, namely, its mainly Christian leadership.

5. Rakah was evidently perturbed by its denominational make-up. Over the years, the pattern of its top leadership gradually changed to include Muslims. The rise of Tawfiq Zayyad to the mayoralty in the "political capital" of Arabs in Israel marked the beginning of this turnabout within the Communist Party. Today, all of Rakah's Arab deputies in the Knesset belong to the Muslim majority; its last Christian member of Knesset was the veteran party leader Tawfiq Tubi, who had served in the Israeli legislature since its first incarnation as the Provisional People's Council. Muhammad Watd himself, the erstwhile caustic tongue, joined Rakah after leaving Mapam following the eruption of the Intifadah during the term of the eleventh Knesset. His career in Rakah, however, was not successful, and his hopes of obtaining a key position there were quickly dashed.

Rakah's organizational power stood it in good stead in contending with the assaults it absorbed from the Right and the Left. In the mid-1970s, its card-carrying membership was estimated at no more than 1,000, but this provided a solid kernel around which a broader circle of supporters gathered. The vast disparity between the number of actual members and the extent of Rakah's electoral support remains one of the features of this party. Rakah tends not to disclose the size of its membership, keeping this "top secret" and a subject for conjecture.

Over the past decade, Rakah has consistently upheld ideological fundamentals, which may be summarized in the following principles:

1. Establishment of a Palestinian state alongside Israel with mutual recognition, and opposition to Zionism.
2. Effectuation of the "right of return" for 1948 refugees who wish to return.
3. Opposition to war as a means of conflict resolution.

4. Inclusion of Jewish players in the struggle to attain the proposed solution, thereby making Rakah not a *purely* Arab party.

The National Committee of Arab Local Council Heads, as the recognized leadership of Arabs in Israel, adopted the principles of the Rakah platform in an official resolution at a conference held on February 8, 1984, following country-wide municipal elections.[22]

The PLO mainstream actually adopted the Rakah ideology in a gradual process that reached its denouement in the Oslo Agreement of 1993. Rakah, for its part, has sought for many years to prove that there is no actual difference of opinion between itself and the "Organization." In his article "Why We Oppose the Independent Arab Party Plan," Emil Toma affirms Rakah's authentic representation of Arabs in Israel, against those who deny this, by emphasizing the "symmetry of platforms" between Rakah and the Palestine National Council in Algiers in February 1983.[23]

The PLO already began sending messages of support to Rakah in the 1970s, undoubtedly due to the influence of the poet Mahmud Darwish, a member of the *Al-Ittihad* editorial board who then emigrated from Israel and joined the top leadership of the PLO information department. The first official encounter between Rakah leaders and PLO personalities took place in Prague in 1977. Since then, the PLO has frequently described Rakah warmly as "the leading vanguard in the war against Zionist ideology."

Rakah considered PLO support especially important in its election campaigns. Therefore, in the year of its first encounter with the PLO, Rakah invoked the meeting as a propaganda tool. In the ninth Knesset elections, it won 55 percent of Arab votes for the unquestionable reason that it was perceived as the only Palestinian representative in the Knesset.

On January 24, 1980, with an eye on the next year's election campaign, a Rakah delegation including Member of Knesset Tawfiq Zayyad met with PLO representatives in Brussels. In this meeting, 'Abd el-Jawad Saleh, a member of the PLO executive, declared the organization's support of the Rakah-led Hadash list in both of the 1981 elections: for the Knesset and for the Histadrut trade-union federation. This time, however, Rakah did not do well. The ultranationalists boycotted the elections on every significant level, causing support for Rakah to drop to 38 percent of the Arab votes. A campaign by newspapers of extremist terrorist organizations in Lebanon in praise of Tawfiq Zayyad in the summer of 1981 did not help. In an interview with him published in *Sawt Filastin*, the Rakah leader emphasized: "There is only one solution to the struggle: recognition of the national rights of all peoples . . . "

Another way that Rakah strengthened its relations with the PLO was by interacting with the Communist Party in the West Bank, headed by Bashir Barghuthi of Ramallah, editor of the weekly *At-Tali'ah* ("The Vanguard"). Rakah gave this party substantial material assistance, advice, and backing.

The PLO was certainly aware of this party's political clout, but beginning in 1984 Rakah had to "share" the PLO's support in the elections to the eleventh and twelfth Knessets with a powerful opponent that emerged from the national camp, the Progressive List for Peace. The PLO attempted to mediate between the two rival movements as a conciliator, without notable success. Shortly before the autumn 1988 elections, PLO leaders tried to arrange a meeting in Bulgaria where Rakah and the PLP would sign a surplus vote agreement; this, too, was to no avail.

At the time of writing (October 1995), although the PLP has in the meantime almost disappeared, Rakah faces a serious threat in the growing strength of the Islamic Movement; furthermore, the Democratic Arab Party has taken a slice of the Arab vote, and the Zionist Labor, Mapam, and Meretz have support, too.

On November 18, 1987, a detailed agreement was drawn up in Moscow setting forth the contours of Rakah–PLO cooperation. The accord provided the Communist Party with general recognition as the chief representative of Arabs in Israel but did not designate it the exclusive mediator between these Arabs and the PLO.[24]

In its struggle to maintain hegemony in the Arab sector, Rakah was hampered by the following constraints:

1. The shackles of its adherence to the Soviet Union, at a time when the latter was no longer perceived as a superpower. The traditional leadership of the Israel Communist Party may be one of the last in the world whose roots extend back to the time of Stalin, who, for them, remained until his death the "Sun of the Nations." The local Communist leadership clung to this mentality precisely when the Soviet Union, its "second homeland," faced disintegration.

2. The revolutionary changes in the Kremlin shook Rakah. The party struggled to adjust to them, and at the same time attempted to justified the blind faith in the name of which

it had imposed a totally alien ideology on its followers, Jewish and Arab alike.

The Rakah leadership continued to use the term "the fathers of Marxism," as if the latter had been the founders of a new religion, ecclesiastic patriarchs whose dogma was as incontrovertible as if handed down by divine revelation.[25] In 1990, however, Rakah's crisis of allegiance to the Soviet Union intensified as the latter moved toward the re-establishment of diplomatic relations with Israel. For the first time, the party leaders began to consider "independence," i.e., divorce from the Kremlin. As *Al-Ittihad* editor Salim Jubran expressed it, "We [in Israel] shall have to learn to live without a father." In an undisguised confession, he revealed to a *Haaretz* correspondent that he had spent many sleepless nights: "The whole attack on the regime, on the system, the market economy, that procession with pictures of the Czar, national conflicts, the Soviet kowtowing to the Likud government in Israel in order to obtain Jewish money and appease the Americans – it's a nightmare."

These are indeed harsh remarks, the likes of which had never been heard from an orthodox conservative Rakah leader who toed the historical party line. A watershed had surely been reached. The Rakah leadership, however, was unwilling to be wiped off the political map. When asked about the conclusions he had reached, Jubran answered in anguish:

> Do I have any alternative?! I live in a reality of national and class oppression, of Intifadah in the territories and dogs at the Soltam factory [allegedly used to put down a labor dispute], and I must continue to struggle with my comrades as Communists *without any connection to the Soviet Union*.[26] [emphasis added]

Rakah had to contend with the nationalist fervor of its rivals as they breathed down its neck, mocking and ridiculing the veteran party. It made repeated strenuous efforts to attract support from the PLO and demonstrate its comradeship with it. Deploying all the strength of its apparatus, it launched a campaign of condemnation against the "iron-handedness" of the Israeli authorities, championing the struggle for equality. It soft-pedaled anything that its rivals might regard as "moderation" and vied with them for extremism. Concurrently, it had to restrain itself in its interaction with the Israeli government and avoid crossing the "red line" in both senses of the word, for this might give the authorities an opportunity to outlaw it. However, Rakah stepped off the safe path on more than one occasion.

In March 1988, Prime Minister Yitzhak Shamir, in his capacity as Minister of the Interior, shut down the newspaper *Al-Ittihad* for publishing articles that "endangered the public order." It was shortly before "Land Day." With the Knesset elections only six months away, Rakah was fighting for its life, its extremist rivals pounding at its vital organs. Rakah argued that Israel's General Security Service ("Shabak") was lying, and complained, as was its wont, of discrimination. Sharpening its propaganda axe excessively, it accused the government of failing to protect Arab workers from thuggery, attacked Defense Minister Yitzhak Rabin with growing intensity, complained that "Labor wants to be a second Likud," demanded a public inquiry into police violence against minorities, organized a commercial strike in Acre that paralyzed the Old City, and sent its organizational apparatus into the field to prove that it had not lost its vigor.

Rakah trod the tortuous middle ground between slogans of sizzling nationalism in order to compete with its more fundamentalist rivals, and more moderate positions in order to remain within the bounds of the law. It strove with all its might to create the image of a militant opposition that also functions as a constructive opposition, thus depicting itself as an option for Arab voters who wished to "have an influence," who tended to vote for parties within the "Israeli consensus," and whose political views on the Palestinian issue did not seem too far from Rakah's.

Rakah succeeded in its task in the 1992 thirteenth Knesset elections, maintaining its support in the legislature. However, it lost sympathy in the struggle for municipal authorities, where it had to contend with the growing power of the greatest menace it faced: the Islamic Movement.

Professor Sammy Smooha of the University of Haifa claims, "If Communism is finished, then the Communist Party is also finished."[27] Rakah is undoubtedly in the throes of an unprecedented crisis, but this does not necessarily imply that the party is on the verge of death. It is still the best-organized party in the Arab sector. Its clear, elastic nationalist policy provides a necessary brake for the destructive fundamentalist trends that are on the rise. It positions itself in the "middle," and its establishment nature, although detrimental to it, justifies its existence.

The rupture of Rakah's umbilical relationship with Moscow does not really threaten its continued existence because of the duality that characterized the party from its very inception. The support that Rakah has always commanded in Arab localities does not originate in the persuasive powers of Moscow. It was neither Lenin nor any of the Secretaries-General of the Soviet Communist Party who convinced voters to cast their ballots for Rakah. Rakah would be compensated for the loss of its "father" in Moscow by the acquisition of a surrogate "father," the Palestine Liberation Organization, with which it maintained close relations. However, the crisis occurred at precisely the time that the struggle within the nationalist camp itself had intensified and the surge toward the Islamic Movement had gathered strength. Therefore, Rakah's rivals closed in from all sides, nibbling and biting continuously, but did not encounter a lost cause, an enemy bereft of the ability to retaliate.

The prognosis, then, is that Rakah will contract but will not die. It has surprising durability and is husbanding all its strength to avoid collapse. Its tactics include more vigorous efforts to win the support of the Israeli Left, flexible maneuvering in the Arab street, vociferous action in support of the Palestinian refugees, tumultuous attacks on the Israeli government, and, at the same time, warnings against extremists whose irresponsible actions do not further the Palestinian cause.

Al-Ard Attempts to Create an Arab Liberation Movement

The Al-Ard group came into being as the result of a protracted effort to create an Arab nationalist organization in Israel, totally free of foreign dependency but inextricably linked to the Arab nationalist movement.[28] Its founders regarded Egyptian President Jamal 'Abd en-Nasser as their *rais* (boss), the patriarch of their movement. They had no need for the Marxist–Leninist forebears whom Maki offered as objects of admiration, and, in fact, they challenged Maki with seething zealotry.

In the summer of 1959, the time seemed ripe to lay the cornerstone of the new movement. The Cairo–Moscow conflict reverberated in the air. The young Arab nationalists of the Maki-led Popular Front fumed about Maki's identification with the Kremlin, which had sided with Iraqi strongman 'Abd el-Karim Qassem. The fourth

Knesset elections were imminent, and election-year fever was raging in the Arab street.

Arab students at the Hebrew University of Jerusalem were enflamed by the events of the time. Many wished to demonstrate their admiration of "Abu Khaled," President Nasser of Egypt, whom they viewed as their supreme leader. Thirstily they absorbed his promise that the "day of liberation" was at hand and that the "oppressor state" would soon be wiped off the map. From their standpoint, Maki was heading in the wrong direction and had subordinated itself to a foreign authority; they wanted to take real action. Arab students' horizons had expanded at the Hebrew University. They had learned about Israeli democracy, which they regarded as broad enough for their purposes.[29] Many of them were law students who believed that their education would help them walk on the fringes of the law in order to circumvent it.

When the Popular Front ruptured in July, a new, dynamic political group emerged on the Israeli scene: *Usrat Al-Ard*, "the Family of the Soil." This group was destined to undergo stormy mutations. From its very beginnings, Usrat Al-Ard took aim at three stronger forces:

1. *The State of Israel.* This was its main target, because non-recognition of Israel was the culture from which the movement grew. The Al-Ard group did not camouflage its intention to change the political map. It decided to fight to attain its goal as an Arab movement from which Jews were excluded. In their nationalist zealotry, its founders eschewed the device that the Communist Party had exploited so well, co-opting Jews in order to disguise its Arab nationalism and strengthen its image among outsiders as a balanced party. The members of Al-Ard seemed unwilling to trust Jews, even those who totally opposed the State of Israel. It also took them some time to understand the importance of explaining themselves to Jews in Israel.

2. *The traditional Arab political array.* The young members of the Al-Ard group regarded the traditional Arab political forces as obsolescent, unsuited to the requirements of the new era and a prop of the Israeli regime. They sought to hasten their collapse.

3. *The Israel Communist Party, the progenitor of the Al-Ard movement.* At this initial stage, Maki was the group's most dangerous enemy because of its proximity.

Practically speaking, the "Family of the Soil" had natural allies within Maki, but as long as they did not join the new movement they could nip it in the bud. They were more experienced than the founders of Al-Ard, had a sophisticated and systematically structured organizational apparatus to call on, and were backed by a world power. They were the first to be on the alert against this new group, fearing that it would affect their standing in the Arab street because it was more extreme, "more Arab," and less tied to foreign elements. At this time, too, Maki opposed the "revolutionary regime" in Egypt because of the USSR's support of 'Abd el-Karim Qassem, the ruler of Iraq.

The Al-Ard group tried to ride this watershed to prominence, hoping to rally nationalist Arab circles around it. Maki was fully aware of the menace.[30] The Al-Ard people stressed the differences between itself and Maki in all possible ways. It regarded the Communist party as its feeding trough and sought to gain support at its expense, assuming that many Arab Communists welcomed it secretly because they shared its goals.

In this context, the two organizations, so similar to each other, felt that there was no alternative to competitive confrontation. Al-Ard's first battle cry against its parent organization was voiced indirectly but had profound practical reverberations. The new movement urged Israeli Arabs to boycott the Knesset elections on the grounds that their participation in these elections amounted to recognition of the Zionist State. This outlook was undoubtedly anchored in the fundamental tenets of this ultranationalist organization, but its practical purpose was to strike a blow at Maki, because Al-Ard was asking the Communist Party's supporters not to vote for it either.

The Al-Ard group regarded its extremism, nationalism, and uncompromising stand as the tools with which it would expand against the forces that stood in its way. With its trenchant, unequivocal style, it rocketed into the Arab public consciousness with a mighty impact.

The first step was the unveiling of a special journal in October 1959, replete with incitement against the state. To circumvent the legal need for a license, its editors attempted to pass off the journal as "nonrecurrent." In fact, they published it several times, giving it a new name each week, between October 1959 and January 1960.

The weekly journal expressed clear solidarity with the United Arab Republic. Its message to the government of Israel was aggressive and threatening: "The rulers of Israel must understand that the time has come to find a just solution to the refugee problem before another sword comes forth to solve it – and what a sword it will be!"

The author of another article rails against the Israeli government in these terms: "Live and let live. Then perhaps you will live!" Ben-Gurion, the prime minister at the time, was ridiculed in the paper as "the dwarf of Jerusalem." All issues contained cartoons in this vein. The editor, Saleh Baransi, and his associates, were indicted for publishing a newspaper without a license. They were convicted, fined, and given suspended prison sentences. From then on, the Al-Ard movement sought to establish organizational modalities that would benefit from the protection of the law. The legal experts among its members pointed it toward the possibilities offered by a democratic regime. In Al-Ard's struggle to create a legal operational framework, the following phases are visible:

1. *The establishment of a trade company.* In June 1960, seven Al-Ard activists submitted an application to register a corporation named Al-Ard, Ltd. The registrar of companies rejected the application, citing "security considerations and concern for the public welfare." A legal struggle ensued for the group's right to associate as a company. Mansur Kardush, one of its leading stalwarts, petitioned the Supreme Court, sitting as the High Court of Justice, to order the registrar of companies to retract his refusal. The court granted the petition, expressing doubts about the way the registrar had invoked his authority in this matter. The order *nisi* became permanent by a majority of two justices against one.[31]

In response, the attorney-general asked for another hearing. His request was granted, and in early 1962 the issue was brought to a broader panel of five Supreme Court justices. Again, the decision of the registrar of companies was struck down;[32] the earlier ruling, ordering the registration of Al-Ard, Ltd., remained in effect. Thus, in the summer of 1962 Israel's list of corporations was augmented by a special company whose main activities had nothing to do with business.

The members of Al-Ard were greatly encouraged by the Supreme Court decision. It strengthened their assumption that the legal framework was sufficiently flexible to satisfy their needs. They tried again to obtain a license to publish a regular weekly, but their application was turned down. When they appealed to the High Court of Justice, the Supreme Court was unwilling to interfere with the prerogatives of the Interior Ministry district commissioner. The group continued to organize and to send memoranda excoriating the Israeli government to international institutions and foreign publications.[33] After this period of internal consolidation, the Al-Ard activists moved on to the next, decisive phase:

2. *An attempt to establish a nonprofit association.* This was the legal framework for Israeli political parties at the time, and the obvious purpose of Al-Ard's step was to create an extremist Arab party that would help promote the goals of the Arab national movement with regard to Israel.

The government decided to foil this attempt. The Haifa district commissioner, to whom the members of Al-Ard presented their application, refused to register the association for the following reason, of which he informed the group's representative, Sabri Jiryis:

> I studied the articles of association attached to your letter, particularly Paragraph 3(c), and the material that was brought to my knowledge. After this perusal, I hereby apprise you of the following:
>
> The association known as the Al-Ard Movement, which you and others presume to set up, is an association created for the purpose of harming the existence and integrity of the State of Israel.
>
> If it transpires that, notwithstanding the above, you act as an organization, legal steps may be taken against you.

A frontal collision was unmistakably imminent; the Al-Ard activists knew they could not avoid it. In an attempt to exploit the law in its dry, literal sense, so that the floor would not be pulled from under their feet, they decided to accept the challenge and petitioned the Supreme Court again to endorse the legality of their association. The fascinating trial that ensued revealed the true nature of the Al-Ard movement, its goals, and its rights in a democratic state.

The attorney-general himself, Moshe Ben-Zeev,[34] appeared together with the attorney Zvi Terlo, a superb solicitor and a sharp-tongued, experienced jurist.[35] They collected various pieces of evidence concerning the subversive goals of the Al-Ard movement with intent to reveal its hostile nature for all to see. They even proposed that the panel of judges peruse classified material which, by order of the Defense Minister, may not be disclosed except to judges for reasons of security. However, the Supreme Court had no need for this evidence.

The court began by analyzing the goals of the Al-Ard group as expressed in its own articles of association, and through them reached the clear conclusion that Al-Ard rejected the state's right to exist and the rights of the Jewish people within it. The three justices unanimously upheld the decision of Haifa district commissioner, ruling that such an organization exceeded the boundaries of Israeli democracy because its intention was to subvert it.

The legal action illuminated the affiliation between Al-Ard and outside Arab hostility toward Israel. The Jordanian paper *Filastin* carried an impassioned article entitled "We're Coming Back – This Is the First Spark:"

> The Al-Ard organization deserves support and encouragement because it is the first spark of a Palestinian revolution in the heart of the plundered homeland . . . It is one of dozens of organizations operating in our occupied land, and we should reach out to them at any price, in any way. It is our duty to organize them and unite them under one Palestinian command. This is not a difficult task for the *fedayeen* ("self-sacrificing fighters" – an Islamic historical term), who risk body and soul to ignite the fire of the Revolution of Return.

The Cairo press wrote in a similar vein. Arab radio stations thundered with cries of solidarity. In the meantime, Egyptian and Syrian intelligence agents began to seek contacts with Al-Ard activists, assuming that they would be eager to cooperate with them in all spheres. It was for this reason that four Al-Ard leaders, Mansur Kardush, Habib Qahwaji, Sabri Jiryis, and Saleh Baransi, were arrested and interrogated. In late November 1964, the Defense Minister signed an order outlawing the Al-Ard group:

> The group of people currently known as the Al-Ard group, under whatever name they may choose from time to time, and the group of people aggregated under Al-Ard, Ltd., created by the joint activities of the shareholders of the aforementioned company or any portion thereof – are an illegal association.

On the basis of this order, the share company was liquidated and the organized activity of Al-Ard came to a standstill. The Arab public was unwilling to be drawn into illegalities. It feared the danger that such an extremist group represented.

Al-Ard activists attempted to resurface by circumventing the Defense Minister's order shortly before the sixth Knesset elections in 1965, when several leaders of the movement prepared a slate of candidates called the Arab Socialist List. Running for the Knesset was contrary to one of the fundamental principles of Al-Ard, which had always viewed participation in elections for the Israeli legislature as a manifestation of recognition of Israel. Having decided that there was no other way, they sought to obtain the protection of the law in this fashion. They hoped to exploit the parliamentary immunity of candidates who would gain admission to the Knesset and operate within the context of the new list; concurrently they soft-pedaled their political goals, which the Supreme Court had condemned so severely.

In the first phase of this gambit, they sought to avoid further confrontation. They had learned from the bitter experience of the past. Without changing their goals, they fine-tuned their methods. The emergence of the candidate list also brought about a revolutionary change in Egypt's attitude toward participation in the Knesset elections. For the first time, the neighboring country did not implore Israeli Arabs to boycott the elections. The Egyptian radio station *Sawt al-'Arab* now urged Arabs in Israel to cast their votes for the Arab Socialist List.

The Egyptian appeal was premature. The Central Elections Committee struck down the list, construing it as a reincarnation of the Al-Ard movement with the same illegal aims. When the list appealed its disqualification to the Supreme Court, the justices accepted the attorney-general's argument that this was "the same dame under a different name."[36] In that appeal, the attorney Yaakov Yerador, counsel for the list, had argued that the elections committee's prerogatives in vetoing lists were so confined as to be virtually non-existent, limited only to the flaws listed in the Knesset Elections Law. Indeed, the law sharply limits the committee's right to strike down lists, as the legislature had deliberately refrained from assigning the committee broad discretionary powers so as to avoid creating an obstacle to the formation of political lists of any shade or hue. Here, however, a majority of Supreme Court justices found that the political freedom to run for office came with a protective constraint, if the goal of a would-be participant was to undermine the state. After analyzing the broader implications of the Basic Law: The Knesset, Justice Shimon Agranat, the president of the Supreme Court, delivered the following ruling:

> I agree that the Central Elections Committee, when exercising its powers to decide whether to approve a list of candidates or not, is usually not empowered to examine the candidates' probity and

political views. This rule, however, does not apply in our case, where the committee's attention was drawn to the fact that the petitioning list is identical to a group of people that the High Court of Justice found to be an illegal association, and to the fact that, pursuant to this ruling, the group was declared an illegal organization.

These facts left the Central Committee with no alternative but to decide not to approve the appellants' list.[37]

After this additional failure, group members continued their activities as individuals and made occasional attempts to resuscitate the organizational cells in one guise or another.

In 1966, the attorney Sabri Jiryis, the aforementioned petitioner in the case, published a book entitled *The Arabs in Israel*, which contained caustic attacks on the Israeli government, embellished with false information and facts quoted out of context. He was subsequently arrested on suspicion of collaborating with terrorist organizations and, at his request, was allowed to leave the country. He emigrated to Beirut, where he began to organize anti-Israel propaganda efforts for the PLO.

Saleh Baransi, another leading figure in Al-Ard, embarked on nationalist activity in the context of "sports clubs" in the Little Triangle. He tried to register one such outfit as a nonprofit association without listing himself as one of the applicants; again, however, the veil was torn off and the true intent revealed. After this failure, Baransi engaged in activities that led to his being charged with security offenses for which he served a prison term. Upon his release, he resumed his ultranationalist activities.

After the Six Day War, former Al-Ard activists displayed a perceptible tendency to join terrorist organizations. Three leaders of the movement were prosecuted, convicted, and, in January 1968, sentenced to lengthy prison terms.[38] The path taken by members of this movement again demonstrated the intentions of Al-Ard and the dangers it posed. The Arab population had reservations about this organization and left it in its marginal position. It was clear, however, that additional efforts of this sort – more complex, more circumspect, but with the same goals – would be made in the future.

In early January 1991, the veterans of Al-Ard formed a movement meant to succeed that of the 1960s. On January 9, 1991, thirteen original members of the movement, headed by Mansur Kardush and Saleh Barnasi, the director of the Institute for the Preservation of the Arab Heritage in Tayyibeh, issued a manifesto declaring the establishment of the National Socialist Front (*Al Jabbah al-Qawmiyyah al-Ishtirakiyyah*)). The pretext for the new organization lay in the fear of mass deportations prior to the anticipated Gulf War.[39] Since then, no special activity has been noted on the part of this front, which joins other tiny extremist organizations in the Arab sector.

Sons of the Village

The movement was conceived in 1972, before the Yom Kippur War, as a means of filling the void left in extremist Arab nationalist activity by the outlawing of Al-Ard and the thwarting of attempts by the Union of Arab Academics to take its place. Its founders were vigorous young people who were sick and tired of lukewarm formulas; many were educated, many in the learned professions. Their leader was Muhammad Tawfiq Keywan, of the village (now town) of Umm el-Fahm, without doubt the fount of the Sons of the Village. Other young Umm el-Fahm men as well, from all the village's clans, were also among the movement's leaders: Hassan Ahmad Jabbarin, Muhammad Salama Mahajna, Ghassan Fawzi Eghbaria, and Rija Muhammad Eghbaria.[40]

It was a new phenomenon: in the municipal elections at the end of 1973, lists of young university graduates appeared in various villages, all under the name *Abna al-Balad* (Sons of the Village), their platforms were similar, and the ties between them were forged in the course of the campaign and afterward. Particularly noticeable that year were their successes in the two large Triangle villages (now towns) of Umm el-Fahm and Tayyibeh. Their momentum accelerated in 1976, when they won additional victories in Nahf, Deir el-Assad, and Majd el-Kurum.[41] They also struck roots in Kabul.

From the outset, Sons of the Village conducted their activities in cells, in the Triangle and the Galilee – extremist, removed, at times arrogant. At the same time, other local organizations bearing a fiery nationalistic message, "free" of foreign impurities, made their appearance. The An-Nahdah (The Resurgence) group was formed in Tayyibeh; in the villages of 'Ara and 'Ar'ara, the Al-Fajr (The Dawn) was created.[42]

The basic ideological outlook of Sons of the Village left little doubt that it stood on the far side of the "red line," in both senses, in blatant opposition to the Israel Communist Party. They clearly challenged the sovereignty of the State of Israel, and unequivocally identified with the PLO, adopting the positions of the "Rejectionist Front" organizations. As far as they were concerned, the Jewish people have no right to self-determination. Their goal was the establishment of a secular, democratic state throughout greater Palestine in its pre-1948 borders. The means, according to their view: "the armed Palestinian revolution," in which the entire Palestinian people would take part, without any dividing line between the Arabs of Israel and the inhabitants of the occupied territories. Their slogan: "One nation, a common struggle and one destiny," or phrased in a flowery Arabic rhyme, *al-Khalil mithl al-Jalil* – there is no difference between Hebron and the Galilee, all regions interweave into the map of one indivisible Palestine.[43]

The idea of the unity of all parts of the Palestinian people everywhere was not merely theoretical, a dead letter. Movement activists set out to forge close links with PLO leaders in the occupied territories, beyond Israel proper. These overtures were kept highly circumspect at first. However, the connections forged at the time with the mayor of Nablus, Bassam Shak'a, believed at the time to be the spearhead of the campaign against Israeli rule on the West Bank, are well known. He himself took part in gatherings organized by Sons of the Village, some of them disguised as cultural affairs, some explicitly political in nature. With his arrest in November 1979, the movement held a mass protest rally in Umm el-Fahm, its "capital," attended by some 1000 people, who angrily demanded the leader's immediate release.

Sons of the Village took a consistent stand against participation in Knesset elections, in full cooperation with the Progressive National Movement (PNM), a sister organization, and with other extremist groups. Together, they attempted to establish an umbrella organization in 1980, the National Coordinating Committee, on the basis of the Umm el-Fahm Covenant adopted on December 21 of that year.

The Sons of the Village movement gradually expanded its activities into the different villages, in a variety of ways, ranging from an attempt to establish labor camps to organization of rallies for the PLO in the Little Triangle, Shefar'am and Galilee villages. They also reached out toward the Bedouin in the Negev, although to a lesser degree than elsewhere. They deliberately instigated confrontations with what they considered the "collaborationist" establishment: the Muslim boards of trustees, parties that run for the Knesset, various prominent figures, and those in contact with government offices.

They were constantly on the lookout for whatever they could use as a means for bringing about a demonstration. The collapse of the roof at the Hassan Bek Mosque served as a pretext for inciting the Arabs of Jaffa. President Sadat's assassination was a cause for celebration; Sons of the Village openly proclaimed their joy over the death of the "traitor." They never miss any of the increasing number of milestone dates in Arab affairs, which are as oxygen to political life in the Arab villages.

It is no secret that the authorities keep them under constant surveillance, and occasionally obtain warrants limiting the movement of extreme activists. Movement activists have been prosecuted for hostile activity, usually consisting of open support for the PLO, under paragraph 4 of the amendment to the Ordinance for the Prevention of Terror, 1948.

In order to safeguard their very existence, the Sons of the Village devote considerable thought to the form their activities take; for instance, it sponsors many local associations the declared purposes of which are cultural and educational. The links between such associations and their sponsor are not always clearly visible. The Lydda Cultural Association and Nazareth's Association for the Advancement of Education in the Arab Sector are but two examples.

Sons of the Village includes a group of nationalists which coalesced in the city with the aim of increasing Palestinian awareness among Israeli Arabs. Its principle economic enterprise is a publishing house, which has undertaken a project to commemorate the Palestinian poet 'Abd er-Rahim Mahmud, who was killed in the battle of Sejera in the summer of 1948, as a soldier in Qawuqji's "Army of Salvation." His fame derives from a poem in which he used the phrase, "How good it is to die for our country."

The association also tried to establish an Arab university in Nazareth. In the summer of 1981, it announced a fund drive to collect one million dollars for a scientific library, laboratories, a research institute, and preparatory courses for young people interested in a higher education. In their request for permission to establish the university, its initiators produced a list with the names of 38 Arab lecturers at universities in Israel, the West Bank, Europe and the United States who were willing to teach in it. The Sons of the Village project in Lydda is registered as a nonprofit organization, the Lydda Cultural Association. In the summer of 1981, it intended to sponsor a work project to refurbish sites in the city holy to Muslims and Christians. However, the local board of trustees of the Muslim *waqf* (religious endowment) refused to authorize the project, as repair of the mosques was within its purview, so the project came to naught.[44]

During Operation Peace to Galilee (1982–85) the Sons of the Village stepped up their anti-government efforts, shoulder to shoulder with the Progressive National Movement and other extremist organizations, such as the Nahdah group in Tayyibeh, Matspen (a left-wing Jewish group), and even the Communist-led Hadash political front. Within the Committee of Council Heads, the Sons of the Village representatives played the role of catalyst in declaring a strike on September 20, 1982, despite their relatively few members on the Committee. The event turned into a commemoration of the Sabra and Shatila massacre victims, accompanied by prayers for the souls of the dead, and cancellation of the traditional celebration of the Feast of the Sacrifice, *'Id al-Adha*. Ever since, the Sons of the Village have striven to steer the Committee onto an extremist path and have frequently tried to cause clashes with the security forces.

Numerous clubs are sponsored by the Sons of the Village. At times they are dormant, and at times effervescent with activity, which ranges from the painting of ceilings in the four colors of the Palestinian flag to demonstrations, burning of tires, distribution of leaflets, memorial services at mosques for some "national hero" or other killed by Israel in Lebanon, the West Bank or Gaza, accompanied by inflammatory speeches and songs.[45] Oft-times public figures who do not belong to the Sons of the Village, or even belong to other parties, participate in such events.

In early 1988, the Sons of the Village began publishing the weekly *Ar-Rayah* (The Flag), giving expression to their world view in the format of ideological debates, painting the Intifadah in rosy colors, and endeavoring to bring its patterns of activity into Israel proper. It ceased publication after a few months, to be succeeded by the weekly *Al-Maydan* (The Arena). The periodical *An-Naqa* (Purity) belongs to the same school of thought.

Not all of the Sons' considerable hostile activity against the State is conducted within their own organization. More than once, terrorist teams whose members belonged to a Sons-affiliated "social association" have been caught. A member of the National Coordinating Committee, which was outlawed in 1981, was one Mahmud Durghal, a leader of Al-Ard in Lydda, who had spent four years in prison for membership in a hostile organization.[46] He had planned kidnappings of Israeli soldiers, either in order to murder them or hold them hostage against release of security prisoners. After his own release, he took up appointment as secretary of the Lydda Cultural Association, which is a Sons of the Village arm engaged in agitation. After the outbreak of the Intifadah, the Sons of the Village, along with the PNM, worked toward exacerbating confrontations with the security forces, developing the doctrine of *tas'id an-Nidal*, or escalation of the struggle.[47]

From 1975, three currents of thought have been competing for control of the Sons of the Village. There are no basic differences in ideology among them, all agreeing with the "strategy for the liberation of Palestine." Differences are over tactics, and involve the questions: Is it permissible to use the Israeli Knesset to help attain their goal? Is it desirable to make use of Jewish anti-Zionist forces, and through them achieve a defensive umbrella *vis-à-vis* the authorities?[48]

The leaders of the first school of thought, which supports parliamentary struggle, are Hassan Jabbarin and Ghassan Fawzi Eghbaria, who had been imprisoned for membership in a Jewish-Arab espionage and sabotage ring. They minced no words in justifying their position: "We consider participation in Knesset elections as one of a composite of various means of struggle. We would not withhold from our people any means of struggle that are at its disposal."

The second school of thought rejected any participation in Knesset elections, which they viewed as tantamount to recognition of Israel. The leader of that current in the movement, Rija Eghbaria, stated his position thus:

In our view, it is not possible to realize the tasks of the Palestinian national organization in the Knesset, although I do not oppose a parliamentary struggle. The experience of the Israeli Communist party over 35 years proves that there is no utility to struggle from inside the Knesset; they have not succeeded in passing a single law to date.

. . . We of the Sons of the Village movement claim that we are an integral part of the Arab liberation movement and the Palestinian national movement.

Our movement is taking full part in the struggle of the masses in conducting the international campaign for liberation, socialism, and unity. This has not been achieved in the framework of solution by stages. (Since no-one among us has spoken about solution by stages.)

We see ourselves as the bridgehead for the strategic solution of the struggle of the Palestinian people . . .

We believe that the Palestinian solution is related to the Arab revolution and the worldwide liberation movement. The war in Lebanon has proven that change comes from the outside, the armed struggle cannot be deferred or cancelled, but rather through a people's war, and that is the war which has brought about an earthquake in Israel for the first time in its history. Even the demonstrations in Israel are a natural result of the Palestinian struggle and the heavy casualties among the Israelis.[49]

The third, intermediate, school of thought favors deferring a decision between the first two, although it seems that many of its members have joined the Jabbarin camp.

The Sons of the Village conference in 1981 decided to participate in elections, although that decision was not implemented. Actually, the decision gave expression to the idea of struggle in stages; recognition of Israel, beside which a Palestinian state would be established, as a first step and without giving up the overall dream.

Still, the Arab public was not called upon to vote in the elections to the tenth Knesset, and the resulting boycott was noticeable by the large number who did not vote.[50] In March 1982, supporters of parliamentary struggle published a red booklet entitled *The Sons of the Village Movement: A Political Program*, which they wanted to bring up at the forthcoming conference, but opponents demanded the matter be deferred. Differences also broke out over how June 5 was to be commemorated as "Israeli Invasion Day." The camp of Ghassan Fawzi Eghbaria and Hassan Jabbarin called for a "national conclave," while supporters of Rija Eghbaria favored a mass demonstration.

The Sons of the Village split at Umm el-Fahm in 1983. Hassan Jabbarin founded the Al-Ansar movement, in honor of the followers of the Prophet Muhammad in the city of Medina, or perhaps as a reminder of the detention camp in Lebanon by the same name. The two wings ran separately in the Umm el-Fahm municipal elections and each won one seat.[51]

It was an election in which the extremist nationalist parties – Sons of the Village, PNM, and local lists in ten Arab villages – attained a relative measure of success. Their voters generally supported the candidate of the Front for Council Head. These lists garnered an aggregate of 3,228 votes, which was approximately 8 percent of the valid ballots cast, and 3 percent of the nationwide Arab total, while in 1978, they had received 1,409 votes in four villages, or 1 percent of the total vote in the Arab sector.[52] In 1981, the nationalists lost the mayor's office of Kabul, which they had won in 1978, and failed to win any council seats. These figures indicate the measure of the popular appeal enjoyed by Sons of the Village and sister organizations, the PNM, and sundry local groups.

The split in Sons of the Village found expression in the contact the Al-Ansar group made with left-wing Jewish groups such as Matspen and Alternativa, among others, as well as with the Progressive Movement in Nazareth, with the aim of establishing an independent Arab nationalist list. Al-Ansar leader Hassan Jabbarin was elected to the preparatory committee at a conference on April 21, 1984, but the group failed to come to agreement with the other parties over a solution to the Palestinian question and over-filling the first several places on the list.

The Al-Ansar group supports the "strategy of stages" for solution of the Palestinian problem, meaning that a Palestinian state in Judea and Samaria would constitute the first step toward its establishment over all of Palestine. In order to achieve the first stage, participation with left-wing Jewish groups is permissible, although it seems that the ground had not been sufficiently prepared for cooperation within a single list. Al-Ansar tried to get the 2,500 signatures necessary to run as an independent list, but failed. Throughout, it was attacked vigorously from all sides, especially from Sons of the Village under Rija Eghbaria.[53]

In the past several years, the Sons of the Village has lost some of its support, particularly to the Islamic movement. In municipal elections in 1988, their vote declined significantly; in Umm el-Fahm they lost their representation altogether.[54] The process of ideological mellowing of the PLO mainstream has had an impact on both wings of the Sons of the Village, although they are inclined toward the radical PLO organizations of the "Rejectionist Front," i.e., the PFLP of George Habash and PDFLP, headed by Naif Hawatmeh.

At the end of their first decade of activity, the nationalist movements in general consisted of small kernels; they failed to expand into broad popular organization, despite vigorous efforts and constantly lying in wait "for the big moment."

The Progressive List for Peace (PLP)

The appearance of the PLP on the Israeli political firmament just before the 1984 Knesset elections was seen as a reopening of the bitter controversy that attended the Al-Ard movement. This was so despite the fact that a reserve major general, Matti Peled, was second on the PLP list, despite its stated platform, and despite the emphasis placed upon its being a Jewish-Arab party.

It is possible that the image of the party's leader, Muhammad Mi'ari, a former Al-Ard activist, engendered this feeling. Perhaps the reason was the view of the defense ministry legal counsel that the Arab candidates had agreed among themselves clandestinely to avoid mention of the borders of the future Palestinian state in the party platform, for fear the list would be disqualified by the Central Election Committee. Perhaps the PLP was simply perceived as the heir of the Nazareth Progressive Movement.[55]

Indeed, the new party's Arab wing included prominent figures of the extremist camp, such as Advocate Kamel ed-Daher and Dr Rashid Salim, both former partners with the Communists on the Nazareth city council, and with them the priest, Riah Abu el-'Asal, who was placed relatively near the top of the list, in an electoral system based on proportional representation. Walid Sadeq, of the Triangle town of Tayyibeh, an experienced politician – he had been a Knesset member with the left-wing Sheli party – was prominent among the PLP's founders. He was fourth on the list; fifth was Nuri el-'Uqbi, who had run for the tenth Knesset on a nationalist list supported mainly by Bedouin in the southern Negev region. The Jews in the group were left-wing activists, members of the Alternativa movement, which continued to maintain a distinct existence as a grouping within the new party.

Alternativa leader Uri Avneri, a well-known figure and former Knesset member, let General Peled take second place on the list, so as to enhance its attractiveness among Jews. Dr Yaakov Arnon, former director general of the finance ministry and a man of pronounced left-wing views, was fifth.

From the outset, the PLP challenged the monopoly enjoyed by the Israel Communist Party (Rakah) as representative of the nationalistic yearnings of Israel's Arabs. The PLP received the backing of *Al-Fajr*, a pro-PLO newspaper published in East Jerusalem. On July 13, 1984, an article by Mi'ari appeared in the paper expounding his world view: "We are different from others. Our Palestinianism is our ideology and point of departure"; an ad supporting the PLP appeared in the same issue. Additional pro-PLP advertisements appeared in the paper during the campaign, until the PLO leadership finally ordered the editorial board to show even-handedness between the PLP and Rakah.[56]

The PLP did all it could to emphasize its Arab-Palestinian character, its emancipation from Marxist fetters and its willingness to employ extreme measures against the Israeli authorities. As with any new movement, its actual identity was not completely clear, yet its nationalistic tendencies were obvious and created expectations for a turning point, for change accompanied by momentum.

The authorities were suspicious of the PLP. Its appearance in an election campaign brought home once again, in bold relief, the problem of freedom of political organization, under the backdrop of suspicions that this party, under the leadership of a lawyer named Muhammad Mi'ari, was simply Al-Ard brought back to life with a facelift.

Mi'ari's activities a few years earlier strengthened such suspicions. The Central Election Committee was, *inter alia*, shown a 1980 affidavit by the commander of the Northern Military Region, laying out the reasons for placing administrative limitations on Mi'ari's freedom of movement, on the basis of the Defense (Emergency) Regulations.[57]

From the affidavit, one learns that Mi'ari was under administrative limitations in the period 1963–73. The affidavit also mentioned that at the time the report was written, he was in contact with former Al-Ard activists, including those engaged in sabotage, and that he maintained links with Arabs in the Territories with the intent of harming the State of Israel, and as such was barred entry into Judea and Samaria. The affidavit stressed his agitation on "Land Day", March 30, 1976, and his participation since then in the organization of violent demonstrations and strikes.

The Central Election Committee disqualified the PLP, which then appealed to the Supreme Court.

The PLP won its appeal, as the three conditions mandated by law as grounds for disqualification did not obtain:

1. The proximate certainty of harm to security or public order.
2. A specific or defined instance in which application of its right would in fact lead to such harm.
3. Categoric consent by the legislative branch to impose limitations on electoral participation.[58]

The PLP would eventually have to defend its existence again against a subsequent amendment to Israel's basic law (clause 7a of Amendment 9 to the Basic Law: The Knesset). That amendment permits the outlawing of a movement which negates any of the three basic premises upon which the State was founded: its Jewish character, its democratic essence, and its abhorrence of racism.[59]

In the meantime, though, the PLP won two seats in the 1984 elections, expanding the base of nationalist Arab support in that body beyond the four seats which Rakah kept. They were two diametrically different men: Muhammad Mi'ari, the former Al-Ard leader, and Gen. Matti Peled. They had sprung from different soils, yet together they put together the new list, which in quick succession overcame the two very substantial obstacles: that of the legal challenge to its very existence, and then that of garnering the minimum 1 percent of the vote to enter the Knesset, actually winning two seats.

The PLP spent its first four years in establishing itself among Israel's Arabs, by means of a constant effort to guarantee the support of the PLO. Toward that end, Mi'ari lent his Knesset appearances an inflammatory nationalist character, often bringing upon himself the outrage of his parliamentary colleagues. The movement's extra-parliamentary activities included violent demonstrations, strikes, and public disorders. The purpose was competitive: against Rakah on the one hand, and extremist nationalist elements such as Sons of the Village, the Progressive National Movement, and the Islamic movement, on the other.[60]

From 1985, relations with Rakah deteriorated sharply, which reflected an internal split in the PLO. The PLP identified with the mainstream of Fatah, while the Communist Party leaned toward the Democratic Union, a left-wing opposition grouping within the PLO, composed of the Popular Democratic Front for the Liberation of Palestine (PDFLP), the Palestine Communist Party and the Popular Front for the Liberation of Palestine (PFLP).[61] At the same time, links were forged with PLO backers in the Territories. Particularly close relations were cemented with Mayor 'Abd en-Nabi en-Natsheh of Hebron, who in the autumn of 1985 hosted a fifty-member PLP delegation headed by Mi'ari. En-Natsheh received many return invitations.[62]

Dissent broke out within the PLP in 1986, with the party's Nazareth periodical passing into the hands of an opposition faction. Subsequently, the central PLP leadership signed an agreement with the East Jerusalem paper *Al-Fajr*, according to which it would serve as a forum for PLP views, along with its other periodical, *Al-Watan*.[63]

From 1984 on, the movement conducted vigorous organizing efforts, consolidating its institutions, bridging differences, and endeavoring to maintain a united front. However, throughout, the tension between its Arab and Jewish components never subsided: the Arab Progressive Movement on the one hand, and its Jewish partner, "Alternativa," on the other.

Father Riah Abu el-'Asal, of Nazareth, proved – as secretary general – to be the movement's outstanding organizer. He resigned, however, at the PLP's third conference in July 1990, under the backdrop of a boycott by Progressive Movement members in Nazareth. That conference also rejected a proposal by Matti Peled to merge the Progressive Movement and Alternativa into a single, egalitarian party, bringing further into view friction between the two partners.

A message of support from Yasser Arafat sent by fax was read by Mi'ari, to the applause of the delegates. It was obvious to all that an expression of support in that manner was intended to enhance Mi'ari's position within the PLP.[64] Mi'ari took a militant nationalistic tone at the conference, going to the extent of hinting that if Israeli Arabs were not given equal rights in all spheres, they would join the Intifadah. The above ostensibly indicates the priority the PLP attaches to equality over broad political goals, which are, of themselves, insufficient to warrant an uprising by Israeli Arabs.[65]

In February 1988, Mi'ari crossed a clear "red line" by attending a PLO press conference in Athens, along with Yasser 'Arafat's spokesman, Bassam Abu Sharif, as part of the attempt to send a boat with returning refugees to Israel. Israel's Attorney General deemed the incident participation in PLO activities, an act far more significant than meeting PLO members, and hence requested the Knesset House Committee to lift Mi'ari's parliamentary immunity. The PLP leader took advantage of the Attorney General's ruling to announce that he would be pleased to be in prison with "Israeli army personnel who refused to serve in the Territories and Palestinian freedom fighters."[66]

Once again in 1988, the PLP had to fight for its right to compete in the elections. Once again, the Central Election Committee disqualified it, and once again, the Supreme Court ruled it a legal party, although this time, not unanimously. The controversy centered on clause 7a of the amended Basic Law: The Knesset, which permits disqualification on ideological grounds. The Court delved into the question of the degree to which the PLP denied the Jewish character of the State of Israel, and apparently did not find its task an easy one. In the end, the justices, by a 3–2 vote, permitted the PLP to run in the elections.[67]

In the ensuing campaign, the PLP stressed its support for the Intifadah, "the revolution of stones." It gave salience to the Palestinian question at the expense of the struggle for equality; it attacked Rakah vigorously for stressing the "Israeliness" of Palestinians in Israel at the expense of their "Palestinianism." In its platform, it gave prominence to its view of itself as a "current" within the Palestinian national movement. It spared no effort to win support from centrist forces within the PLO.

An election advertisement in the newspaper *As-Sinarah* announced unequivocally that "The Progressive List for Peace has one national platform. Even the supreme Palestinian authority (i.e., the PLO) has endorsed the platform. Leader Yasser 'Arafat has signed it, after writing on it in hand, 'Together with our holy land.'"

> "Can the leadership of the Israel Communist Party, atrophying, failing, two-faced, tell the Palestinian masses who has signed their platform . . . "[68]

All along, the PLP's Arab leaders, Mi'ari and Father Abu el-'Asal, boasted about their being branded "PLO agents" in the Knesset.[69] PLP election posters displayed the slogan "A Palestinian heart, Arab faces, and human aspirations," under the party logo. Pictures of Yasser 'Arafat were shown alongside those of Mi'ari, or with the greeting, "You in the Progressive Movement are a noble Palestinian current, which we are proud of . . . "[70] The PLP retained only one seat that year. It lacked 3,431 votes to retain its second. It also could have done so by means of an agreement with another party to transfer excess votes.[71]

Support for the PLP declined in 1988 compared to 1984 by virtually every possible yardstick. Among urban Arabs, its vote declined from 20.4 to 15.9 percent; in the villages, from 15.2 to 6.1 percent; among Bedouin in the Negev, it virtually disappeared, declining from 11.7 to 1.1 percent.[72] It transpires that the hard nationalist line hurt, rather than helped, the PLP, yet it continued to be given prominence. The PLP leadership, above all Mi'ari, supported Saddam Hussein's invasion of Kuwait, as a means of bringing about unity in the Arab world.[73] The PLP paper *Al-Watan* published an editorial on August 17, 1990, which left little room for varying interpretations. Its heading was to the point: Yes to Saddam Hussein's Initiative, Yes to "*sumud* of Iraq."[74]

Knesset Member Mi'ari violently denounced the United States. Appearing in Umm el-Fahm, he lashed out against the attempt to impose a new dispensation on the Middle East and called for the building of one Arab nation, with a higher culture, to deal with events with a unified strategy.[75]

The Progressive Movement for Peace is currently in a moderate decline. Its strength already declined in the twelfth Knesset elections in 1988. The list ran in the elections for the thirteenth Knesset in 1992, but was divided and weakened and failed to win any seats. Support for it among rank-and-file Arabs is currently very slim. This trend, however, could be reversed with a renewed nationalist awakening among Israel's Arabs.

The Democratic Arab Party

The Democratic Arab Party (DAP) was established for the purpose of competing in the November 1988 Knesset elections. Its founder, 'Abd el-Wahhab Darawshah, had resigned from the Labor Party, which had originally given him his Knesset seat, furiously slamming the door in Labor's face and glorifying his Palestinian Arab nationality and the Intifadah, but without forfeiting the option of joining a future government. He chose to announce his resignation at a mass demonstration in Nazareth, organized by the Supreme Monitoring Committee, on the day that Palestinian independence was declared by the PLO in Algiers (January 15, 1988).

"Rabin is a murderer!" he shouted passionately as the masses roared with enthusiasm. He ordered Arab members of Labor to "return their membership cards to the Minister of Defense."[76] The new party did rather well. Its approximately 27,000 votes earned it one and a half Knesset mandates; the surplus of votes was lost.

For the first time, an all-Arab party, i.e., one with no Jewish members, joined the political tapestry represented in the Knesset. Obviously this party had no Jewish candidates; furthermore, almost as a deliberate gesture, it refrained from seeking Jewish support, in contrast to Rakah and the PLP, which went to great lengths to woo Jewish voters.[77] The emergence of the DAP at the height of the Intifadah gave it an incentive to clothe itself in a mantle aglow with fiery nationalist hues, leaving no room for Jewish members.

Unlike the Rakah-led Hadash and the PLP, the DAP emphasized its Arabism. The composition of the DAP's Knesset list was also notable for its Muslim complexion; Christians and Druze were hardly represented.[78]

The DAP platform is not very different from that of Hadash or the PLP in its focal advocacy of a Palestinian state throughout the occupied territories, including eastern Jerusalem, under the PLO flag, and its emphasis on the goal of full equal rights for Arabs in Israel.[79] As if to augment its Arab nationalist foundations, the DAP platform includes a call to "return previously expropriated land" to its "legal owners." Elsewhere it aspires to develop relations with dispersed Arab and Palestinian communities in pursuit of "common goals."[80]

The DAP flaunted its all-Arab nature in its election propaganda, warning, "The Arabs do not need Jews to represent them."[81] It proudly called itself *Hizb al-'Urubah*, the party of Arabism, and informed its constituents that its electoral success would represent a triumph for the Palestinian people.[82]

The President of Israel attended the party's founding convention. After he left the hall, Redwan Abu 'Ayyash, secretary of the Association of Arab Journalists in the Terrories, was called to the podium. He gave an impassioned speech that he introduced as follows: "I bring you greetings from the land of the Intifadah." The audience was asked to observe a moment of silence in memory of the victims of the Palestinian uprising.

DAP publications are replete with slogans such as: "No to the Iron Fist," "No to Occupation," "We Identify with Our People's Legitimate Nationalist Struggle." The party also stresses its Muslim nature, imploring believers to vote for a leader who repeats the traditional Islamic testimony that *"La ilah illa Allah, wa-Muhammad rasul Allah"* (There is no god but Allah, and Muhammad is the messenger of Allah).[83]

Despite all of this, the DAP made it clear that it would not boycott the government resulting from the elections because of its interest in wielding real political influence, in contrast to the sterile opposition of Hadash and the PLP. Its slogan in this regard was "Vote for Influence, not Dissidence."

The DAP list had to fend off the criticism of its sparring partners, Hadash and the PLP, to the effect that it was actually a Labor satellite. Darawshah's political origins fueled propaganda alleging that "he left Labor through the door in order to re-enter through the window." Darawshah bided his time, hoping – in vain – that Labor would attack him furiously and thereby cleanse him of this "stigma." Labor, however, did not bother to help its ex-stalwart. Consequently, he had to intensify his nationalist statements and emphasize the security-related details in the record of his party's candidates. Two of them were lawyers who had specialized in defending security prisoners in the Territories, one of whom had been forbidden by the army Southern Command to enter the Gaza Strip. Another one of the DAP's first five candidates, a business-man from Majd el-Kurum, flaunted the month-long administrative detention that he had served in 1956 under the military admin-istration. The DAP platform stressed these "vital" biographical details.[84]

But the competing parties, Hadash and the PLP, had an even more appealing history in this respect and they condemned the DAP in the strongest possible terms, although, as 'Abd el-Wahhab Darawshah himself put it, all three were peddling the same mer-chandise."[85] Because of the competition for the same target popu-lation, the PLP refrained from concluding a surplus-vote agreement with the DAP in order to deny it the national approval that this would confer. This rivalry made losers out of both parties' voters, for it impaired their ability to realize a very similar platform.

The DAP's deployment in the Arab sector reflects common sense and detailed knowledge of the political map. The fledgling party sought niches that had not been adequately represented by Hadash or the PLP. Therefore, the DAP turned to the Muslim sector, which had been under-represented in the other parties. The head of the Jat local council, a former teacher and academician from the Galilee village of Iksal named Ahmad Abu 'Isba, was placed in the number two slot on the list after Darawshah. Abu 'Isba was undoubtedly an excellent choice, not only because of his Muslim identity but also for his personality, rich experience, eloquence, and the reputation he had built up in his struggle for equality as a member of the Committee of Arab Local Council Heads.

The DAP also focused on the Bedouin, who had been unrepres-ented in the Knesset since the murder of MK Hamad Abu Rabi'a in 1981. The DAP placed a Bedouin lawyer from the Qudeirat es-Sane' tribe in the third slot, and he brought in 6,000 Bedouin votes, 43 percent of Arab votes in the Negev. Representation was also given to small localities, which were usually crowded out of the other parties' lists.

A majority of the DAP electorate was Muslim. The new party evidently bit most deeply into Labor, which lost about 10 percent of its voters; although the PLP only lost 4 percent, it also lost its second Knesset seat. In certain localities, there was an interesting correlation between the number of votes that Labor lost and those that the DAP won.[86] Interestingly, according to Darawshah, the DAP, despite its all-Arab nature, received more Jewish votes than the PLP. The party leader's decision to emphasize this fact indicates his desire to have the "best of both worlds." Indeed, although the DAP wished to paint its banners in bold nationalist colors, it did not want to position itself beyond the pale of candidacy for participation in government. It wanted genuine political influence and feared the dilution that the absence of power centers and ability to act would cause. This combination might give it an edge over its competitors, but it also contained a contradiction that the DAP's rivals cited in their efforts to undermine it.

The results of the elections, as announced the night after the balloting, were construed by the DAP's leader and founder as a resounding victory for Arabism. Thus he proclaimed his credo haughtily:

> We have made history in the State of Israel. This is the first time that a nationalist Arab party has succeeded in entering the Knesset as an independent list, not as a satellite of Zionist parties. We have accomplished this even though the Zionists and the Communists spent many months fighting us. Our party with one mandate will be far more active and effective than older parties with five mandates. We are the true victors, and our Arab people is on the right path.[87]

Practically speaking, the DAP was not greatly enhanced in its activity by its single parliamentary deputy, unlike the experienced Hadash and the PLP, the latter also with a single seat in the twelfth Knesset.

In the Likud–Labor rivalry that followed the collapse of the National Unity government in 1990, the DAP stance was essentially no different than that of Hadash and the PLP. All three were willing to form a bloc to prevent the formation of a right-wing government, provided that two conditions were met: the continuation of the peace process, in accordance with the points set forth by U.S. Secretary of State James Baker, and the assurance of equal rights for Arabs in Israel.

The DAP did not encumber the leftist bloc and seems to have

reached an agreement with it that was never fully disclosed. In retrospect, this understanding came to naught when Shimon Peres failed to set up a government and Yitzhak Shamir assumed leadership.

Because it is outside the government's sphere of operation and lacks centers of power, the DAP has to fight for its existence in the Arab street. It vacillates as to how to underscore its uniqueness. It is threatened by the possibility of the independent entry of the Islamic Movement into the electoral system, because this would certainly lessen its influence among Muslims.

The occupation of Kuwait by Iraqi forces forced the DAP to make a difficult choice. It sensed the mood in the Arab street and responded to its constituency's feelings by expressing its support for Saddam Hussein's forced "unification," stressing its disgust with the corrupt regimes of the oil emirates, which had "squandered the Arab nation's money."[88] By the same token, MK Darawshah underwent contortions *vis-à-vis* the Jewish public to avoid identifying with support of Hussein's threats against Israel. However, another DAP leader, Shukri el-'Abd, explained that

> it will be impossible to impose peace on Israel without force, and countries cannot interrelate soundly without the element of fear. I want a strong Arab nation. The State of Israel wants a weak, divided Arab nation, because only thus can it avoid having to make peace.[89]

Ahmad Abu 'Isba, the second on the DAP list, was more moderate:

> We oppose forcible annexation; we favor peaceful resolution of all Middle East conflicts; we favor the Kuwaiti people's right to decide its own fate and to liberate itself from the decadent rulers who sit at the oil tap like America's faithful watchdogs.[90]

The DAP needs solid internal organization, a means of expression, and the ability to make broad public inroads in order to strike roots in the Arab sector. Only thus may it obtain the niches of support with which it will take its place in the variegated political spectrum. It has its finger on the nationalist pulse, is building its chances of making various breakthroughs, but faces the danger of corrosion by rivals to its right and its left.[91]

In the thirteenth Knesset elections in 1992, the DAP won two seats. Its leader, 'Abd el-Wahhab Darawshah, kept his seat in the Israeli parliament and was joined by a Bedouin MK, attorney Talab Abu Sane'.

The Islamic Movement

The "Young Muslims" were the last to join the tapestry of political currents in the Arab sector. This is a large movement with a special character: neither a party nor a list, neither an ideational caucus nor an operational entity. It is not even a "body," but rather a multi-faceted phenomenon that perhaps embraces all these definitions in a complex combination.

It rocketed onto the Israeli Arab scene in 1988, signalling the maturation of a growth process that originated after the Six Day War, when it became possible to cross the "Green Line". This barrier, which had previously kept Israeli Arab youth who wished to study Islam from probing these religious intellectual horizons, was shattered all at once. At the height of the secularization trend, the weakening of traditional frameworks, and rampaging westernization, Arab high-school students suddenly had the option of attending Arab institutions of higher education in the Muslim faith.

Initially, the enrollment of young Israeli Arabs in religious studies in the West Bank was not considered very important. There was still only a trickle of students at that stage, and the transition itself was regarded as a natural outcome and manifestation of the growing contact with the occupied territories.

Only in retrospect will researchers identify the first step in the career of the Israel Islamic Movement's spiritual leader, Sheikh 'Abdallah Nimr Darwish of Kafr Qassem, in his application to enroll for studies at the Islamic Institute in Nablus. Darwish, born in 1948, entered this institute at the tender age of twenty-one to spend the next four years acquiring a broad religious education. Israel had no institution of its kind, because the Muslim religious elite had been truncated in the mass flight of 1948 and could not be renewed without importing *'ulama*, religious leaders, from abroad.

Darwish was the first to choose this direction of higher studies, but he was not the only one. He was followed by young Muslims who would become leaders of the Islamic Movement in Umm el-Fahm. Sheikh Khaled Muhanna, Sheikh Raid Salah Abu Shaqra Mahajna, and Sheikh Hashem 'Abd er-Rahman, all three born in 1958, attended the Islamic Law College in Hebron from 1976 to

1979, and after graduating undertook the mission of disseminating Islamic religious teachings in Israel.[92]

It is absolutely clear that this group set out to arrest the spread of secularism among Muslims in Israel at the right time, in two senses: the danger, as perceived by these religious intellectuals, of estrangement from the wellsprings of Islam, and the readiness of many Israeli Arabs to "return to the faith." The latter sentiment was fueled by the following frustrations:

1. Disillusionment with Arab secular political bodies, such as Rakah or other fringe national organizations (Al-Ard, the Progressive National Movement, and the Sons of the Village) that came on the scene with great *élan* but faded when faced with difficult political decisions. On the other hand, the attempts to integrate into the Zionist political constellation also seemed either pointless or indicative of disloyalty or egotism on the part of individuals or families. Thus, the only way to improve the conditions of Israeli Arabs politically and otherwise seemed by many among them to be passing through the (still untested) Islamic political organizations.
2. The failure of the Arab states or, in a larger sense, the Arab national movement, to solve the Palestinian problem.
3. The daily existential struggle of Israeli Arab citizens amid serious basic problems in the fields of house building, development, education, and employment, coupled with issues of equality and discrimination, which the existing political organizations could not solve.

These factors created a hunger for religion as a framework of new hope. It came about at the right historical moment, when Israeli Arabs were given the opportunity to go on the *hajj*, the pilgrimage to Mecca and Medina; to attend Friday public worship in the mosques on the Temple Mount (*al-Haram ash-Sharif*) in Jerusalem; to attend Islamic colleges in Judea and Samaria; to consult libraries bursting with religious writings; and to maintain two-way contact between religious sages, preachers, and effervescent religious political parties, including some outside of Israel: the Muslim Brotherhood, *Hizb at-Tahrir al-Islami* (Muslim Liberation Party), and charitable associations in eastern Jerusalem, Judea, and Samaria. The success of Shi'ite Islam in Iran and Lebanon may have some bearing on this phenomenon.

Under these circumstances, the call for an Islamic revival did not go unheeded. The core of the movement took shape in the Triangle, whence it spread to the Galilee, principally to Nazareth. Its current swept up both the masses and the intellectuals, including doctors such as Suleiman Eghbaria of Umm el-Fahm and Khaled Diyab of Nazareth, editor of the religious journal *Al-Bayan*. Along with them came educators, journalists, and engineers, who held important positions in their localities.

Its strongholds are the charitable associations that form integral parts of the movement, principally those known as *Ar-Rabitah al-Islamiyyah*, which operate in Umm el-Fahm, Nazareth, and Tayyibeh. They sponsor a network of public services such as kindergartens, libraries, summer camps for youngsters, and sports associations incorporated in the Union of Islamic Sports, *Al-Ittihad ar-Riyadi al-Islami*. The movement put out a lavish newspaper, *As-Sirat* (The Path), edited by its leader, Sheikh 'Abdallah Nimr Darwish. Darwish also disseminated his ideas in books, letters, and sermons, making use of printers in Nablus, Tulkarm, and the towns of the Triangle.[93]

The Islamic revival did not coalesce into a solid bloc from its outset. A review of its development points to quarrels between opposing factions, and several metamorphoses took place before it reached its present format. As it evolved, it rejected the extremist dogma of its initial phase under the name *Usrat al-Jihad* ("The Family of Holy War"), led by Farid Abu Mukh, which operated in the underground in the Triangle until it was detected and disbanded in the early 1980s.[94]

The movement clearly perceives itself as bearing a national mission *vis-à-vis* the Arabs of Israel as an integral part of its religious message, in the light of the Islamic slogan *"din wa-dawla taw'aman"* – religion and state are twins. This is why some fear that this movement will slide into intransigent national fundamentalism of the kind manifested by Hamas or by the Qassamiya, a Muslim fundamentalist organization under Sheikh 'Izz ed-Din el-Qassam that surfaced in Palestine in the 1930s.

The image of the movement's leader, Sheikh 'Abdallah Nimr Darwish, appears different at present: more moderate, down-to-earth, sophisticated, and pragmatic. He has avoided Khomeinism and, unlike Dr. Khaled Diyab, rejected the doctrine of Sa'id Hawwa, the ideologist of the Muslim Brotherhood in Syria, who advocates violent opposition to the regime there. In the same spirit he has criticized the Jihad group in Egypt.

In other words, Sheikh Darwish wishes to display his intent to attain his movement's goals not by bloody confrontation but by preaching steadfastness in a protracted struggle for Palestinian national aspirations, including effectuation of the "right of return." Darwish's sermons plainly suggest an attempt to keep his teachings free of too extremist a stamp, aware as he is of the dangers that such an image would create.

Nevertheless, there is no doubt that the Islamic Movement fervently supported the Intifadah. Its newspaper, *As-Sirat*, repeatedly stressed its solidarity with the Islamic nature of the uprising and its encouragement of the "Intifadah, favored by Allah." The leader of the movement himself, Sheikh 'Abdallah Nimr Darwish, urged Arabs in Israel to identify with their brothers in the Territories and provide them with food and financial support. The movement has gained considerable political momentum in recent years by emphasizing action. It has established a cultural and educational network that includes private schools; it offers substantial economic assistance to the disadvantaged; and it promotes the idea of fulfilling the commandment of *zakat* (charity), one of the Five Pillars of Islam. It also demonstrates that its activities are of genuine benefit by campaigning against corruption and vice, including western cultural innovations such as movies, television, and rock music.

In the 1988 Knesset election campaign, the Arab parties had already become aware of the movement's vast influence and attempted to enlist its support. Sheikh Darwish, however, was not keen to commit himself; only at the last minute did he instruct his followers to support 'Abd el-Wahhab Darawshah's party and the PLP. The Islamic Movement participated in its first round of municipal elections with tremendous panache that led to impressive successes, both in the "capital of the Triangle," Umm el-Fahm, where it captured the mayoralty, and in Nazareth and many other Arab localities.

Today, no one doubts its real power, its solid infrastructure, and the growing admiration of its leader. Darwish does not hesitate to appear in the Hebrew mass media to seek Israeli public approval of his movement.

The Islamic Movement evidently exploits its successes to enhance its strength and wealth by fundraising in Israel and abroad. Its financial resources are steadily expanding, its socio-educational activities making new inroads, and its political influence intensifying.

The main rival of the Islamic Movement in the Arab sector is Rakah. The movement denounces Communism fiercely but also snipes at other factions, such as the Progressive List for Peace and Darawshah's Democratic Arab Party. It seized the mayoralty of Umm el-Fahm from Rakah, trimmed Rakah's support in Nazareth city hall, and has not stopped there.

The attempt by secular Arab political movements to form an opposing coalition does not seem to have slowed the movement's spread, and the complexity of its opponents' attitudes toward it is perceptible. Alongside fear, anxiety, and effort to curb it, there have also been attempts at appeasement, conciliation, and currying of support, or, at least, prevention of hostility.

The movement navigates cautiously and misses no opportunity to appear as a "superpower," as if viewing the local political struggle from above. For example, it granted its followers absolute freedom in voting in the November 1989 Histadrut elections, as the movement's spokesman, Sheikh Hashem Mahajna of Umm el-Fahm declared, so as to refute rumors that an order to vote for Labor had been given.

The Islamic Movement won about 3,500 votes in elections for the Nazareth Workers Council even though it did not participate in these elections. It is self-evident that the movement's voters did so knowing in advance that their votes would be disqualified in order to express protest or mockery of the other lists.

Islamic Movement leaders belong to the Monitoring Committee and take an active part in its decisions. They have proved to be excellent tacticians, both in their attempts to accumulate political power against their adversaries and in their skirmishes with the Israeli government.

The mayor of Umm el-Fahm has become a leader whose oratory resounds in current issues. In the spring of 1990, he led the struggle to obtain NIS 100 million (then $50 million) from the state budget in order to solve the problems of the Arab municipal authorities. It was he who proposed sending a delegation to the UN to complain of discrimination and to meet with representatives of the foreign diplomatic corps in Israel. The decision was shelved when the Interior Minister agreed to earmark a substantial sum for these municipal authorities.

With typical sophistication, he expressed his opinion on Jewish immigration from the USSR not by direct opposition but by protesting that the government, so swift to raise billions to integrate

these immigrants, found it difficult to provide the Arab authorities with a mere "hundred million," as if Israeli Arabs were
stepchildren.

When crisis erupted in the National Unity government in 1990,
the leadership of the movement lost no time in deciding to set up a
new party that would participate in the general elections and, it was
hoped, become a factor that could tip the scales. The decision was
made on March 13, 1990, with the movement expressing willingness
to join a united Arab list, mainly in partnership with the DAP and
the PLP, in a Muslim alliance against the Rakah-led "red front," i.e.,
Hadash.

Serious obstacles soon emerged. Many members of the movement opposed this step, stressing the contradiction that arose from
pledging allegiance to the State of Israel and its laws, as movement
leaders would have to do if elected to the parliament. Could Israeli
legislation possibly be reconciled with the precepts of the Muslim
faith? Thus the Islamic Movement decided not to participate in the
thirteenth Knesset elections in late 1992.[95]

Christians and secular Muslims who do not favor the fundamentalist Muslim movement vote for the PLP and the DAP. There is no
doubt, however, that both parties need the blessing of the sheikh
from Kafr Qassem. Be this as it may, the Islamic Movement is
obviously a rising political force. Its image has not yet come into
full focus, and it constantly reshapes its attitudes in accordance
with circumstances. It certainly threatens Rakah's pride of place in
the Arab sector.

As the 1996 elections come into sight, the movement seems to
have changed its mind and will probably participate in the polls,
perhaps in alignment with other Arab factions. The movement may
tumble into schism on these grounds.

The Emergence of a Country-Wide Political Leadership

The Committee of Arab Local Council Heads

The Committee was established as a national body dedicated to
promoting Arab municipal interests. Within two years, though,
its explicitly political character stood out in bold relief under the
backdrop of "Land Day," on March 30, 1976, an event upon which
it left its stamp of leadership. That date was a milestone in the

relationship between the State and its Arab minority. From that day on, none doubted the political significance of the Committee, which had attained recognition as *national* leadership, as a force that initiates and reacts, as an ultimate address and supreme authority.

A general strike was declared for "Land Day" in reaction to a decision by the government to expand the city limits of the Jewish townships of Upper Nazareth and Karmiel, by sequestering land from the Arab villages of Arraba, Sakhnin, and Deir Hanna. The Committee as a body had not declared the strike, although central figures on it participated in the organization of the strike.

On May 24, 1976, a meeting took place between the Committee and Prime Minister Rabin. The Committee was represented by a number of particularly influential local council heads: Ibrahim Nimr Hussein, of Shefar'am; Hanna Muweis, of Rama; Jamal Tarabey, of Sakhnin; Mis'ad Qassis, of Ma'ilya; Zaki Diab, of Tamra; Ahmad Masalha, of Daburiyya; Tareq 'Abd el-Hayy, of Tira; 'Abd er-Rahim Hajj Yahya, of Tayyibeh; and Jalal Abu To'meh, of Baqa el-Gharbiyya. It was a heterogeneous group, composed of traditional figures and educated young people, extremists and moderates, Rakah members and the unaffiliated. "Land Day" had been a turning point for a number of them, who came to the conclusion that it behooved them to keep a distance from the regime.

A case in point is Tira mayor Tareq 'Abd el-Hayy, who until then was considered close to the regime. On "Land Day," a mob marched on his home and denounced him as a traitor. He felt like a traitor, and "crossed the lines," joining Rakah, with which he had hitherto been at sword's ends.

The group prepared a position paper for its meeting with the prime minister. It was an acid document, emphasizing the lack of any action in solving underlying problems, and at the same time protesting the seizure of land and justifying the events of "Land Day". The paper stated that thousands of acres which had been

> under private ownership for generations were transferred to State ownership on the pretext that they were uncultivated or rocky lands. These actions are a perversion of justice. The Arabs see these actions as a means of dispossessing them of their land. The fact is that Israel's Arabs, who constitute some 14 percent of the State's citizens never enjoyed [land] seizures such as this, but only the opposite. A Jewish moshav or kibbutz that rents land to Arabs for seasonal cultivation

is punished by the appropriate institutions. The events of March 30 of this year contain not a little bitterness that has been pent up inside the country's Arabs. The height of bitterness, which has been given expression on March 30 of this year, is the latest seizure of land, and reports of plans for seizure in the future, even if 10 or 15 years hence, and not as certain parties in the media or newspapers have tried to explain, as if this is a continuation of the incidents of 1936.[96]

The Committee demanded a rescinding of land seizures in the Galilee and Triangle; transfer of State lands situated in Arab villages to those villages; return of land designated for the State under the terms of an arrangement reached with holders of those lands during the last 15 years; payment of an indemnity, in land, for land that had been sequestered; and transfer of *waqf* land to a committee to be chosen by local councils in the Arab sector (namely, the Committee of Arab Local Council Heads).

A disbanding of "Arab departments," which "in the eyes of Arab citizens are a symbol of discrimination," was also demanded, as well as the "establish[ment of] a coordinating committee, in the Office of the Prime Minister, which should include representatives of the elected Arab local governmental authorities, which would deal with all issues related to the integration of the Arabs into the life of the country, in all facets of life, and with ways to close the social, educational, and economic gaps within a period not to exceed two-three years."

Subsequent to "Land Day," the Committee had appealed to the prime minister to cancel charges being brought against demonstrators, to rehire those who had lost their jobs, and even to appoint a board of inquiry.

After the meeting with the prime minister, a letter was sent him summarizing the Committee's positions, and for the first time, protesting the non-recognition of Israeli Arabs *as a national minority*, expressing concern for the prime minister's assertion that Israel is a Jewish state the primary goal of which is the realization of the hopes of Zionism. "We request that the honorable gentleman take note of our feelings, that we are equal partners in this country, and that it is not reasonable that the Israeli-Arab conflict should justify any lessening whatsoever of equal rights for Arabs and recognition of our national reality, which is a historic reality." This chapter in the Committee's history, under the backdrop of that first "Land Day," was a cornerstone in the process of its becoming the national leadership of the country's Arabs. From the outset, a transformation was discernible on the Committee. It was similar to that which had taken place in the composition of local councils in Arab villages with the ascendancy of the young and educated. The establishment of the national Committee gave expression to the trend toward a national leadership, which had hitherto not managed to take form. The Committee itself did not immediately assume that role; a process involving several stages was required before it could strike roots as a national leadership.

Rakah attempted to control the Committee. Hanna Muweis, a Knesset member of the Rakah-led Hadash list, headed the Committee until his death in early 1981. On June 9 that year, Shefar'am mayor Ibrahim Nimr Hussein was unanimously elected to replace Muweis and immediately announced that the Committee would preserve its independence and not be involved in partisan politics. After Hussein's election, Rakah influence waned on the Committee, which went on to reject a proposal by Nazareth mayor (and Rakah leader) Tawfiq Zayyad to elect three deputy Committee chairmen and add three more Rakah supporters to its membership.[97] Hussein (also known as Abu Hatem) has kept his position as Committee chairman ever since.

The government had not recognized the Committee as the representative of the local councils. It does seem that Hussein's election was intended to clear the atmosphere for such recognition. Hussein himself promised to coordinate the Committee's activities fully with the Local Government Center. Both sides, however, were entirely aware that the Committee arose as an organ of national leadership for Israel's Arabs, and not to deal with such mundane matters as sewage, water, and electricity.

In 1981, the Committee adopted articles of association, spelling out its activities in the realm of municipal affairs and emphasizing its intention of working with the Local Government Center. It also includes political clauses, among them a demand to realize "the legitimate rights of the Palestinian people."

Virtually every year, the Arab municipalities declare a strike over their straightened finances and discrimination in distribution of government funds. Sometimes the councils themselves go on strike, which tend to be for longer periods each year; sometimes a general strike in the Arab sector is declared. The Arab councils went on strike in March 1990, in accordance with a Committee decision of March 24, 1990, a week before "Land Day". In the summer of 1991, Arab council heads staged a sit-down strike opposite the

Knesset.[98] Committee chairman Hussein stressed that the local councils would not go back to work until a solution was found, "so that the public could see the neglect and deprivation we live under."

The Committee organized the March, 1991 "Land Day" without demonstrations, and the day in fact passed without untoward incident. That summer, though, the Arab councils went on strike, to back up their demand for increased government subvention of their depleted coffers. The council heads demonstrated opposite the government office complex in Jerusalem, and dispersed only after their demands had been met. They had achieved their aim with the aid of the Local Government Center, with which they had come to work closely, including with right-wing Likud representatives. At the same time, in the periods preceding "Land Days," police officers and Committee representatives meet to work out ways of maintaining order in the course of a general, national strike. Thus, the Committee has combined two levels of local and national activity without anyone taking notice anymore.

The struggle for Arab equality in Israeli life is without doubt a central aim of Committee activity. However, alongside it is its broad political activity, with the aim of strengthening the Committee's standing as the national leadership of Israeli Arabs. Hence, Committee denunciations of Israeli intervention in Lebanon; collection of contributions for war victims; aid for people in the Territories during the Intifadah; denunciation of the bloody incident on Temple Mount during the Feast of Tabernacles, in October, 1990; and the sending of a Committee delegation to worship at the al-Aqsa Mosque in times of tension, either to denounce Israeli policy or give open support for some Palestinian goal. Relations within the Committee are not uniform over time. There are, of course, various political power struggles, as well as struggles of a personal nature. The positions of Rakah constitute something of an "average," or "meeting ground," within the Committee; this does not, however, indicate domination of the Committee by Rakah. There are also individual council heads who take moderate, pragmatic positions, rather than go along with provocative demands.[99]

After the March, 1989 municipal elections, a new 20-member National Committee of Arab Council Heads was chosen. Eight of its members were Communists, three members belonged to the Islamic movement, and one member each belonged to the Progressive List for Peace and Democratic Arab Party. Seven members refused to divulge their political affiliations, although a number of them were known to have links with Zionist parties. Sons of the Village and the Progressive National Movement also had representation on the Committee.

Rakah influence had declined on the Committee, while there was a strengthening of a pragmatic tendency. The Committee indicated an increasing degree of political maturity, a capacity to direct affairs in time of crisis, and ability to enter into alliances beyond its own parochial setting. During the contest between the Labor Alignment and the Likud for chairmanship of the Local Government Center, the Committee was courted by both.

Abu Hatem came to be called "the president of the Arab sector," and indeed spared no effort to bridge over differences between the various forces active in that sector. At his initiative, efforts were begun to put together a common list for elections to the Histadrut Labor Federation. That list's platform would give prominence to planks calling for equality for Arabs, two states for two peoples, recognition of the PLO as representative of the Palestinian people, and the rights of Palestinian workers.

The guiding principle of the new National Committee was formally announced in May 1989, shortly after its election: "Complete solidarity with the heroic Intifadah," along with "strict care that the said solidarity be expressed only within the law and giving due consideration to the fact that the [Israeli] Arabs are citizens of the State of Israel." In other words: The Intifadah, as it is, must not cross the "Green Line," notwithstanding the unqualified support given it as a just uprising of the Palestinian people in the Territories.[100]

The Joint Monitoring Committee

The Joint Monitoring Committee was established from the Committee of Arab Council Heads following the Israeli invasion of Lebanon in June 1982. The war in Lebanon caused a storm among Israel's Arabs, which created the need to broaden their national leadership by including those who represented them in the Knesset and Histadrut. With their blood affinity with refugees in nearby camps, they felt called upon to raise their voices, particularly in view of the danger to which the refugees were exposed during the invasion and the ensuing bloody incidents. And they felt much freer to do so, given the internal controversy in Israel over the issue.

The Committee met in Shefar'am on June 19, 1982 and issued a sharp statement:

> The Committee vigorously protests the war of extermination against Lebanon, against the Lebanese people, and against the Palestinian people in Lebanon. We demand an immediate cessation of this war and the removal of the Israeli army from Lebanese soil, without condition . . . The Committee calls for a collection of contributions and [the extension of] help to the war victims in Lebanon and requests that the Arab powers take part in this humanitarian effort.[101]

However, the war continued, reaching a grisly climax with the massacre at the Sabra and Shatilla refugee camps in Beirut, which was perpetrated by an Israeli-backed Christian Lebanese militia. In the wake of this massacre, violent demonstrations took place on September 2. It was then that additional status was required for the national leadership, a symbol of its national scope.

At this juncture, the Joint Monitoring Committee was established, as somewhat of an upper house. It was composed not only of Committee members, but also of Arab Knesset members of all parties and Arab members of the Histadrut Central Committee. The move coincided with the ambitions of the Arab Knesset members, who needed the new body to help them keep their seats, just as that new body was strengthened by their presence in it. The same was the case with the Histadrut officials. The new body engendered a degree of tension between the various political currents, but also brought about a closing of ranks.

The Monitoring Committee's first meeting, on October 30, 1982, was held in Shefar'am, which became the leadership's quasi-capital, and whose mayor became its chairman. The agenda included a number of practical items, such as the deplorable financial condition of the Arab municipalities; opposition to expansion of the Misgav regional council's limits at the expense of Arab jurisdictions; and expansion of the areas of those jurisdictions, which did not have sufficient reserves of land for development. The Monitoring Committee serves as the sounding board for the central topics that are raised from time to time in the Arab sector, such as land, master plans for local development, and allowances for large families.

The principal thrust of the Monitoring Committee's activities has been toward equality for Arabs in all spheres of life. However, alongside its practical positions, it conducts a ceaseless effort on behalf of the national aspirations of Israel's Arabs, to denounce government policy, to warn, to call for action to help the needy in the Territories. Time and again, the Committee had to guide Israeli Arabs in respect of the Intifadah, while making no bones of its identification with it, and affording it material aid. However, when events are near a boiling point, such as during a general "Land Day" strike, the Committee always sees it as incumbent upon itself to restrain, so as to avoid bloodshed and upsetting the fragile balance between Jews and Arabs.

At the same time, one must not forget that it is the Committee that calls the strikes in the first place, the strikes during the course of which tempers flair and Molotov cocktails are thrown. The Committee, however, is between the hammer and the anvil, and must guard against either of two pitfalls: it must prove itself a fighting national leadership, lest it be perceived as too "establishment"; on the other hand, it bears responsibility to prevent matters from getting out of control, and to stay the pragmatic course. That latter course is the only way to blend into the life of the country.

The "middle way" consists, on the one hand, of restraint in actual employment of the general strike weapon, and prevention of incidents during strikes. On the other hand, the middle way involves threats of strikes, to bring Arab wishes to the attention of the powers that be, particularly the wishes of the young. It also involves the initiation of protest activities, such as those against the curfew in the El-Bureij refugee camp in the Gaza Strip in October, 1990; the organization of aid to camp inhabitants; taking militant political positions; and continued efforts to find common denominators between the various elements that make up the leadership.

An outstanding example of such a middle way was the reaction of Committee chairman Hussein to the Persian Gulf crisis. In August 1990, he said,"We oppose any conquest and any belligerence perpetrated by one country against another. The use of force does not solve problems . . . Why do the Americans insist on coming in? Where were they from 1967 till now?" He explained that the Arabs see the United States as an enemy, and that sympathy for Iraq emanated from an expectation of deliverance, when people were tired of waiting and Arab regimes were seen to have contributed nothing to the solution of the Palestinian problem.[102]

In March, 1995, the Monitoring Committee decided not to call a general strike on "Land Day," but to demand that the peace process be speeded up and that the municipal boundaries of Arab local authorities be enlarged.

Arab Voting Patterns

General Characteristics

Voting patterns among Israeli Arabs certainly reflect the soul of this complex sector of the country's population from a variety of standpoints. Analysis of these patterns is necessary for an understanding of basic processes taking place in it. A breakdown of election results is insufficient for an understanding of socio-political trends. It behooves one to acquaint oneself with the forces at work within this divided population, before coming to conclusions about the purport of dry numerical results. The contest itself constitutes a critical element, as it is a reflection of the entire compendium of currents in conflict.

Israel's Arabs refer to an election year as *sanat al-marhaba*, or the year in which they are favored with many visits, greetings, and *promises* by the Jewish parties. Afterwards, there is a deep silence. Their generous visitors collected their booty, large or small, and vanished, to take stock. Gone are the cars bringing dignitaries to make speeches; the "home circles," where issues are discussed in depth. The courtship period between elections has shortened over the years; in the distant past, election year had also been called *sanat al-'asal*, "the year of honey." Israel's Arabs are adapting to a changing reality. Their eyes are open, yet, disillusionment has left its stamp upon them, and characterizes the approach of the Arab voter.

Arab influence in the Knesset is relatively small. While 18.5 percent of the country's population is Arab, only 5–6 Arabs, or roughly 5 percent, have sat in the legislature over the past decade. The reasons for this are as follows:

1. The percentage of Arabs eligible to vote is 6–7 percent below the Arab percentage of the population:[103] (a) Almost all East Jerusalem Arabs, who make up some 17 percent of Israel's Arabs, do not have Israeli citizenship. Hence, unlike their status in municipal elections, they cannot vote for the Knesset. (b)

Israeli Arabs and Druze have a higher birth rate, and hence are younger: the median age of Israeli Muslims is approximately 17.5 years, while that of the Jews is 27.9.[104] This of course explains the large percentage of Arabs who cannot vote. (c) One can assume that administrative errors in the voter rolls are more numerous for the Arab than the Jewish sector, or perhaps that in that sector there is less feeling of urgency to correct mistakes. There are no data for this matter and its magnitude is a matter of conjecture. There is no doubt, however, that the impact is marginal.

2. The rate of non-voting is relatively high, as a result of the boycott by extremist groups such as Sons of the Village, the Progressive National Party, and the An-Nahdah group of Tayyibeh. In addition there are also feelings of bitterness, frustration, and helplessness without connection to political groups. These are material factors in the higher Jewish turnout, which is approximately 80 percent, and which since 1981 has exceeded the Arab turnout by at least 6 percent.[105]

3. A splintering of votes across the political spectrum.

4. Loss of votes, given a non-inclination of the parties that derive their principal support from the Arab sector to enter into surplus-vote-sharing agreements.

5. Arab votes for Zionist parties, which do not allot realistic places on their lists of candidates to minority members; and the relatively high representation for Jews on the Rakah list, which derives most of its support from Arabs: two of Rakah's four members before the 1992 elections were Jewish, although it is to be stressed that they, too, support the party line, which is determined by its Arab leadership. On the other hand, Arab voters who supported Mapam in the 1988 election did not "justify" the inclusion of an Arab on its list, by a proportional calculation. Still, there is no doubt that Mapam's 3.7 percent of the Arab vote then was impressive. The Citizens' Rights List won 4.4 percent of the Arab vote, and Shinui 2.7 percent. Even the National Religious Party won 3.1 percent. The latter three parties, who between them in 1988 won over 10 percent of the Arab vote, did not allocate a single Knesset seat to members of that population segment.

The relative weight of these factors rose over the past decade, resulting until 1992 in a reduction in direct Arab representation in the legislature. In the elections during the period 1951 to 1981, eight and then seven Arabs had been sent to the Knesset (except for the elections of 1973). Later, their number was reduced to six. In the 1992 elections, seven Arab MKs were elected, and an eighth one joined later to fill a vacancy in one of the Zionist parties.

It is noteworthy that the Arab voter turnout had declined over the years from a high of 91 percent in elections for the third Knesset in 1955, to 74 percent in 1988, for the twelfth Knesset.[106] Had that 17 percent decline not occurred, and on the assumption that the distribution of votes remained what it was and that the factor of agreements for sharing of surplus votes remained constant, the Arab camp would have received additional seats. One may assume however, that most non-voters would have supported the Arab lists.

Table 3.1 Arab Participation in Knesset Elections as Voters and Members

Knesset	Years	% of Total Voters	% of Voter Participation	No. of Knesset Members
First	1949–51		79.3	3
Second	1951–55		85.5	8
Third	1955–59	8.19	91.0	8
Fourth	1959–61	7.73	88.9	7
Fifth	1961–65	8.34	85.6	7
Sixth	1965–69	8.34	87.8	7
Seventh	1969–73	8.35	82.0	7
Eighth	1973–77	8.35	80.0	6
Ninth	1977–81	9.19	75.0	7
Tenth	1981–84	9.75	69.7	6
Eleventh	1984–88	10.00	73.6	6
Twelfth	1988–92	11.00	73.9	6
Thirteenth	1992–	12.00	73.0	8

Note: The data are taken from Yehiel Harari (ed.), *Elections in the Arab Sector, 1977* (Giv'at Haviva, 1978), p. 11; and *The Arab Sector in Israel and the 1988 Knesset Elections*, pp. 52, 61, *Review*, 6, 41–42 (all in Hebrew).

The phenomenon in its entirety reflects the complex position of the Arab minority to a fuller extent than other characteristic contours of election results in that sector. It is abundantly clear that its principal reasons are not "technical." While hundreds of thousands of Jewish voters have emigrated or are outside the country during an election, Arab emigration is marginal. Hence, the disparity between the turnouts of Arab and Jewish voters is more meaningful than can be reflected in dry statistics.

In the past, the PLO command to boycott elections bore considerable weight; now, however, the PLO orders participation, lessening the impact of such groups as Sons of the Village and Progressive National Movement. Further, Arab participation in local elections has been much higher than for the Knesset. Among minority groups, the Druze have a very high rate of voter participation and the Muslims a very low rate, with the Christians in between. To date, no definitive study of the reasons for this phenomenon has been conducted. However, it seems to be the result of loss of faith, frustration, and a sense of estrangement, alongside constant agitation by extremist elements, which itself accrues from the above factors.

Another material factor on the political map is the lack of agreements on sharing of surplus votes. This factor is a reflection of the intense rivalry between parties that compete in the Arab sector, and whose platforms on critical issues are not clearly different. Rakah will not enter into such an agreement with either the PLP or the Democratic Arab Party (DAP). Neither have the latter two new parties seen fit to enter into such an agreement. The PLP has reviled the DAP as a Labor Alignment satellite, stressing the past of its founder, 'Abd el-Wahhab Darawshah as a Labor MK. The result was two Knesset seats that were lost, besides the two lost because of a low Arab turnout at the polls.

In the intense parliamentary maneuvering subsequent to the break-up of the National Unity Government in 1990, for example, those additional four seats would have been of material importance to the anti-Likud block. Those seats would also have conferred immense leverage to the Arab parties, beyond the actual number of seats held. Ten Arab Knesset members, even if some belonged to the Labor Alignment and Mapam, could have constituted a powerful lobby on behalf of the struggle for Arab equality. This "blocking majority" was indeed formed in 1992; at the time of writing (October 1995), the left-wing government depends on it and has made historic, revolutionary changes through the peace process with the PLO and Jordan, as well as profound changes of policy toward the Arab minority in Israel, with a view to closing the economic and social gaps existing between it and the Jewish majority.

It seems that the following trends can be expected, in the future, to gradually enhance Arab representation:

1. A constant increase in the number of young Arab voters. They are not likely to bring Arab electoral weight beyond the Arab percentage of the population, though, because of Jewish immigration from the former Soviet Union. Without that immigration, the relative Arab weight in the population would *double* in two generations or less, assuming that the disparity in birthrates between Jews and Arabs was preserved: already in the early 1990s, Arabs constituted half of Israel's population under 25![107]

2. One may assume that the day will come when the Islamic movement will decide to contend for Knesset seats, bringing thousands who have hitherto boycotted elections to the polling stations. Islamic entry into politics would undoubtedly not leave currently active Arab parties unaltered; such parties would probably merge, experience splits, spin off onto other groupings or have other forces join them. On balance, the net result could be either accelerated cleavage among Arab parties, or more of an inclination to work together.

3. The lesson of lost votes through a failure to reach surplus vote agreements has been fully learned.[108] The amended Basic Law: The Knesset, of October 1991, raising the minimal share of the vote required to enter the Knesset to 1.5 percent (from 1 percent), is also expected to be a powerful catalyst toward amalgamation, as a party now needs at least 40,000 votes. The amendment has already left its imprint on Knesset representation in general, and particularly on Arab parties, which tend to be small.[109]

4. The Zionist parties will have to think of new ways to attract Arab voters. They will invest most of their efforts among Druze, Christians, and the Bedouin. They will have no choice but to give these sectors more representation. In the case of the Druze, the large parties have the added incentive to keep satisfied a population segment that has given them strong support in the past.

5. The Christians may very well succeed in increasing their representation, given the expected appearance of an Islamic list, or if Muslim extremists manage to leave a deeper imprint on their voting patterns.

In brief, the percentage of Arabs who vote is likely to increase, and more Arabs are likely to be elected to the Knesset, including with the Zionist parties.

Arab Voting Trends since 1949

The distribution of Arab votes since the race for first Knesset in 1949 indicates the following:

1. A bitter struggle between the Communist Party (Rakah) and the Labor Alignment, or Mapai, as it was called in the early period. Until the ninth Knesset elections in 1977, when Rakah garnered 50.6 percent of the Arab vote and the Alignment only 27 percent (down from 41.7 percent in 1973), the Alignment had outpolled Rakah among Arabs.

2. The 1977 elections was also the turning point of Arab support for Rakah, which has continued to gradually decline.

3. Nationalist Arab lists sprouted up in the resulting vacuum, taking votes from both Rakah and the Alignment. In addition, other Zionist parties began taking larger portions of the Arab vote, as well: even the right-wing Likud took some, as did the National Religious Party and left-wing Meretz.

4. The Zionist parties achieved an aggregate of about half the Arab vote; the rest went to the Rakah-led Hadash front and to the DAP, which was seen as likely to stake out a comfortable middle ground: a nationalist Arab party, yet flexible and likely to bring Arabs into an Alignment-led coalition.

5. There appears to be a "floating" vote of some 10–15 percent, which is likely to support a party that appears inclined toward a middle ground.

6. In certain circumstances, Rakah may be perceived as centrist in the Israeli-Arab context: moderate, established, well-organized, sober, yet requiring a nationalistic dilution of its Marxism and an infusion of new blood.

     A process of internal fragmentation may prevent that from happening, though.

7. The Islamic movement is currently seen as Rakah's most dangerous enemy, although it also looms as a strong competitor for all other political lists. Rakah would have trouble competing with the Islamic movement among the Muslim

An Arab newborn baby is brought to his mother by a nurse in one of Israel's hospitals. Today almost no Arab woman gives birth at home.

The village of Barta'a in the Little Triangle was bisected by the 1949 armistice "Green Line" until 1967.

A meeting in the shadow of expected collapse. MK Fares Hamdan listens to the promise of Commerce and Industry Minister Pinhas Sapir, who tried in vain to save the food-canning plant in Baqa el-Gharbiyya.

A meeting in the *shiq*, the Bedouin hospitality tent: Gen. Moshe Dayan, then Chief of the Southern Command, often used to tour the tribes' camping areas, sometimes accompanied by his wife Ruth.

A rare meeting of Ben-Gurion with Christian notables. Teddy Kollek then served as Head of the Prime Minister's Office.

In 1963, the first Jewish-Arab Youth Camp was held, in which Arab girls participated as well. Abba Eban, then Deputy Prime Minister, lectured in literary Arabic so eloquently that it brought smiles to the faces of his Arab listeners.

Muslims praying at the mosque in an Israeli Arab village.

Easter ceremony performed by members of one of Israel's Christian-Arab communities.

Druze clergymen with President Zalman Shazar in Jerusalem, 1963.

A traditional house in the Arab village of Musmus in the Little Triangle, 1959 (left). Since then, much has changed there, as well as in other villages, as can be seen in the other photo: a house in the village of 'Ara, also in the Triangle, 1983 (below).

Bedouin in the Negev, 1949.

Bedouin harvesting their field in the early 1960s; modern machinery is already being used.

Bedouin dwelling in the Negev, 1991.

A street in Nazareth, 1984.

By the 1980s, women had already become full participants in political activities: women taking part in a demonstration for the establishment of a Palestinian state alongside Israel, held in the Arab town of Tayyibeh in 1988.

Arab students at Haifa University's library, 1974. The Hebrew sign says: "Arabic catalog."

Women and a man in traditional garb, as well as youngsters in modern clothing, in the 1988 Knesset elections in Kafr Qassem.

A traditional leader: the late Seif ed-Din Zu'bi with Chaim Weizmann, first President of the State of Israel, and Mrs Weizmann, in 1949.

Anti-government riots in the Arab village of Qalansawa, in the Little Triangle, on the first "Land Day," March 30, 1976, which signalled the growing rift between the Arab minority and the Jewish majority in Israel.

The Arab city of Umm el-Fahm in the Little Triangle has become a stronghold of the Islamic Movement, which runs various social projects there. The emblem of the annual Islamic Work Camp is painted on a wall in one of the city's sections.

Young demonstrators waving makeshift PLO flags in the Israeli-Arab village of Deir Hanna in Galilee in 1983 as a token of Palestinian identification.

A joint Communist-Islamic rally in the Israeli Arab town of Tayyibeh in 1988, in support of the Intifadah.

majority, although most Islamic votes may come from current non-voters, floating votes (mainly at the expense of the PLP and DAP), and even votes given to Zionist parties.

8.   Arab politics are not subject to rigid formulations. They move in circles of time, are sensitive to regional fluctuations, to events in Israel, and are influenced first and foremost from developments among the State's Arab population.

9.   Non-concurrence of elections to the municipalities and the Knesset constitute a factor which must be taken into account.

Table 3.2   Arab Support for the Communist Party versus its Zionist Opponents (in percentages)

Knesset	Year	Rakah	Align./Mapai and Satellites*	Mapam	Likud
First	1949	22.2	61.3	0.2	
Second	1951	16.3	66.5	5.6	
Third	1955	15.6	62.4	7.3	
Fourth	1959	10.0	52.0	12.5	
Fifth	1961	22.7	50.8	11.0	
Sixth	1965	22.6	50.1	9.2	
Seventh	1969	28.9	56.9	–	
Eighth	1973	38.7	41.7	–	
Ninth	1977	50.6	27.0	–	3
Tenth	1981	37.9	29.0	–	7†
Eleventh	1984	33.0	23.0	–	5
Twelfth	1988	33.0	20.4‡	3.7	7

Notes: * Governing party until 1977, when the Likud came to power.
† Likud appears in Arab sector for first time as governing party and doubles its strength.
‡ Actually, the Labor Party received only 16.7 percent of the Arab vote. Mapam, which broke from it, received 3.7 percent.

Since the 1960s, a salient fact of electoral life in Knesset elections has been the weakness of the traditional political forces. Internal conflict cause fragmented votes, and, as has been mentioned, clan and confessional community heads can no longer deliver the votes of their communities, as there is no immediately discernible connection between a decision at the polls and the particular clan or communal interest.

On the other hand, in local council elections, clan members are inclined to vote for their representative. Hence, thousands of Arabs tend to split their votes, with significant differences between the way they vote for the Knesset and for local councils. When election for the two levels of government are concurrent, deals are often made between political figures of local and national lists, trading votes for the Knesset for endorsements in the local race.

4

Relations with Arabs Abroad

The "Green Line" Breaks Down

The 1967 Six Day War broke the barrier of the "Green Line," which since 1948 had set apart neighboring Arab villages and had created, in a land that had been until 1948 a single entity, two separate societies albeit of the same origin. A reverse process seemed now to take place: Arabs from both sides of the former border resumed their contacts by visiting each other, going on excursions in both directions and holding meetings. This interaction took place on many social, political and economic levels.

The Widening Horizons of Israeli Arabs

Once the Armistice Line previously drawn up in Rhodes in 1949 had collapsed, and free passage eastward was allowed, residents of Tira, Kafr Qassem, Qalansawa and other Arab settlements in the Little Triangle flocked to visit their formerly close neighbors in the nearby West Bank. They renewed old ties, looked about to see what had happened since 1948, and compared their respective standards of living and opportunities. Many located family members whom they had not seen for many years. At the same time, numerous Arabs from all over Israel – the Galilee, the Negev, Jaffa, Lydda, Ramle and other mixed towns – also set out to look for relatives in the refugee camps, in the Big Triangle towns (i.e., Nablus, Jenin, Tulkarm), in Gaza, Rafah, and Khan Yunis.

Very soon this flow of people turned into an immense encounter. Once again, people from Tayyibeh or Baqa el-Gharbiyya could be seen sitting in cafés in Tulkarm, which gradually reinstated itself as the focus of attraction for the residents of the Little Triangle, a position formerly taken over by the Jewish city of Netanya. In these cafés, people discussed various issues, making comparisons, drawing conclusions; the higher level of development reached by Arab villages in Israel was juxtaposed with the better opportunities for advancement in the sociopolitical ladder offered to Palestinians in Arab countries. It turned out that in the West Bank there were a great many more people with higher education than among Israeli Arabs, and that the former were much more mobile and in great demand in the oil-producing countries.[1] At first, the firm economic situation of Israeli Arabs made an impression, but first impressions later gave way to different understandings.

The new circumstances sometimes opened the way for meeting with relatives in other Arab countries. The policy of "open bridges" has helped to extend such opportunities. Meetings took place in various ways – within the law as well as bypassing it – encouraged by a sense of diminishing distances and weakening prohibitions. A characteristic case was that of Fahima Zeitawi Abu Warda, a 40-year-old woman, the mother of eleven, who without much ado set out in August 1967 to visit her family in Jordan. She crossed the "Green Line," then the cease-fire line, spent one day with her relatives behind the lines, then went back home. She was intercepted only on her return trip and sentenced to a token one-day imprisonment. The judge, believing her story that she had only wished to visit relatives, ruled: "A day for a day."

The "new geography" gave rise to a growing pressure for family reunification. Since the war there had been a constant flow of requests to allow refugees to reunite with their families. In some special cases, permission was granted. Thus, the government of Israel allowed several refugee families who had fled from the village of Abu Ghosh during the fighting in 1948 to return to their village. Shortly after the Six Day War, the Arabs of Israel rallied to help and rehabilitate economically their kindred in the Territories; research conducted in the Little Triangle region showed that the expenses for hospitality, gifts, and financial aid had depleted the resources of the local inhabitants.

For the first time, Israeli Arabs were allowed to take part in the *hajj* pilgrimage, one of the five basic precepts of Islam. Thousands of them merged with millions of other Muslim pilgrims from different continents streaming toward Mecca and Medina. This opened the way for contacts between the Arab minority in Israel and the great majority of Arabs in the Middle East, of whom they are part. During the *tawaf* ceremony in Mecca in which the Qa'ba is circled, believers from Qalansawa, Tayyibeh, Nazareth, Jat, Tel Sheva, and Bir el-Maksur would meet with co-believers from Damascus, Cairo, Baghdad, Khartoum, and from villages, townlets and tribes from all parts of the Muslim world. This historical encounter had its influence on the Israeli Muslims' outlook.

Also, delegations of Israeli Arabs began set out to participate in various events in Arab countries. The first one was a condolence delegation to King Hussein on the occasion of his wife 'Alia's death in 1977. This was initiated by the director of the Istiqlal *waqf* in Haifa, Suheil Shukri.[2] A similar delegation of condolence met with President Assad of Syria following his son's death in a road accident in 1994. Activity in this field has not been particularly extensive, owing, perhaps, to some coolness on the part of Arab governments.

The Formation of Socioeconomic Contacts

The weakening of the political barrier led to the renewal of former contacts and the formation of new ones in both the social and economic areas. Arab workers from the Territories found work with their brethren in Israel, commercial connections were established, yet at the same time economic frictions were kindled. Thus, for instance, Arab quarry owners from Galilee who were suffering damages from competition with Judean stone formed a delegation headed by Arab Knesset members, demanding to impose tariffs on such imports, a demand that was complied with. Cheap agricultural products from the villages of Judea, Samaria and the Gaza Strip reduced the profits of Arab farmers in Israel. Sometimes the dumping of markets left no choice but to destroy surpluses.

Cheap labor from Gaza, Rafah, Halhul, Artas and other places in Judea, Samaria and Gaza pushed out Israeli Arab workers, who were not prepared to work for such low wages. Thousands of Arab workers from the Territories became employed in construction sites, building houses for newcomers from the former USSR; in the words of a Gazan journalist affiliated with Hamas: "I am ashamed to say that many of our people are hoping to make money from this building boom for the newcomers from Russia."

The competition with the Territories was becoming noticeable even in the sensitive area of dowry. Right after the end of the 1967 war, the Arab male population of Israel discovered the advantages of the new situation: the "Green Line" was being flooded by surges of weddings, threatening to swallow it up completely, mainly because of the comparatively low dowry rates in the West Bank. This offered a solution to the difficulties of many Israeli Arab bachelors who had not been able to afford the "market prices" prior to June 1967. Young brides from the Territories, for their part, were sometimes pushed into marriage to enable them to live in Israel. The pressure in this direction was substantial, with the accumulation of many applications for permits for permanent residence in Israel. These ramifying ties have deepened, extended and strengthened the blood relationship already existing between people on both sides of the "Green Line." Brides from Gaza were especially preferred. A case in point was that of Ni'ma 'Awda – whose family, Bedouin by origin, had become sedentary on the outskirts of Lydda – who lost her fiancé owing to "comparing prices":[3]

First came Hilmi (of the Abu Reqayq tribe), who was then studying with my sister at a teachers' seminary in Jaffa, a gentle guy and a poet. We met just once and fell in love with each other; we exchanged love letters in poetry. He used to send his letters care of the Weisses in the neighboring [Jewish] village, and they kept them for me. Later we met several times in Tel Aviv in great secrecy . . . I urged him to come to my father to ask for my hand, and after the 'Id al-Adha festival at the beginning of 1972, they came. My sister prepared my mother and my mother arranged with my father. My father did not ask them for anything [did not name a figure for dowry], stating only that he would not give his consent unless they gave me a house. Springtime they came to say that they had put us down for an apartment in a public housing development in Tel Sheva. On that occasion my father demanded IL 12,000 [about $2,500], which was a lot of money. They argued that housing was highly valuable, to which he answered that his daughter was more valuable to him. Meanwhile some people came from the Embarek family of Tira [formerly Bedouin], who were working with a cousin of mine in groceries. They said that he [the intended bridegroom] was educated and a good fellow. My father asked for IL 14,000, to put them off, as he said, while waiting for the Hilmis' answer. They agreed to pay only IL 13,000, and agreement could not be reached . . . Shortly afterwards came people from the Abu Libda family [*fellahin* – non-Bedouin peasants – from the Triangle]; this one [the intended bridegroom] was teaching in Lydda at the same school as my second sister. She was the one who had arranged it. A truly pleasant, well-educated person; I had heard and also seen him several times. Then, when they [the Embareks] finally agreed to pay him [her father] IL 13,000, he demanded IL 15,000 from the others, although the man already had an apartment. Actually, my father did not want them because they were *fellahin* . . . He said 15,000, upon which they cleared out at once. Toward the end of the summer the others from the Negev came back, saying they were prepared to pay. My father, my brother and my uncle followed them to look over their housing conditions. On their return my father firmly said, "This is not for you." I said that for his sake I was prepared to live at first even in a tent and that we would gradually better our conditions, but my father now demanded from them IL 16,000 and they went away. They had come here driving a new Peugeot pickup. Then, when they were already on the pickup ready to drive away, they shouted to us: "What do you think, that your daughter's . . . is more valuable than that of a girl from Gaza?" . . . Poor Hilmi, he wrote to me afterwards desperate letters, saying he wished he was dead. Later, we heard that they married him off to one from Rafah for IL 4,000. It almost came to blows here . . .

Throwing Off the Suffocating Cultural Bonds

Despite some factors that tended to blur the "Green Line" in the consciousness of Israeli Arabs after the 1948 war, they still seemed to feel as if they were enclosed within walls that were barring any cultural contact both with their own people and with the residents of their country. In fact, they "were cut off from anything that was going on at all levels of contemporary Arab culture," to quote the agonized words of Anton Shammas in his *Reading Diary*.[4]

They recoiled from the Hebrew language despite the fact that the two languages were related, as the language of the supercilious conquering foreigner. This reservation was not easily overcome.

In the meantime there was a depressing feeling of suffocation, or as Michel Haddad of Nazareth put it in one of his poems: "Farewell to thee, ability to breathe." The more sensitive among the Arab intelligentsia in Israel felt as though they were being twisted in the grasp of a triple loop, to paraphrase the words of the Hebrew poet Yehuda Amihai in a different context; three languages, "Hebrew, Arabic and Death," were clasping them, and they were being squeezed between them. As Shammas cried out angrily:

For twenty years the Arabs have lived in this country with a single lung. The system of Arabic education in Israel, at least in my school days, bred tongueless people who felt a greater affinity with a seventh-century poet than with a twentieth-century one. These are people with no cultural past and no future, only an improvised present and a weak personality. The tongues of these people have been cut off, just as in the case of that old Arab in "Facing the Forest," whom no one will allow to speak in his own language, until he finally resorts to speaking in fire.[5]

The Six Day War brought down this wall, allowing access to the books published in the West Bank, the Gaza Strip, Amman, Cairo, Damascus and Baghdad; people were able to read all the poems written there, to leaf through all the newspapers issued there. And so, the young Arab intelligentsia eagerly turned to drink from the fountain of a culture they had known to exist, but which hitherto had been out of their reach. Nowadays the bookstands are overflowing with newspapers, magazines and books from all over the Arab world. At the same time, the works of Israeli Arabs are finding their way to Arab capitals.

An undeclared boycott seemed to have been lifted after the 1967 war; before that war, the works of Israeli Arabs were pointedly ignored in the Arab world; they could not be found in magazines or books, nor were they mentioned in literary conventions, as if they were foreign to Palestinian literature. It is true that the Palestinian writer Ghassan Kanafani had broken through the "blockade" already before the war, coining in 1966 the term *Adab al-Muqawamah* ("resistance literature") in his research on Israeli Arab writers and poets. But this was an exception.[6]

Since the war, the Arabs of Israel have become desirable guests in all literary circles. Literary critics sing their praises, with special attention given to the poets Mahmud Darwish, Samih el-Qassem, Tawfiq Zayyad and Salem Jubran. The works of Israeli Arabs are infiltrating all channels of expression, both in Arab countries and in the organs of the Palestinian Liberation Organization; the interaction between Palestinian writers from all "three circles" – Israel, the Territories, and the Diaspora – is becoming more and more pronounced, together with the impact of Arab literature in general.

However, just when the language was beginning to regain its strength, "speaking in fire," in the sense attached to it in the story "Facing the Forest," started too. Terrorist activity became more intense; the fire rose higher and higher.

The Beginnings of Joint Efforts to Organize Radical Activities

After the Six Day War radical nationalistic tendencies grew stronger among the Arabs of Israel, owing to the combined forceful effect of several causes. As a result of their diversified contacts with their brethren in the Territories, Israeli Arabs began to feel more deeply the inner contradiction of loyalties. With the obliteration of the "Green Line," their consciousness of "Palestinianism" grew stronger, finding also outlets that had not been acceptable or possible before the war. The terrorist organizations realized that Israeli Arabs, who were part of and familiar with life in Israel, were valuable for their struggle. Inspired by the conflicts that made these Arabs feel divided, they offered them a way of identification with the said organizations. At first, clandestine contacts were formed between radical nationalist activists. Gradually they also drew in Arab youth, who until then had not been swept into radical circles. This tendency has been greatly influenced by the growing prestige of the terrorist organizations in neighboring countries and their formal status there.

These elements have been working against the background of forceful agitation coming from Arab countries, and reaching the Arabs of Israel through the media, particularly television. The effects of this process could be seen at first in the incitement to organize students' strikes, in painting hostile slogans and passing on information, but at the same time, terrorist units were being organized. Their actions revealed the full force of the potentially explosive pent-up attitudes within the Israeli Arab community.

The effect of these accumulated forces, born from the new reality, was to intensify the potential security risk of this minority, which had been caught up in the turbulence of opposing currents.

Yet the same terrorist actions exposed the reluctance of the Israeli Arab population in general to embark upon this road; they were fully aware of its potential dangers to the community. True, the radical nationalist tendency gained power, but the Arabs of Israel seemed to sense at once the need to draw the line beyond which disaster lurked. This aversion to radical actions, with their obvious implications, was clearly demonstrated by large sections of the Arab population. Denouncing announcements by Israeli Arab leaders, organizations and institutions were not merely lip service.

A substantial concentrated effort was made to stop young Israeli Arabs from joining terrorist organizations, in the midst of a strong struggle within the Arab society in Israel. The general success of Israel's security forces to expose terrorist networks has undoubtedly had a crucial effect in this combat between conflicting tendencies.

Meanwhile, the terrorist actions had two grave consequences:

1. An increasing tension in Jewish-Arab relations, with an upheaval that led to an inevitable chain reaction: a growing bitterness and deepening frustration within Israeli society as a whole.
2. A tendency to change attitudes among moderate leaders, who found themselves in an awkward position in the wake of nationalistic waves which had tainted the atmosphere among the Arabs of Israel. They were increasingly forced to adapt themselves to a clear-cut, uncompromising nationalist Palestinian line based on absolute recognition of the PLO as the sole legitimate representative, which could not be criticized publicly. Its positions had to be adopted without question, and even when practically bypassed, no *declarative* reservation was allowed.

On the eve of "Land Day" on March 30, 1976, the process that had started right after the war ripened. The stormy events merely expressed poignantly the significance of change. It hit in the face of leaders besieged by an unruly mob that wanted to tear them to pieces. Their weakness was exposed, as was the government's inability to back them up. This was the end of the "collaborating" generation. From that time on, even members of Zionist political parties would bow before the "Organization" (i.e., the PLO), making statements that were almost identical to those of their political opponents.

The PLO "Discovers" the Israeli Arabs

During the first few years following its establishment in 1964, the PLO completely ignored the Israeli Arabs, who were considered citizens of the state it was pledged to destroy; they were strangers to the organization which had committed itself to liberate Palestine. Almost inadvertently, the PLO adopted the attitude of the Arab states toward those Arabs who had "stayed behind" and had "accepted the yoke" of Zionist rule. They had become the "bondmen" or "servants" of Zionism, indifferent to the Palestinian national struggle, or at best incapable of contributing to it.[7]

Some nationalist circles from among the Arab minority were eager to seek ties with the PLO, but the latter was reluctant to pursue this course and only tried to make use of Israeli Arabs for terrorist operations, as if their only advantage was being located inside Israel and able to reach Jewish centers or shelter terrorists from beyond the border. A few joined terrorist cells, mostly from Al-Ard (which meanwhile had been banned). The moving spirit among them was Saleh Baransi.

Some young Israeli Arabs, of no specific political affiliation and mostly with little education, joined the militants in the Territories soon after 1967, but they remained marginal, and were unable to carry with them any sizable group from among the Arab minority in Israel. In some cases, they were recruited by PLO agents. From 1967 until 1973, 320 Israeli Arabs were indicted for security offenses. Some 30 acts of terrorism were committed in Jewish centers during this period, most of them by Israeli Arabs.[8] The perpetrators were usually caught quickly, and tried. Some were deported; of these, most made their way to Beirut, eager to join the PLO.

At first, in the eyes of their PLO hosts, their main asset was their knowledge of Hebrew. But the PLO soon found out that they were also useful for their intimate knowledge of Israel's home affairs and their ability to analyze internal events there correctly. This greatly assisted the PLO's operational planning and, later, mapping out its political strategy. The most prominent of those who fled from Israel to Beirut were three intellectuals who, despite their youth, were soon appointed to senior positions in the PLO's hierarchy: Sabri Jiryis (a lawyer); Habib Qahwaji (a former leader of Al-Ard); and the writer Mahmud Darwish (the Israeli Communist Party, in which Darwish had held important positions, initially condemned his "desertion," but later took a more lenient view).

All three had no hesitation in leaving their homeland in order to promote their anti-Israeli activities. At PLO headquarters they came to form "The Israeli Arab Lobby," enthusiastically trying to persuade the PLO top echelon of the vital importance of integrating the minority in Israel into the wider Palestinian struggle on an equal footing with the other segments of the Palestinian people. Initially, their prime contribution was within the PLO's propaganda staff – a direct consequence of their knowledge of Israeli affairs and their personal experience of discrimination against Israeli Arabs by Jews. Later, they succeeded in making the PLO more aware of the Israeli Arabs' usefulness for the organization, not necessarily with respect to terrorist operations. This had not been understood prior to the 1967 war, let alone translated into action.

But the 1967 war marked a major change which can be accounted for by consideration of the following:

1. Almost overnight, the Arabs of the West Bank and the Gaza Strip came under Israeli administration, and their contacts with Israeli Arabs multiplied rapidly. The "Green Line" was thrown open in both directions. More than that: because of the policy of "open bridges" across the Jordan River, Palestinians from elsewhere, entering the West Bank for family visits, turned into a massive stream of Arab tourists visiting Israel. On their return to Jordan or other areas of the Palestinian diaspora, they took with them first-hand information about Israel as well as the situation of the Arabs there.

2. The conquest of the Territories, inevitably seen by the PLO as yet another catastrophe falling to the lot of the Palestinian people, did in fact open up – for the first time – lines of communications linking all parts of the Palestinian people: the refugees, the inhabitants of the West Bank and the Gaza Strip, and the Israeli Arabs. It was only now that the PLO actually came to see all three as a single unit – a view that existed previously as an abstract theoretical consideration only. In this way, the concept of the "three circles" came into being.

   Israeli Arab personalities told me "off the record" – making me swear that I would not expose them – that one reason for the PLO's "discovery" of the Israeli Arabs was the fact that financial aid received by the PLO from the oil-rich Arab states was graded according to the size of the population the organization claimed to represent. In other words: payment was *per capita*. Counting in the Israeli Arabs was therefore a profitable exercise. The Israeli Communist Party and other nationalist political groupings soon demanded the "share" of the Israeli Arabs, or at least part of it, for themselves.

3. The Israeli Arabs themselves started breaking out of their former isolation; their Palestinian consciousness grew as contacts, previously unfeasible, became easier and more frequent. A natural tangential point was created at which the two populations, constantly striving to draw closer, could meet.

The vibrant mutual relations existing today did not come about all at once. They emerged gradually, beginning with the 1967 war when the image of the Israeli Arab first started to be discerned in its "natural colors." Back in 1972, still before the 1973 war, the Palestine National Assembly (the PLO's quasi-parliament) resolved fully to support the Israeli Arabs' struggle for their national rights. The "Green Line" seemed to have dissolved as the Assembly spoke of the "need for national unity between the masses of our citizens in the areas occupied in 1948 [i.e., Israel in the old borders] as well as in the West Bank and the Gaza Strip and outside the occupied homeland."[9]

The 1973 war acted as a catalyst, accelerating processes that had already begun. A further layer to this development was added during the stormy events of "Land Day" of March 30, 1976. Quite possibly, this is the more decisive date, the real road sign, the baptism of fire during which the Israeli Arabs were put to the test of violence, paid with their blood, and proved their national loyalty.

If, for a variety of reasons, the 1973 war propelled the PLO to a much more widely recognized position as the true representative of the Palestinians, the Israeli Arabs certainly joined the chorus and acknowledged it as such with fervor. The PLO gained an added advantage with the Israeli Arab community when, at a later stage, its mainstream elements acknowledged the need to develop a moderate image, following the PLO's declared readiness to accept the existence of Israel. This readiness increased with the signing of the Oslo accords and the subsequent progress in the peace process.

Very slowly, and with a great deal of vehement internal argument, the new political strategy was worked out by the PLO, ostensibly in contravention to its own Charter. Without actually revoking it, a new "theory of stages" was formulated: no longer relentless, uncompromising all-out war for the sake of Palestine in its entirety, implying the conquest of Israel, but rather a certain readiness to compromise, at least temporarily, and to set up a Palestinian state first of all in the occupied territories from which the Israeli armed forces would withdraw. The further struggle, aiming at the liberation of all Palestine, would be relegated to the "second phase." A political struggle – so it was realized in the PLO – must be carried out gradually: it requires adaptation to realities rather than attempts to act out dreams. Pragmatically possible partial gains must not be turned down because they do not offer the totality of one's aspirations. These new concepts saw the light of day amid painful birth pangs. The old attitudes, forbidding as much as mere lip service to the possibility of recognizing Israel, were not easily shed. To renounce even a fraction, it was feared, might eventually cause the Palestinians to lose all. If the old doctrine was even temporarily diminished, it might never revive again.

But realities dictated change. The adamant resistance of the PLO's so-called "rejectionists" could not alter that. The military balance being what it was, the prospects for conquest, even by the method of the "long haul," were dim. The old truth that "the better is the enemy of the good" seemed to reassert itself once again.

In this new constellation, the importance of the Israeli Arabs was greatly augmented; they turned into the "bridge" linking the two phases; they became the guarantee that the struggle would be carried on by means of the pressures they would bring to bear on Israel from the inside, from within its own confines. The realization of the "right of return" would reopen the borders of Israel to a massive stream of returning refugees which would increase their strength within the Zionist state and make it practical politics for them to strive to become the majority and "inherit" the state altogether.

According to this view, the Israeli Arabs are that part of the Palestinian people whose area was occupied in 1948, yet whose liberation must be delayed until the second phase. They are an inseparable part of the Palestinians and no substantive difference exists between them and the people of the West Bank and the Gaza Strip, occupied almost twenty years later, except that, under the overall plan, the liberation of the latter will take place first.

Even before that doctrine was fully adopted, the Israeli Arab "ambassadors" in Beirut – the three intellectuals mentioned above – had made it clear to the PLO leaders that the Arab minority in Israel was indeed capable of becoming a major strategic asset in the political struggle. The right attitude toward them would enable the PLO to act against Israel from the outside, while they themselves, the citizens of the Zionist state, would direct their blows against it from the inside, in the manner of the Trojan horse.

The 1976 "Land Day" demonstrations attested to the strength of this third Palestinian circle, and West Bank and Gaza inhabitants hurried to identify with the Israeli Arabs by means of widespread violent clashes. The date of "Land Day" became, from then on, one of the fixed days in the calendar of political anniversaries of the Palestinian people, whether on this or that side of the "Green Line."

As these trends emerged, the self-confidence of the Arab minority increased; nationalist groupings emerged and endeavored as best they could to establish links with the PLO. They were no longer satisfied with verbal declarations on the part of their Israeli Arab leaders of different political persuasions, recognizing the PLO as the legitimate representative of the Israeli Arabs, or with carrying slogans of identification in processions and demonstrations. Nor were they satisfied with flying the Palestinian flag or symbolically using the Palestinian colors on shirts or copybooks. Their leaders began meeting PLO personalities, at first covertly, later with greater publicity and with increasing frequency. The meetings, symbolic to begin with, became more and more substantive and significant. At first, the very fact of their meeting was the important thing; but during the last ten years or so, these meetings became more like actual conferences at which the PLO conveyed information, advice, guidance, perhaps even outright instructions. Patterns of cooperation were set, the desired frequency of such meetings was established; 'Arafat endorsed certain Arab lists running for the Knesset, supporting them publicly and advising the Israeli Arab public how to use their electoral power when inserting their envelopes into the ballot boxes marked with the official emblem of the Zionist state. He sent greetings to the congresses of parties he considered "positive," using the technology of facsimile transmission to do so.

PLO personalities began mediating between various Israeli Arab factions in order to promote the "unity of ranks," and pressured them to conclude Knesset surplus vote agreements among themselves.

All this marked a veritable revolution in the PLO's tenets, both with regard to Israel and with regard to its Arab minority, two bodies no longer seen as separate entities. Presumably, in their closed meetings, PLO representatives told their Israeli Arab interlocutors that it has become possible to agree to the establishment of a Palestinian state alongside Israel, to reconciliation with Israel and to recognizing it, on the assumption that the Arab minority on the inside will ensure that the next phase eventually comes to pass. That phase will then bring about the realization of the Palestinian state extending over the entire area for which it was, and is, destined. Accordingly, there is no point in boycotting Knesset elections (as some nationalist groupings had demanded, arguing that to vote in the election was tantamount to recognizing the legitimacy of the official Zionist institutions).

Such arguments led to the conviction that the PLO was capable, from the outside, of exerting some influence on Israeli politics by making use of internal forces, i.e., the electoral leverage of the Israeli Arabs. The latter need the PLO's backing, seek its endorsement, and regard it as its supreme leadership of the "state in the making" to which they wish to belong – even though for the time being they reside outside its direct domain, in an area destined to be dealt with only in the "second stage" (as the extremists among them hold).

The *Al-Ittihad* newspaper, the Arabic-language organ of the Communist party, took the matter a step further: on November 15, 1988 – the day the PLO proclaimed in Algiers an independent Palestinian state – it termed the West Bank and the Gaza Strip "the Palestinian State" and called 'Arafat its president, as if the regime and the presidency of this as yet non-existent state had already been determined.

There was something strange in a situation in which the State of Israel negated the PLO to the point of refusing to sit at the same negotiating table with it, while one group of its citizens set up a multitude of significant ties – direct and indirect, covert and overt – with it. Israeli democracy is shot through with contradictions, and not always aware of their full import. This contradiction diminished when Israel recognized the PLO in 1993.

It is worth noting that, unlike the line it took in the Territories, the PLO did not encourage subversive activities on the part of Israeli Arab citizens. It did not call for civil disobedience or for an uprising. Its contacts with local Arab leaders or political bodies touched on the latters' participation in Israeli elections, a subject entirely within the bounds of Israeli law. It is as if the PLO, in this particular regard, subjects itself to Israeli sovereignty, or else as if it were reluctant to make demands on the Arab minority in Israel which the latter is bound to turn down; the PLO is obviously aware of, and accepts, the existence of "red lines" which Israeli Arabs will not cross.

It is further worth noting that the Arab political groupings who turn to the PLO to enhance their own political leverage conduct themselves independently even on matters on which the PLO takes an express stand, often regarding that organization's views as no more than recommendations they can accept or ignore. An example is the refusal of the Communist Party to enter into a Knesset elections surplus vote agreement with the Progressive List for Peace, despite the PLO's urgings to do so. The texture of relations is complex and sensitive and not always easy to interpret; but there can be no doubt that it exists and is spreading.

In a process which began at the time of the 1967 war, the Israeli Arabs and the PLO have gradually got to know each other and have arrived at a point of "mutual recognition." The PLO recognizes their "Palestinian dimension" and has come to think of them as a component, equal to others, in the overall Palestinian struggle; they claim that the PLO alone has the right to represent the Palestinians wherever they may be, including the Israeli Arabs themselves.[10]

The 1982 War in Lebanon

The entry of Israeli troops into Lebanon in June 1982 created yet another trauma, comparable – for all its differences – to that of June 1967. Again, there was a warlike breakthrough across the border of a neighboring Arab country: again, contact was re-established with kinsmen and friends in places inaccessible for many years, dating back to before the "deluge": contacts with co-religionists and with the inmates of refugee camps.

This time, communal tensions played a greater role, tensions which divided different segments of the nation in Lebanon and led Israeli Arabs to identify with one side or the other, according to their own communal affiliation. Israeli Druze and Christians found themselves ranged against each other for the first time, as if compelled to emulate the hostility existing over there, in the Shuf Mountains of central Lebanon. This strange war thus gave rise to inter-communal tensions among the Israeli minority for which there was no precedent in its earlier history. For the first time, Druze soldiers in the Israeli army went into action wondering what policy their army was following *vis-à-vis* their co-religionists, furious at Israel's preference for the Maronite population in the territories seized in the heat of battle.

Israeli Druze protests grew more vocal as their contacts with the Druze in Lebanon intensified, including meetings with relatives and pilgrimages to places holy to the Druze. When the situation of the Druze in Lebanon deteriorated markedly, a hue and cry to rescue them arose among their Israeli brethren throughout the villages inhabited by local Druze. The Israeli Law of Return (the law enabling any Jew from anywhere to immigrate into Israel) was suddenly subjected to a sharp, cold scalpel probing the equality of its application when Lebanese Druze demanded the right of asylum with their co-religionists in Israel.

The Druze author Salman Natur illustrated the problem when he wrote:[11]

> After the war, I discovered my *hamulah* in Lebanon, some ten thousand people, Druze and the descendants of Druze, spread out over several villages, from Beirut in the north to Hasbaya in the south. Some of them came to visit us, told us about the bloody civil war, the suffering, the hunger and the fear. And we told them about the quiet here and the economic prosperity. They saw [our] villas, and just as they had heard the Arabic transmission of the Israeli radio speak about democracy here, we told them about it, too, and we said that the state relates to us with great respect and that we have schools and that every time a Druze soldier falls, the representatives of the authorities swear in their eulogies that they will grant us full rights, just like the Jews.
>
> Our relatives were of course glad to hear these things and envied us. Someone threw out an idea: "Perhaps you can arrange with your government for us to come and live on Mount Carmel; you have enough room; we will set up a village next to yours and live together in peace. Thus you will rescue us from death and from the shame of war." They did not ask for much – just that we should rescue them. "Is this possible?" they asked.
>
> We said: "Certainly! After all, the government sees to it to bring in Jews in distress from all over the world and issues them identity cards before they even board the plane, according to the law. Surely they will look after you, too, because there is no difference between us and the Jews. Wait patiently, and we shall write to the Prime Minister, and they will keep their promises."
>
> I sent the letters and asked in all innocence for the same rights as those the Jews enjoy under the Law of Return. The Prime Minister at that time, Shimon Peres, wrote to me that he had read my letter with great attention. I, too read his reply with great attention.

In some ways, the war in Lebanon opened fissures in the texture of national cohesion of the Arab minority by arousing contradictory communal loyalties. But, unlike the 1967 war, it does not seem to have left deep scars. Communal tensions remained subject to restraints, and did not lead to confrontation. When things quietened down, they too abated. In retrospect, the decisive aspect of the 1982 war seems to have been the "Israeliness" of the minority as against their communal loyalties. Had this not been so, we might have witnessed violent clashes in mixed (Druze–Christian) localities or cases of insubordination on the part of Druze soldiers. But such cases did not occur.

All in all, tensions mounted in the Arab sector during the war in Lebanon, and there were more frequent acts of violence. The note of hostility displayed during the protest demonstrations on September 22, 1982 against the massacre in the Sabra and Shatilla refugee camps were even more severe than those of the 1976 "Land Day."[12]

The elimination of the PLO's footholds just north of Israel's borders and the uprooting of its leadership from Beirut augmented the relative importance of hostile activities in the occupied territories, and consequently the support of Israeli Arabs for them. The withdrawal of Israeli forces from Lebanon, after paying a heavy price in casualties, demonstrated the sensitivity of the Israeli public to the loss of life and in turn aroused hopes that the same result might be achieved in the West Bank and the Gaza Strip. In some respects it would be accurate to say that the Intifadah was born from the war in Lebanon, an avalanche snowballing gradually over the intervening years.

The Impact of the Intifadah[13]

Despite the general policy of the Israeli Arab leaders not to let the Intifadah and its attendant violence penetrate into Israel, there can be no doubt whatsoever that it did, on some occasions, penetrate deeply. This was most clearly felt at the time of general strikes or demonstrations called for by the Monitoring Committee, on occasions such as "Peace Day" or the "Land Day" anniversaries or on other dates commemorating days of bloodshed. One such date was the anniversary of the murder of seven Arab laborers at Rishon Letziyon; another, that of the fatal clashes with Israeli Police on the Temple Mount in Jerusalem in October 1990 after stones had been hurled down at Jews praying at the Western Wall.

But also on ordinary days, individuals or small groups from among the Arab minority carried out acts showing the obvious imprint of the Intifadah: throwing incendiary bottles, stoning buses or private cars, blocking major roads, cutting telephone cables, setting forest fires, destroying agricultural crops, property and equipment, as well as hoisting Palestinian flags and inscribing hostile graffiti. From time to time, groups of masked men, so well known from the Territories, appeared in Israeli Arab villages, eager for violent encounters with members of the security forces. Young people exhibited a tendency to imitate the action of their peers on the other side of the "Green Line," though this was often no more than the spirit of youthful mischief.

On many occasions, Israeli Arabs rescued Intifadah activists from the Territories from measures the security forces were taking against them. They responded to the desperate call by the "United National Command" in the Territories to help them prepare the public announcements they wished to distribute, but were prevented from printing there. Some Nazareth printing shops refused to do so, but in the Triangle the United Command found support. It became known that "Announcement No. 11" and "Announcement No. 12" had been secretly printed in one of the larger villages of the Triangle. Leaflets and booklets on behalf of the Islamic Resistance Movement (known as *Hamas*, its acronym in Arabic) were printed in Umm el-Fahm.[14] When telephone lines in the Territories were cut off from the international exchange, Israeli Arabs put their private telephones at the disposal of Intifadah activists for making overseas calls. It appears that some Israeli Arabs also helped to circumvent the "financial embargo" against Intifadah groups by allowing them to use their personal bank accounts to receive money transfers from abroad, whether for the United Command or for Hamas.

These were not mass phenomena, but rather actions taken by a few, wishing to cause a wider popular conflagration by means of the Popular Committees for Assisting the Intifadah, in which political rivals found they could sit together to promote what had become a common goal. They engaged primarily in fund-raising and in collecting clothes, blankets and food for Intifadah victims. Occasionally, they organized convoys of heavily loaded vans to go to selected spots in the Territories.[15] On other occasions, they organized blood donations or sent out Israeli Arab doctors to hospitals in the West Bank and the Gaza Strip to help there according to their specialization.[16] The Monitoring Committee called several times for fund-raising operations for the purpose of sending food, medicines and money into the Territories. It also responded to requests from the Red Crescent organization in the West Bank and Gaza for medical aid.[17]

It would appear, however, that no comprehensive organizational framework was set up and no executive apparatus formed; support and aid for the Intifadah remained sporadic and limited in scope.

Only at the time of the second anniversary of the eruption of the Intifadah in December 1989 was an umbrella organization set up which assumed control of local bodies. It was called "The Monitoring Committee for Aid to the Intifadah" and was headed by Dr Hatem Kana'na. Its founding convention was held the following March and was informed that Israeli aid to the Territories was so far estimated at IS 500,000 (then $250,000).[18]

More massive food shipments were made on the occasion of '*Id al-Fitr* (the holiday ending the month-long Ramadan fast) in April 1990. The *mufti* of Jerusalem, Sheikh Sa'd ed-Din el-'Alami, issued a *fatwa* (a religious ruling) instructing Muslims to use all charitable sums given during the month of Ramadan for the benefit of the inhabitants of the Territories.[19]

At the political level, meetings were held to protest against the measures taken by Israel to fight the Intifadah: demonstrations expressed identification with detainees and refugees or with specific localities in the territories then under curfew or subject to prohibition of entry or exit.

Already on December 21, 1987, barely two weeks after the eruption of the uprising, the Monitoring Committee called for a general country-wide strike in support of the Intifadah as part of the events marking "Peace Day." "Nobody can prevent Israel's Arab citizens from expressing their identification with their brethren residing in the Territories," asserted Ibrahim Nimr Hussein, the chairman of the Committee of Arab Local Council Heads (sometimes referred to as the "president" of Israeli Arabs). And indeed, his constituency responded to the strike call with tremendous enthusiasm which gave vent to their immediate sentiment, only a short time after the beginning of the Intifadah.[20] Some young hot-heads were not satisfied with the mere closing of shops and offices in the Arab sector and – in contravention of the express instructions of their leaders – launched acts of disorder copied from the practice of the Intifadah: burning of tires, stone-throwing, clashes with the police and the blocking of roads. Near Umm el-Fahm, a stronghold of the "Sons of the Village," demonstrators became unruly and blocked the Hadera–'Afula highway with huge stones, throwing incendiary bottles and destroying whatever they could find. They did so in total disregard of the pleas of Umm el-Fahm mayor Hashem Mahamid (of the Communist Party leadership) who tried in vain to restrain those who, by their actions, perverted the purpose of the day: to hold quiet nationalist-Palestinian demonstrations avoiding violence.

Similar actions continued from time to time, though on a smaller scale. Occasionally, hand grenades were thrown; stabbing of Jews became rather more frequent. Pro-Intifadah leaflets, in the style of the "announcements" in the Territories, were occasionally distributed in this or that Arab village.[21] Palestinian flags were hung on electricity poles and state emblems vandalized. The leadership of the minority condemned acts of violence, but continued to call for strikes from time to time. One such strike was timed to coincide with the proclamation of the State of Palestine (in Algiers, on November 15, 1988). The connection was not officially acknowledged, yet symbolized the fusion of the two aims of the struggle: equal rights for the minority and the establishment of a Palestinian state.[22] On February 25, 1990, another general strike was held to protest against the difficulties which had befallen most Arab local authorities because of the lack of government grants. Later, a strike of the local councils themselves was proclaimed, to last for an indefinite period.

Several "Land Day" anniversaries occurred during the period of the Intifadah, and there can be no doubt that it influenced the way they were marked. The second one, in 1989, was commemorated by a mass rally at Nazareth attended by 40,000 people. Despite signs of unrest, there were few infringements of the law. Knesset members who, in their speeches, had proclaimed the victory of the Intifadah, were carried shoulder-high by the crowds. At a mass rally on January 23, 1988, Knesset member 'Abd el-Wahhab Darawshah shouted that Yitzhak Rabin (then Defense Minister and as such responsible for the Israeli measures against the Intifadah) was a "murderer" and that he, Darawshah, could no longer belong to the same party with him.[23] He subsequently resigned from the Labor Party and set up a party of his own. Other pro-Intifadah demonstrations in the Arab sector were of lesser scope and not quite so stormy, and the different approaches of the various political trends among the minority left their mark on them.

During the Intifadah period, the struggle for equal rights for the Arab minority was not neglected; on the contrary, it spread and intensified, accompanied by the customary means of protest: strikes, demonstrations, shut-downs of local authority offices, petitions, appeals to the Knesset, the President and other official figures. Proposals were made for complaining to the UN and other international bodies, but such ideas seem eventually to have been dropped.[24]

There was a sharp increase in acts of terror within the "Green Line," beginning with the eruption of the Intifadah: arson, throwing of incendiary bottles, destruction of property, laying explosives, knifings, assaults, use of fire-arms and hand-grenades. These peaked in 1988, then subsided somewhat, though knifings and the use of fire-arms continued and even increased. The annual police report for 1988 stated that from the beginning of the Intifadah and until the concluding date of the report "infringements of law and order have not ceased, [such as] throwing incendiary bottles, forest arson, burning of motor vehicles, and throwing stones at civilians and members of the security forces."25

Israeli Arab leaders, including Knesset members, traveled abroad and made speeches in support of the Intifadah, sometimes at rallies organized or sponsored by the PLO.

The Arab Knesset members, regardless of their party affiliation, jointly formed a sort of lobby on behalf of the residents of the Territories, pointing to their distress, demanding the cessation of stern measures, pleading for easier conditions for detainees, voicing their complaints, and representing their viewpoints in meetings with security officials or representatives of the civil administration in the Territories.

Israeli Arab lawyers frequently attended trials of Intifadah-related security offenders in military or other courts, or visited police detention barracks. They were the ones who petitioned the Supreme Court on their behalf, often together with Jewish colleagues from leftist or non-Zionist circles.26

The Arabic-language press in Israel throve on the Intifadah, covering it fully, publishing photographs of its heroes, of detainees and victims of Israeli army actions or of sealed houses. *Al-Ittihad* carried a daily account of all Intifadah events under its main headlines. Ironically, Israeli Arabs, from the Galilee or the Triangle, turned all the more Israeli in the eyes of the stone-throwers or arsonists the moment they crossed the "Green Line."27 Their cars had Israeli license plates, but they tried to display their different identity by such means as traveling with a single headlight on, a sort of tacit signal to the "children of the stones" lining the roads. They also tended to "amend" their dress when entering "Intifadah country" and donned the traditional Arab headgear which, back home in Israel, they had shed years ago.

Political action in support of the Intifadah peaked with the affair of the so-called "Ship of Return," meant to help build that vital bridge by which the PLO was trying to link the Palestinian Diaspora with the Arab minority in Israel. It was to symbolize the aim of al-'awdah (return). Tens of thousands of Israeli Arabs were to come to the slopes of Mt. Carmel to applaud as the ship carrying refugees would try to enter Haifa Bay. The Monitoring Committee responded to the call of the PLO to cooperate in that venture, and demanded emphatically that the Israeli authorities allow the "historic" ship to enter Haifa Port. A mass demonstration was to take place opposite the Haifa Municipality at the time the ship was approaching its destination, while the leaders of the Communist Party, the Progressive List for Peace and other political groupings were to join the refugees on the ship. Knesset member Muhammad Mi'ari even went to Athens and took part in the press conference the PLO held there in connection with the scheme. There was a plan to hire an old ferry boat belonging to a Galilee kibbutz, to be paid for from contributions of wealthy West Bank residents, for a delegation of Israeli Arab leaders to meet the "Ship of Return" at sea. The plan fell through when a mysterious explosion opened the side of the boat at its moorings in the port of Piraeus before it put out to sea. The ferment its voyage had threatened to unleash abated, yet the widespread support of the plan was indicative of the Israeli Arabs' readiness actively to cooperate in ventures planned and launched by the PLO against the state whose citizens they were.

But the force of the conflagration also induced grave doubts among Israeli Arabs. Since 1967, thousands of workers from the Territories had moved into Arab localities in Israel, penetrating the rural economy and the labor market of the Arab towns, and threatening the complex and sensitive texture of the local society. Attempts by the Israeli authorities, in 1990, to make these workers go back to their former places in the West Bank and the Gaza Strip were perhaps not unwelcome to the veteran population who had always referred to them as Daffawi or Ghazzawi ("West Banker" or "Gazan") with a note of derision and haughtiness.

Quite possibly, there was a feeling of relief among Israeli Arabs that the flames threatening to engulf them seemed to be dying down. After all, for all the verbal cloud of enthusiasm surrounding it, the Intifadah remained something undefined in their eyes, like a code that had not been quite deciphered. Who had launched it? By what force was it continuing? Which way was it going? What shape would it acquire tomorrow and the day after? Would it end up by doing away with the "Green Line"? What would be its final price? Israeli Arabs despaired at the "message" coming from the Territories, and even West Bankers began to lose their faith in the Intifadah's rationale.

An influential and highly-educated person from Bethlehem stated some time before the Temple Mount incident in October 1990 that the real power directing the Intifadah was the Israeli security service. "Your *Shabak* [Hebrew acronym of the General Security Service, Israel's internal security branch] pulls the strings. Its men hold the key posts in the command of the uprising. They draft the public announcements, and they issue the instructions."[28] Such views reflect the "conspiracy theory" often found in the Middle East, which sees events as being orchestrated by a clever, sophisticated, virtually omnipotent adversary. At times of despair, the inclination increases to tell of the enemy's deceptive tricks, to regard him as larger than life, a giant among dwarfs; amorphous suspicions spread, there is a feeling of being caught in a dead-end street, and the heady pride characteristic of the first phase evaporates.

More and more often, there were complaints of corruption at the top, such as the greed for money on the part of lawyers who ostensibly did everything to defend Intifadah offenders, but took fat fees and then left them in the lurch. The east Jerusalem newspaper *An-Nahar* spoke scathingly, in June 1990, of the anger against leaders from the "aristocratic" families (the Nusseibas, the Husseinis, the Tarifis) who made headlines at the expense of the simple peasants.[29] Israeli Arabs heard such mutterings, too; they did not wish to become partners in failure. In mid-1990, it appeared as if the Intifadah was losing momentum. But then the Gulf War seemed to offer a new "redeemer." Having well-nigh despaired of the Intifadah, they turned to the new "hero of Arabism" who was defying the entire world. Nearer home, the Temple Mount Incident of October 1990 stoked the fires of the Intifadah afresh.

The Intifadah upset the delicate balance which the Israeli Arabs had arrived at in the preceding forty years, catching them amid new and contradictory constraints, reducing the ability for sober consideration and threatening the leadership with loss of control – a leadership still young, unstable and inexperienced. It placed the leaders in the middle between chain reactions of violence in two sectors, as extremists from both peoples seemed to work together to create a vicious circle of mad pursuit of violence bound to break down the fragile bridges built over several decades of joint efforts by the state and its Arab citizens.

The transition from stone to knife after the Temple Mount incident exposed the Israeli Arabs – individually and collectively – to existential dangers. The killing of a Jew in Israel immediately calls forth reactions of vengeance from young hot-heads against any Arab that comes their way. This has become the gravest threat to the integration of Arabs in the life of the state since the latter's inception.

Not only did the knife replace the stone – making the latter a sort of relic from an earlier geological period – but the use of firearms was now also on the increase. A period of individual assaults began: single persons try to attack Jews, whether civilians or soldiers, to knife them to death, unlike the "stone age" when stones were thrown from a distance, without hand-to-hand fighting and usually not by single attackers but by crowds. Only few Israeli Arabs joined the knife-wielders, but the lunatic fringe among them, as well as those overcome with bitterness, were in danger of being carried along.

Undoubtedly, the Intifadah did cross the "Green Line," but with respect to its dimensions of violence, it also made it a "red line" of caution. While in many ways it demonstrated the common fate and attitude of the Arabs in the Territories and the Arabs in Israel, it also, at one and the same time, sharpened the latters' perception of their own particular identity, facing them with the fact that their minority–majority problem had a coloration all of its own. They had one foot in each camp, and were beset with doubts, dilemmas and ambiguities, or else went about their daily lives with a certain "division of labor" between the "three sectors" of the Palestinians worldwide.[30]

Some leaders from the Territories also appealed to Israeli Arabs not to join the Intifadah, defining their task as that of influencing Israeli public opinion and the Knesset on behalf of a political settlement. Dr Faysal Husseini, for instance, said so very clearly in the course of a lecture at Giv'at Haviva on January 22, 1990.[31] As a rule, prominent figures from the Territories refrained from taking part in the ceremonies marking the "Land Day" anniversaries. When one of them mounted the speaker's dais on such an occasion at the Bedouin settlement of Rahat, a major riot threatened to break out.[32] A Haifa University lecturer, Dr Majed el-Hajj, spoke, in July 1989, of the Israeli Arabs as "standing on the 'Green Line,' examining anew their status and their strategy of existence in the State of Israel."[33]

At times, the Intifadah turned into a means for Israeli Arabs to achieve their own particular aims, by way of implicit or explicit threats. Illustrative of this is the following statement by Dr Majed el-Hajj: "If the Arabs in this country are pushed aside even further, there is no telling how they will react. Will they adopt the strategy of the Intifadah or will they find different patterns to attain their goals as citizens?"[34]

From its very beginning, the Intifadah was like an earthquake, both for the majority and the minority in Israel, though each felt it in a different way. It made palpable the dangers of living on a volcano liable to erupt and shatter Jewish-Arab relations at all levels, including the level of personal human relationships. A single person, overwhelmed by bitterness, may leave for work early in the morning, a knife hidden on his body; hours later, his victim may chance onto his path, anonymous, except for belonging to the enemy nation: young or old, child or soldier, walking near his or her home, unaware of any danger. They happen upon their murderer who does not know them, of whom they have never heard. He sentences them to death with the blind hatred of vengeance, thinking of himself as fulfilling a national mission, perhaps himself not having known beforehand that the moment of the ultimate outburst was at hand.

In short, the Intifadah with its many facets became a unique stage in the Jewish-Arab confrontation in general, and in Jewish-Arab relations in Israel in particular. With tremendous force and against their own will, it placed the Israeli Arabs at a dangerous crossroads, regardless of their apparent desire to maintain the balance so laboriously built up over forty years.

In retrospect, we can look at it by comparing it with the uprising which took place half a century earlier in the years 1936–39, called "the rebellion" by the Arabs and referred to as "the incidents" in Jewish history books. The word Intifadah did not enter Israeli parlance in the media, the Knesset and the government all that easily. For a long time, official spokesmen tried to avoid calling it thus, preferring circumlocutions like "the disorders." Words have a weight of their own in history. But eventually, even the Jewish right wing gave up calling it anything else, even though they continued to demand its total and relentless suppression.[35]

No doubt the two periods call for a comparison. For all the undeniable differences, there are certain features they have in common: the suddenness of the eruption; the means employed, such as strikes; the attempt to hit road traffic in particular; the assaults on casual passers-by; the internecine struggles in the Arab camp, including the liquidation of opponents. But the differences are no less obvious: the much greater force of the initial eruption, despite a much inferior starting point; the self-imposed restraint of the early phases, particularly the abstention from the use of firearms; the international resonance, completely lacking in the earlier instance; the absence of "gangs" or of a group like the "Army of Salvation"; the empathy on the part of the Zionist left; and most of all, the overall political situation, with all that this implies.

A comparison of the two periods should be comprehensive and thorough – a venture which remains beyond the scope of this book. Yet it seems possible to point to the following features as characterizing the latter uprising:

1. It was no doubt an unprecedented, multifaceted new phenomenon in the history of the Jewish–Arab conflict.

2. It was a form of war, yet very different from all preceding Arab–Israeli wars.

3. The Israeli Arabs were experiencing such a type of event for the first time, making it impossible for them to remain on the sidelines, or to say that they wanted to be left out, for the Intifadah defined itself as the national uprising of the Palestinian people to which they see themselves as belonging, flesh of its flesh.

4. This time a direct confrontation developed between Israel and the Palestinians, involving no other side, while the earlier uprising was directed against the British as much as against the Jews.

5. Unlike all previous wars, no Arab army appeared in the field.

6. The vehement debate among the Zionist parties themselves softened the impact of the Intifadah on the Israeli Arabs to some extent, allayed the feeling of isolation, allowed for discerning some backing from segments of Jewish public opinion, though within certain rather narrow limits.[36]

7. Its relatively long duration was unprecedented in the annals of the Jewish–Arab confrontation so far. The Intifadah did not seem to let up; it demanded taking a stand toward it; the Israeli Arabs felt called upon to make a choice. It was as if they were being asked: Who are you, after all? Israelis or Palestinians? And in answering that they were both, they found themselves once again between the hammer and the anvil, searching for

a formula to bridge the opposites and release them from their dilemma.

The Israeli Arabs and the Gulf War

The Iraqi occupation of Kuwait made the Israeli Arabs face the question of their place on the map once more, at a time when the regional map had changed beyond recognition. It was no longer a map showing Israel opposite the Arabs, with the trenches clearly marked. Now there was a major Arab country which had swallowed a small, weak neighbor. And there were two Arab camps opposing each other, with the United States taking an ever more decisive part in Middle Eastern affairs. While the governments of most major Arab states regarded Iraq as a dire threat to themselves and welcomed western aid and intervention, many of their peoples were thirsting for a great, powerful Arab leader to fight a foreign culture, comparable to Khalid Ibn al-Walid, the seventh-century Arab conqueror, or to Salah ad-Din (Saladin), the victor over the Crusaders, or to Jamal 'Abd en-Nasser, "the boss," who had driven the British out of the Suez Canal Zone.

Unlike in the past, Israel was suddenly altogether marginal in a warlike situation, even though Saddam Hussein tried to draw a parallel between the invasion of Kuwait and the 1967 war, and to create a linkage between his retreat from there and Israel's withdrawal from the occupied territories. To bolster his image as an all-Arab leader, ready for immediate war against Israel, he threatened to "burn" half of it, yet it is clear that Israel was not his real enemy and that all he did was to try to embarrass his Arab adversaries by making them appear indifferent to the Palestinian cause. When they failed to react, he berated them as traitors. But to the Palestinians he appeared as the only Arab leader genuinely eager to go to war for their just cause. The PLO immediately made the Iraqi position its own. 'Arafat hurried to Baghdad and clothed himself in the mantle of the mediator (yet was unmistakably siding with Iraq). His mediation attempts were seen as sheer hypocrisy by all who opposed the seizure of Kuwait.

Taking a longer historical view, one cannot help remembering how, on the eve of World War II, the *mufti* of Jerusalem, the Palestinian Arab leader Hajj Amin al-Husseini, courted Hitler.[37] Similarly, 'Arafat made his decision on the strength of a judgment about who was the stronger. Yet in his innermost heart he must have known that he could not condemn the seizure of territories by Israel and, in the same breath, praise the occupation of Kuwait. But Saddam's "linkage" provided the end which sanctifies the means. This, 'Arafat seemed to be saying, was not the moment for moral considerations; it was a time for the language of force.

The PLO thus took its stand unambiguously alongside Saddam. As far as it was concerned, the occupation of Kuwait had come – even though unintentionally so – at the proper time, at a moment when the Intifadah was slackening and the population of the Territories beginning to falter under its weight. Now the appearance of a new "boss" carrying the banner of Arab heroism fanned the flames again, bringing new hope with it.

The Arabic papers of east Jerusalem supported Saddam most vocally; Arab residents called new-born babies after him; in the narrow lanes of the *suq*, traders used rude language to condemn Saudi Arabia for letting foreign troops onto its soil, virtually "occupying" it, in order to attack a "hero of Arabism."[38]

At such a time, the Israeli Arabs could not keep aloof. They listened to the voices, heard the thunder, sensed the rejoicing in the Territories at the "redeemer" who was ready to take on the whole world. In view of such earth-shattering events, they had to take sides. They too longed for a legendary, archetypal national leader who would lift above themselves and do away, at a single stroke, with all the present sad, grey, frustrating realities. There would be no more need to try to find one's convoluted path amid conflicting currents.

First reactions were sober, realistic, true to the logic that had developed gradually over the years since the establishment of Israel, forged on the anvil of experience. The leading political groups condemned the invasion of Kuwait and negated this kind of "solution" to political problems. *Al-Ittihad* pointed to the dangers for the Palestinian cause liable to spring from support of Iraq. At a colloquium on the Gulf held at the Galilee village of Tamra on November 11, 1990, the paper's editor came out strongly against the invasion.[39]

But the waves of enthusiasm in the Territories and among Palestinians abroad began to undercut sobriety. The greatest anger was turned against the United States, the hated foreign power which now became the focus of furious criticism. To quote *As-Sirat*, the organ of the Islamic Movement:

There was a crisis called the invasion of Kuwait which lasted for a few days and was over. Now we are facing a crisis which is the invasion by the United States of our honor, our soil, our Holy Places and the Arab natural resources. That is the real crisis through which we are living today.[40]

The Progressive List for Peace, the Democratic Arab Party, the Sons of the Village, the Progressive National Movement, and other radical groupings began supporting Iraq, though with somewhat differing degrees of emphasis. DAP leader 'Abd el-Wahhab Darawshah explained that he viewed the event as the "union" of two Arab countries, stressing his loathing for the corrupt regimes of the oil principalities, while trying to evade the issue of Saddam's threats against Israel: these were unimportant – the main thing was the linkage with the need for an Israeli withdrawal from the Territories. This linkage provided a basis for negotiations capable of resolving both crises.[41]

PLP leader Muhammad Mi'ari also asserted his support of Saddam, speaking of the occupation of Kuwait as an "inevitable" step on the road toward comprehensive Arab unity which – much to his regret – could not be achieved without the use of force.[42] It was the United States which was to blame for the terrible bloodshed meant to exterminate Iraq. The US "did not want a political solution," and acted to gain time to complete its preparations so as "to drown the region in blood and gain control of the Arab nation's natural resources."[43]

Even more moderate Arab leaders felt obliged to join in, putting particular emphasis on the struggle against "degenerate" Arab rulers. They depicted the war as a Western assault against the Arab nation to rob it of its resources. Samir Darwish, head of the local council of Baqa el-Gharbiyya and a well-versed former television reporter, asserted in mid-war:

What we appreciate in Saddam is his fervent fight against the curse of the West and of Imperialism and against the decadent money-oriented life of corrupt sheikhs. All this is most impressive. He is the only [leader] who does not waste money on belly dancers and casinos.[44]

The editor of *As-Sinarah*, Lutfi Mash'ur, known for his flexible formulations, found a way of evading the charge of dual loyalty: "The Israeli Arabs," he wrote, "support Saddam Hussein against other Arab rulers, *but not against Israel*."[45]

The man on the street was also impressed by Saddam's heroism, capable – so they thought – of allaying their fervent longing for restoring the lost honor of the Arabs. A young man from Umm el-Fahm put it like this: "This is the first Arab president to say 'No' to someone stronger than himself. He is ready to die for his principles and that makes him a hero in Arab eyes."[46]

The Israeli Arabs did not hide their admiration for the *sumud* ("steadfastness") of the Iraqi people in the heavy fighting, were furious at the shedding of the blood of civilians in the air attacks, and felt with the Iraqis in their great suffering. The bombing of an air-raid shelter in Baghdad produced very sharp reactions. It was at this time that Dr Ahmad Tibi exclaimed:

> Even Arabs who, like myself, oppose the occupation of Kuwait, give top priority, above all else, on their public national agenda to the issue of the destruction of Iraq . . . My voice is a resounding Arab voice; not many Israeli voices have sounded the same note.

When the fighting broke out in the Gulf, an order banning Tibi from leaving Israel was issued only a few hours before he was to fly to Egypt for a family vacation. During his stay there, he was to meet Usama el-Baz, Egyptian President Mubarak's political advisor.[47]

Sympathy for Iraq expressed itself in a multitude of ways: some Israeli Arabs suddenly "discovered" family ties with prominent Iraqis. Thus it was found that Iraqi Foreign Minister Tareq 'Aziz had a grandfather coming from the Galilee village of Kafr Kana. For a while, his little house, long abandoned, attracted attention as a "historical site." Members of the family drew up a genealogical tree and asserted that 'Aziz was entitled to claim large tracts of lands from his grandfather's legacy. This sensational news item was carried by the Nazareth paper *As-Sinarah* and elicited a great number of excited reactions from its readers. Those who could claim kinship with the Iraqi minister found their prestige considerably augmented.[48] At times, heads turned a little too hot. Soon after the Temple Mount incident, three young Galilee Arabs were sentenced to prison for having carried slogans saying: "With our souls and our blood, we will redeem you, oh Saddam."

In a few cases, there were attempts to take action to aid Iraq, rather than merely support it verbally. Thus, the security service uncovered, immediately after the outbreak of the fighting, a cell engaged in espionage on behalf of Iraq. It was made up of a number of young Arabs from various places in central and northern Israel.

They had been recruited by a Fatah activist, an Israeli Arab who had lived in Baghdad for a time and had been enlisted by the Iraqi intelligence services. Members of the cell took photographs of security-related installations, were told to buy periodicals dealing with military topics, and to report on the exact locations hit by Iraqi missiles.[49] It would appear that several more people cooperated with Iraq in locating missile hits. Dr Sari Nusseiba of east Jerusalem was arrested on the same suspicion.

The "United Command" in the Territories made occasional attempts to stir up disorders against the background of the Gulf War. Masked men from beyond the "Green Line" entered through the Triangle village of Tayyibeh, waved PLO flags and shouted slogans in support of Saddam, but the inhabitants turned against them and called in the police.[50]

On the whole, Israeli Arabs avoided acts of violence. They did not dance on the roofs as SCUD missiles came down; rather, like all the rest of Israel's citizens, they sat in their shelters. Many responded to the call of Jewish organizations to assist the victims of the bombings, offering blood donations as well as volunteering work days for rebuilding destroyed houses of Jewish families. The local council of an Arab village near Haifa launched a campaign of good-neighborliness and offered to take in Jews from the city.[51]

The fact that Saddam's missiles were threatening Arab localities just as much as Jewish ones did not call forth any particularly sharp hostile reactions against him, but there can be no doubt that the common danger gave rise to different sentiments, as opposed to the trend of admiration for Iraq. Once again, a complex attitude emerged, a confluence of contradictory emotions ostensibly incapable of being entertained simultaneously by the same group of people. But the Arab minority in Israel managed to do so: pro-Iraqi feelings apart, it took its share in the measures of civil defense, occasionally complaining that the Arab sector was neglected with respect to the distribution of gas masks, the location of warning sirens and the allocation of materials to seal classrooms.[52]

Many Arabs were critical of the occupation of Kuwait. The Communist party came out against it consistently, calling it a "grave error." *Al-Ittihad* wrote unequivocally:

Iraq must withdraw from Kuwait and restore its sovereignty; even if, historically speaking, Kuwait is part of Iraqi soil, the problem must not be solved by the use of force.

But the United States, despite being engaged in driving the Iraqis out of Kuwait, was condemned by the Communists. Even the vote of the Soviet Union in the Security Council in favor of an ultimatum for the withdrawal from Kuwait came in for criticism in the Communist press.[53] The official party position notwithstanding, many Communist sympathizers defied the party during those turbulent days, hoping for Iraq to stay in Kuwait so that Saddam's victory would become their own.

In some ways, the Gulf War turned into a test of unprecedented severity for the Arab minority in Israel. They were asked to identify fully with two opposing sides: on the one hand, there was the feeling that Saddam's heroism in facing the entire world must bring about an Arab renaissance. Obviously, they understood that he would not "redeem" them, but they wanted to share in the dream, though without experiencing the pain of awakening. As against this, the missiles "lit up the situation in the cold light of reason," and the Israeli Arabs did not let themselves be carried away, like so many Arabs elsewhere. Any show of sympathy with Saddam was interpreted by Israel's Jews as a sign for the minority having "failed the test." Their being strangers to the emotional dilemmas of the Arab population pointed up the fact that war – any war – carries these complexities to the point of acute pain.

Here we have one of the reasons why a longing for peace is common to all trends among the Israeli Arabs, regardless of their particular political persuasion. In the final analysis, the Gulf War demonstrated – once more – the need to adapt to realities and to shy away from mere dreams. In doing so, it added one more layer to the growing understanding that Israel must be recognized as an existing fact.

Evoking the Palestinian-Arab Heritage

Wide circles from all parts of the nationalist movement of Israeli Arabs are demonstrating a growing desire to cultivate historical awareness based on memorial days, battle heritage and commemoration of heroes from the near and far past who were killed in battle or executed – *shuhada*, martyrs of Holy War.

In this vein, the "As-Sawt" society initiated the establishment of publishing houses for the literature of the Palestinian heritage. In Tayyibeh, former Al-Ard activist Saleh Baransi established, after his release from prison, the Institute for the Revival of the Arab Heritage (*Markaz Ihya at-Turath al-'Arabi*), which has also published books and magazines. In 1991, a monthly called *Kan'aan* appeared with essays on current issues, as well as various historical ones, such as a discussion on "The Deir Yassin Massacre in Zionist Thought and Policy."[54]

This memorial culture taps generously on the British Mandate days, bringing up heroes such as Sheikh 'Izz ed-Din el-Qassam, whose name is engraved on all Palestinian commemoration plates as a national hero; his commemoration day has been declared by the Intifadah's United Command as a day of general strike. Hamas units were named for him and Muslim groups proudly hold services in his memory.[55]

His successor, Sheikh Farhan es-Sa'di, hanged by the British in 1937 during Ramadan, was also made a saint whose picture decorated the walls of Arab houses in those days. Yusuf Sa'id Abu Durra, a gang commander in northern Samaria, is also regarded as a martyr deserving of commemoration.[56] He was executed in 1940 after his flight to Jordan and being turned over to the authorities. Geoffrey Morton, a British police officer, recounts in his memoirs that Abu Durra walked to his death with his head high, convinced that he had acted properly in his people's cause. In the 1970s, a PLO unit infiltrating Israel from Lebanon bore his name.

Other figures enveloped in eternal glory are the fighters of the *Thawrah*, or the Rebellion of 1936–39 which was followed by the war of 1948, which is regarded as the "Holocaust" of Palestinian Arabs; still, from the darkness of this later war stand out fighters such as 'Abd el-Kader el-Husseini, Faisal Husseini's father, who was killed in Qastel village near Jerusalem.

Cited are the last words of the poet 'Abd er-Rahim Mahmud from 'Anabta, killed in the battle of Sejera in the Lower Galilee in the summer of 1948, while serving in the "Army of Salvation": "I'll carry my life in my hands and throw it into hell, if my death leads to victory".[57] The "As-Sawt" society in Nazareth initiated a project to commemorate this fighting poet.

To the pantheon of Palestinian national heroes were added figures who won their glory after the establishment of Israel, among them Israeli Arabs and writers contributing to the struggle literature, and PLO fighters and leaders. Former Al-Ard activist Mansur Kardush initiated the establishment of the "Society for Commemorating the Heritage of Rashed Hussein," which has published his poetry.[58]

The writer and critic Ghassan Kanafani, killed in an explosion in Beirut in July 1972, has become the hero of George Habash's PFLP. He shares glory with 'Ali Salameh, killed by Israeli agents in the capital of Lebanon, and with the poet Kamal Nasser, Yusuf en-Najjar and Kamal 'Adwan, PLO activists killed in an IDF raid on Beirut in the 1970s.[59]

At the top of the list stands Khalil el-Wazir, "Abu Jihad," the PLO's operations officer, who was shot to death in his home in Tunis during a raid in May 1988, and next to him is "Abu Iyad," 'Arafat's right-hand man. These men are the subjects of heroic tales; thousands of Palestinian babies born around the time of their deaths were named after them, and their names are also used for various operations, organizations and literary works. Alongside the cultivation of individual famous heroes, there is also a web of commemoration woven for the anonymous dead who fell in Deir Yassin, Kafr Qassem, Sabra and Shatilla and on the Temple Mount in Jerusalem in October 1990. Their remembrance days are commemorated by strikes and mourning processions, black flags are raised, prayers said for them, and in times of unrest these ceremonies are accompanied by violent disturbances.[60]

Beside national holidays, such as "Fatah Establishment Day" and "Declaration of Palestinian Independence Day," the Palestinian calendar is becoming overcrowded with memorial days drawn from history, from current events, and shared by all Palestinians, whether in Israel or abroad. Among these memorial days are "*Nakbah*," the 1948 disaster, and "*Naksah*," the 1967 defeat, alongside the Israeli Arabs' "Land Day." This is a diversified web, richly expressed also in various literary creations.

5

Minority Rights under Israeli Law

The Basic Concept – Equality of Rights

The principle of guaranteeing the individual rights of citizens of Israel, along with the minorities in its midst, found expression in the Declaration of Independence as follows:

> The State of Israel . . . shall uphold absolute social and political equality of rights for all its citizens, without distinction of religion, race or sex; it shall guarantee freedom of religion, conscience, language, education and culture; it shall preserve the holy places of all religions; and it shall be true to the principles of the Charter of the United Nations.

Further on in the proclamation, a call to the Arabs in Israel was voiced:

> We call, even in the midst of this bloody onslaught which has been carried out upon us these past months, to the sons of the Arab people who are residents of the State of Israel to maintain peace and to take part in the building of the State on the basis of full and equal citizenship and on the basis of appropriate representation in all its institutions, provisional and permanent.

The Declaration of Independence was not born as a constitutional law. The People's Council, which made the ceremonious proclamation, was not empowered to legislate laws. This was a special body, created by virtue of the unique historical circumstances, amidst the turbulence of the War of Independence of the Jewish People. But planted in those few lines was the seed of the essence of Israel, as its founders wished to see it at that fateful hour in history.

Accordingly, the Declaration of Independence was ascribed a

special status, which in the course of years made its mark on the Israeli Law regarding basic rights of citizens of the State. In one of the first rulings of the Supreme Court, Chief Justice Moshe Zemorah states with regard to the legal significance of the proclamation:[1]

> It expresses the vision of the nation and its conviction, but it does not constitute a constitutional law prescribing an actual ruling with regard to the existence of various ordinances and laws, or the revocation thereof. The institution, which was temporarily empowered to legislate laws is the Provisional State Council which was established with the proclamation of the State . . .

Later on, it seems that the effect of the proclamation was broadened, and it took on the significance of a kind of "guide" in interpreting the laws of the State, as expressed by Justice Agranat in considering the question of freedom of expression in the State:[2]

> . . . The system of laws in accordance with which the political institutions were established and function in Israel demonstrates that this is indeed a state built on democratic principles. What is stated in the Declaration of Independence, and particularly with regard to founding the State "on principles of freedom" and guaranteeing freedom of conscience – means that Israel is a freedom-loving state. It is true that the Declaration "does not constitute a constitutional law prescribing an actual ruling with regard to the existence of various ordinances and laws or the revocation thereof" (HCJ 10/48 . . .), but to the extent that it "expresses the vision of the nation and its conviction" (*ibid.*), it is our duty to heed its manifestations when interpreting and giving meaning to the laws of the State, including the legal provisions enacted during the period of the British Mandate and adopted by the State, following its establishment, via the channel of Article 11 of the Administration of Government and Justice Ordinance, 1948; after all, it is a known axiom that the law of the people must be learned as reflected in its national life.

This concept struck roots in other rulings. It seems that the declaration became a sort of "test lab" for the acts of the executive authority in order to make sure that all those rights determined therein are preserved, explicitly and in general, including full equality of rights for the minorities in Israel, both individual rights and their rights as a national minority.

Lacking the status of a constitution, the declaration does not have the power to cancel a contradictory law; however, it does seem to serve as a brake mechanism against the passing of any legislation contrary to its principles. Such being the case, through the broad interpretation it is possible to guarantee that the laws of the State are in harmony with the basic principles manifested in the Declaration of Independence.

The culmination of this process is with the passing of the Judicial Foundations Law, 1980, which gave these principles full legal significance, serving as a foundation for the entire system of laws in the state, as laid down in Article 1 of the law: "the principles of freedom, justice, integrity and peace [which are the principles] of Israel's heritage."[3]

This may be a winding road for the purpose of safeguarding the basic rights in a democratic state, although this has unquestionably proved its strength up until now in view of the strong position of the Supreme Court's adjudication.

In the light of this basic concept, there is no doubt of the equality of the minorities before the law. This is a basic principle interwoven in the very essence of the Israeli Law. There is no legal provision expressly dealing with this, apart from the Declaration of Independence. It seems that any further mention of such equality is superfluous, and any discrimination toward an Arab citizen, as an Arab, shall be ruled out by the Court impromptu. But the very determination of this equality before the law is not sufficient.

The complex position of the Arab minority, struggling to define itself and pulled in various directions by opposing forces, creates for itself a special status also from the legal point of view. There is no mention of this uniqueness among the written rights, where the equality is set forth without requiring special emphasis, but it is particularly conspicuous on the level of obligations.

The main implication is that Arab citizens in Israel are not required to serve in the Israel Defense Forces (IDF). This is apparently the only matter within the system of rights and obligations in Israel which expressly distinguishes between citizens of the State according to a nationalistic cross-section. Exempting Arabs from serving in the IDF stems from a realistic view of their unique position. It is intended to prevent the inner contradiction of their existence from becoming more acute and to guarantee that they will not have to fight their brethren, serving in Arab armies or among the ranks of terrorist organizations.

This exemption may also be seen as an expressed recognition of both the nationality of the Arabs in Israel and of the special right of this public in general not to fulfill the duty imposed upon the rest of the citizens of the State, due to the existing political circumstances.

And indeed, this exemption corresponds with the feeling of Arabs in Israel, as already expressed many years ago in a series of articles by a Muslim Arab, who called himself 'Abd el-Muta'al. He emphasized:[4] "I am simply against Israeli Arabs serving in the army. I am not prepared to fight against my brothers in Arab countries, since I am an inseparable part of the Arab nation." And he adds a high-flown declaration in order to clarify that his lack of willingness is not an expression of alienation from the State of Israel: "I would be willing to fight for the country should danger be imminent from a foreign power; Russia, the United States, Britain, France."

Obviously, he is well aware that willingness to go to war against the United States or France has no real meaning, but he emphasizes it in order to underscore the same basic line that causes the disturbing predicament of the Israeli Arab in view of the hostility of Arab countries towards his country. He therefore concludes: "If I say that I am willing to serve in the Army in order to prove loyalty, then I loudly declare that I am a hypocrite, and a hypocrite I do not wish to be."

This silent consent, which exists till today, is a reality laden with contradictions; it is not possible to achieve full equality in the realm of security. In recent years, some Israeli Arabs have demanded that the Arab citizens of the State be recruited into the IDF. Even though a comprehensive poll has not been conducted on this issue, there is no doubt that the majority of the Arabs of Israel would *not* wish to assume this duty, despite the feeling that as long as equality does not include the duties, the weight of the rights on the scale is reduced.

Accordingly, a middle road is proposed – mamely, applying a duty of "national service" to young Israeli Arabs. This topic is raised from time to time, but until now no real steps have been taken to implement it. Minister David Magen decided in 1990 to establish a committee in order to clarify the various possibilities of voluntary recruitment. In late December 1990, the Monitoring Committee of Israeli Arabs decided that the principle of *civil* service of young Arabs should not be ruled out, "subject to adopting a detailed plan, the object of which is to guarantee full civil equality, including development budgets to integrate the Arab population in the country's economy." It was also decided to absolutely object to the existing mandatory recruitment of certain Arab youths into the IDF, such as Druze. This position was presented in a meeting of Arab Knesset members with the minister.[5]

Another special problem related to the integration of Arabs in Israel on the basis of equality is the declared nature of Israel as a Jewish state. The Law of Return, 1950,[6] expresses this basic concept in granting to every Jew the right to immigrate to Israel, with certain restrictions. This law deals with the manner of naturalization in Israel and it grants to Jews special rights, due to the nature of the State, but it does not contradict the equality of rights of its Arab citizens, as there is no other law or legal provision granting privileges to Jews as citizens.

The Law of Return unquestionably gives clear and distinct preference to Jews whoever they may be to immigrate to Israel as part of the historic yearning for an ingathering of the exiles and due to the very essence of Israel in accordance with the Zionist vision, which is expressed at the beginning of the Declaration of Independence.

This is not discrimination against the Arab citizens of Israel, but rather a clear statement of the desire to realize the idea of turning Israel into the national homeland of Jews from the Diaspora. Indeed, this does emphasize that the Arabs of Israel do constitute *a minority* within the boundaries of the State, without prejudicing or derogating civil equality.

One should not ignore, though, other possible implications of the concept of Israel as a Jewish State in everyday reality, in which there may be situations that could give rise to "so-called" discrimination on this background. For the purpose of analysis, let us imagine a hypothetical case that could lead to a charge of discrimination on a nationalistic basis: an Israeli Arab citizen, who declares that he objects to Jewish immigration to Israel, participates in a tender for a high-ranking position in the Ministry of Absorption, which is wholly aimed at assisting the absorption of Jewish immigrants. The tender committee disqualifies him because of his opinion, despite the principle of freedom of thought and freedom of expression, and he petitions the High Court of Justice to cancel the disqualification of the tender committee. It is not inevitable that the Supreme Court will dismiss the petition and support this consideration of the tender committee. However, the disqualification of a candidate in this case is not because he is an Arab, but rather because of his views, which are liable to interfere with his identifying with the tasks assigned to him.

The situation described above is a case of pseudo-discrimination from a purely legal point of view. It also seems unrealistic, since it is hard to imagine an Arab, who publicly objects to Jewish immigration, to especially insist on working in the Ministry of Absorption. Nonetheless, here lies a key point in the feeling of discrimination of Arabs in Israel. Even the most moderate Arabs would hesitate before offering their candidacy to positions calling for absolute Zionist awareness. Such being the case, we cannot ignore the fact that in reality the Israeli Arab minority does not exhaust its legal rights, both in view of the tense security situation and due to the very nature of Israel as a Jewish state. On the political sphere, this initial factor restricts any movement aimed at excluding this basic principle from the essence of Israel as a Jewish state. By the nature of the political circumstances, it is precisely Arab organizations which tried to rise against this line in the definition of the State.

In Elections Appeal 1/65 *Yerador vs. Chairman of the Central Elections Committee of the sixth Knesset* this question was raised in all its intensity. The Arab Socialist List, which requested to participate in the elections to the sixth Knesset, strictly complied with all the requirements of the Election Laws, but it challenged the existence of Israel as a Jewish state. The question was raised whether the Central Elections Committee has the authority to disqualify the list in view of its identification with the animosity of Arab countries, without granting the committee such authority in one of the laws.

Chief Justice Shimon Agranat adjudicated an unequivocal positive response in determining that the State of Israel was not only established as a sovereign, independent, freedom-loving state, but also "as a Jewish state in the Land of Israel" and this is a constitutional basic fact, "which Heaven forbid should any authority of the State – be it an administrative authority, a judicial authority or a quasi-judicial authority – deny it in exercising any of its powers."[7]

Nevertheless, the very nature of the State does not limit the equality of rights of the minorities in its midst. There are various minorities in many countries which define their national character, and there is no contradiction between their essence as a democracy and their national definition, although many difficulties crop up in reality in implementing the principle of equality toward minorities, who at the same time are entitled to be different, to preserve their national character and religious faith, to speak in their language and cultivate their culture, while maintaining their loyalty to the State. Against this background a great deal of constant tension exists in many enlightened countries regarding the relations between the majority and the minority living among them.

Preserving this line of distinction in Israel is even harder in view of the hatred expressed towards it by Arab countries and the tendency of radical, mostly Arab, groups within Israel to identify with them. This reality has increased the need for extensive security measures as a means of prevention and deterrence. These measures were indeed directed at Arabs, but not because of their being Arabs. The defense forces feared their hostile activity and were not more lenient in their treatment of Jews with similar tendencies. However, because subversive trends concentrated primarily in the Arab sector, those wishing to contradict the faithfulness of the Israeli law to the principle of equality and preserving the rights of the Arab minority look for support here. This trend has grown more acute since the outbreak of the Intifadah.

These groups can point to Arab detainees who were put under administrative arrest pursuant to Regulation 111 of the 1945 Defense (Emergency) Regulations, later replaced by the 1979 Emergency Authority Law (Detentions),[8] or to areas which were closed off pursuant to Regulation 125, including Arab villages. These regulations, which were exercised in the Arab sector, serve to them as clear-cut proof of the lack of equality in the Israeli Law or the implementation of laws by way of discrimination. *Prima facie* they are justified, and there are undoubtedly statutes that were chiefly exercised against Arabs, but this is still a far cry from the conclusion that they were discriminated against because of their being Arabs, unless it be said that by their being Arabs they could not, for the sake of their self-integrity, refrain from preparations to harm the security of the State.

Administrative arrest has not been exercised against Arab citizens, unless due to the concern of a security risk. The way of exercising the regulation or the need to modify or limit its use is debatable, as well as with regard to the need for creating another level for appeals of each personal warrant issued in accordance with these regulations.

The extent of the actual use of administrative arrest is relatively limited; there is a great deal of sense to the argument whether it is at all necessary for the well-being of the Israeli democracy, but by no means should administrative arrest or another restraining exercise of the Defense (Emergency) Regulations be regarded as a deviation from the equality toward the minorities.

The Military Administration was abolished in 1966, following a gradual relaxation of various restrictions imposed within its framework. Since then every security measure has been meticulously scrutinized in order to prevent the feeling of discrimination. Nonetheless, there is no doubt that under the existing circumstances, there may be unjustified measures, steps and an overly broad exercise of the regulations which by their very essence are adopted as a last resort security measure.

Those wishing to prove that the government authorities consistently adopt a clear line of discrimination are grasping at isolated cases or steps limited in scope. They are searching for a peg to hang on in citing rulings of the Supreme Court in which a certain measure adopted by the defense forces is criticized, but they ignore the very implication of the ruling as proof of the separation of the authorities and the faithfulness of the Israeli Law to the basic principles in the perception of the minorities in the State. They are hanging on to the exceptions in order to prove that the rule does not exist.

Even more complicated are the questions pertaining to the problem of land. Extensive areas in Israel were handed over to the custodian of absentee property by virtue of the Absentee Property Law, 1950.[9] There is no doubt that the absentees, as defined in Article 1(b) of the law, are Arabs, but this fact is a consequence of the circumstances surrounding the establishment of the State and not a result of national discrimination.

The law defines an absentee as any person, who at any time since the United Nations resolution on the partition of Eretz Yisrael (Palestine) on November 29, 1947, was the legal owner of property within the territory of Israel, or occupied it, and was a citizen or subject of one of the Arab countries, or resided therein, or in part of Eretz Yisrael (Palestine) outside the territory of Israel, or was a citizen and left his regular place of residence in Eretz Yisrael (Palestine):

1. For a place outside Eretz Yisrael (Palestine) before the 27th of Av, 5708 (September 1, 1948); or
2. For a place in Eretz Yisrael (Palestine) which was occupied at the time by forces wishing to prevent the establishment of the State of Israel or who fought it following its establishment.[10]

The basic logic of the law is not contestable.

The political reality facing Israel required that it prevent people, who were subjects of the enemy or who were within the borders of a hostile government, to remain the owners of property in Israel. Many countries in the world adopted similar legal measures in a time of war or during a time of emergency.[11] Both Jordan and Egypt issued similar laws regarding Jewish property in the West Bank and Gaza Strip after 1948.

The expropriation of absentee property from their owners was a necessity of the hour. It was eased by articles, giving the custodian discretion to release transferred properties, and indeed properties were released and returned to their owners by virtue of the recommendations of a special committee appointed for this purpose.

The ownership of the custodian was restricted with the aim of guaranteeing the use of the property for the purposes prescribed in the law, that is rehabilitation, settlement and development. In this way, *waqf* (Moslem charitable endowment) lands were also transferred to the custodian, since throughout most of the Mandate period they were administered by the Higher Muslim Council that was declared an absentee. In this way, the Muslim community in Israel gained assistance in financing religious, educational and charitable activities and for construction, on a wider scale and in a much more efficiently organized way than under the administration of the Higher Muslim Council. The Higher Muslim Council served for a long period as a political tool in the hands of the Jerusalem *mufti*, Hajj Amin el-Husseini, both in order to attack his enemies and to finance the struggle against the Jews.

In 1937, the Higher Muslim Council was dispersed by the British High Commissioner, and since then *waqf* property has been administered by a government-appointed committee.

Following the 1948 war, not one of the members of the Higher Muslim Council remained in Israel. They all fled the country, including those who administered the family *waqf* properties, which was handed over to the administration of the custodian of absentee property. By virtue of the 1953 Acquisition of Land Law (Confirmation of Deeds and Compensation), *waqf* properties were transferred to the development authority so that lands should not remain uncultivated, but the proceeds from these properties essentially financed the original objects of the Muslim religious trust; orphanages, schools, kindergartens, health centers and clinics were built and even student aid funds were established for Muslim students. Substantial funds were allocated for Bedouin tribes in the Negev.

With the rehabilitation of the Muslim community, claims were

voiced to return the *waqf* properties to the administration of independent Muslim organizations. Indeed, pursuant to an amendment
of the Absentee Property Law, 1965,[12] Muslim trust committees
were established, which constitute corporations qualified to purchase and transfer any right, to sue and be sued, and they are
authorized to administer the properties in their possession. These
committees are independent, although subject to the criticism of the
State Comptroller.[13]

The Muslim community in general enjoys very broad judicial
autonomy. Its courts of justice have unique authority in everything
pertaining to consecrations and the personal status. Article 9 of
the *Qadis* (Muslim Religious Judges) Law, 1961 releases the *qadi*
from any dependence, and his appointment is for an unlimited
period.[14]

The judicial autonomy demonstrates the right of the minorities
to be *different*. Nevertheless, it was imperative for the legislator to intervene on basic questions, mainly involving the nature
of the government in Israel.[15] Young Muslims sometimes protest the "intervention" of the Israeli legislator, which is meant
to reinforce the position of the Muslim woman and grant her
equality, constituting a basic condition for the development of a
modern society. This "intervention" is essential for the socioeconomic advancement of the Arab society, so that the gap will not be
a stumbling block in the way of implementing equality in practice
– in employment, in education and on the social level.

The Right to Be Different

In many countries that define their national characteristics, there
exist different minorities, without any contradiction between the
national definition of those countries and their essence as a democracy. Nor is there any doubt that many difficult problems arise in
the manner in which the principles of equality are applied with
respect to the minority group, which at the same time is entitled
to be different – in preserving its national identity and religion, in
speaking its own language and developing its own culture – while
remaining loyal to the state. It is against this background that in
many enlightened countries there exists a constant state of tension
between the majority, and the minority living in its midst.

In the Burkan ruling, HCJ 114/78, the Supreme Court was

requested to examine the concept of equality in the course of its implementation against the background of the right to be different reserved unto Arabs living in Israel.[16] The picture became sharper as described by Justice Meir Shamgar in stating:

> It is noteworthy here in general that an automatic transfer from one place to another of the entire range of modes and ways in which the rules of equality were to be implemented, without considering the conditions and the special circumstances, may be to no small degree misleading: For instance, the compulsory integration of students elsewhere [meaning the reference of the petitioner to a ruling of the United States Supreme Court regarding the prohibition of segregation in housing and education – (author's note)], thus imposing the English language and Anglo-Saxon culture on every student, which is considered there to be *the height of equality*, may be considered here *compulsory assimilation*, if an Arab student is forced to forego studying in a separate school in which the studies are conducted in his language and according to his culture: And there were special circumstances in which this court gave its seal of approval to provisions forbidding Jews to pray on the Temple Mount and did not regard this, due to these special circumstances, as a prohibited violation of freedom of religion and freedom of religious worship.[17]

The Burkan Ruling is undoubtedly a milestone in Israeli adjudication in outlining the application of the right to be different, while emphasizing that it does not derogate from the principle of equality. In the words of Justice David Bekhor:

> A rule held sacred is that, Heaven forbid, should we take part in anything smacking of discrimination between people because of their religion or nationality, but at the same time in applying this big rule, we must not ignore the reality and the situation in the field, and we must be careful not to create discrimination of another kind in the opposite direction and not violate the security of human lives.[18]

The set of facts that served as a background for this ruling was undeniably unusual: The respondent, the Company for the Restoration & Development of the Jewish Quarter in the Old City in Jerusalem Ltd., a state-owned company, offered to the public apartments that it built in new buildings in the Jewish Quarter. Within that offer of apartments to the public it was determined that only one of the following was entitled to participate in the offer: either an Israeli citizen who is a resident and served in the IDF or received an exemption from service in the IDF or served in one of the Hebrew (Jewish underground) organizations prior to May 14, 1948, or a new immigrant who is a resident of Israel.

Supreme Court Judge Hayim Cohen clarifies at the beginning of his ruling: "The petitioner admits that he is neither an Israeli citizen nor did he serve in the IDF, nor is he a new immigrant: he is a Jordanian citizen, and according to him he has always been a resident of the Old City of Jerusalem. Hence, this Court has issued him an order *nisi*, requiring that the respondents also give grounds why this instruction should not be rescinded in accordance with which the offer of apartments is limited to citizens of Israel and new immigrants only . . . The petitioner contends that the apartment of his desire was built on his ancestors' land, where he and his father lived since 1947, and that the building where they lived 'since the beginning of time' has been a Muslim's property, and 'Jews never lived there'. It has been ascertained that this building passed from Jewish hands to Muslim hands during the period of the 1938 bloody incidents; and that already several years ago the petitioner and his family moved to a new home, which they bought in Beit Hanina (an Arab neighborhood outside the Old City)."[19]

Judge Hayim Cohen determined that it was not necessarily wrong to discriminate between citizens and non-citizens regarding benefits from the Nation's property or other economic rights, based on Article 3(2) of the International Convention on Economic, Social and Cultural Rights, approved by the General Assembly of the United Nations on December 16, 1966. However, with regard to the matter at bar, his third reason is particularly significant, which is: "The need for restoration of the Jewish Quarter in the Old city arises only because the armies of Jordan invaded it and expelled the Jews and robbed them of their property and destroyed their homes. By the nature of things, the restoration is intended to restore the glory of the Jewish settlement in the Old City, so that Jews may have, as in the past, a special quarter next to the Muslim and Christian and Armenian quarters. There is nothing wrong in discrimination that sets apart these quarters, each quarter and its community."[20]

In other words, national unity which creates a closed circle is not necessarily discrimination, although the question is undoubtedly raised whether this ruling gives rise to the need to also preserve the distinctiveness of the other quarters in the Old City. Judge Shamgar indirectly responded in emphasizing: "Having regard to the fact that this concerns a very unique set of facts, i.e., the restoration of a notable historic site – while preserving its character and identity – and not to a small extent in restoring it, it's no wonder that the respondent did not find it possible to sell the apartment in the quarter to the petitioner, and it was entitled so to do."[21]

Politics and Law

Israeli Arabs were already defined in the Declaration of Independence as "sons of the Arab people," without ignoring their national identity as part of the nation that waged war on Israel and with the clear recognition of their status as a separate national group, whose sons are entitled both to full and equal citizenship and to representation in the State institutions. The perception from the outset was unequivocal: Israeli Arabs should not be assimilated or estranged from their nationality, or be denied of their right to cultivate their culture, to develop their religious frameworks and to use their language in accordance with Article 27 of the universal declaration regarding human rights, passed at the General Assembly of the United Nations on December 10, 1948.

The language of the Declaration of Independence from the political point of view is general and perhaps even ambiguous. Sons of the Arab people, residents of the State of Israel, are called on "to maintain peace and to take part in the building of the State on the basis of full and equal citizenship and on the basis of appropriate representation in all its institutions, provisional and permanent."

What is the meaning of this "appropriate representation," mentioned at the end of this passage? It seems that there was no intention of guaranteeing "reserved" seats for Arabs in the Israeli Knesset, or a fixed percentage of representation, corresponding with their share of the population, but I have already heard such an "interpretation" from an expert of political science, claiming that in the Declaration of Independence, Israel's Arabs were promised proportional representation in the Israeli Knesset, according to their percentage of the State's citizens. This is entirely unfounded. The "appropriate representation" was nothing but an expression of willingness to integrate Arabs as members of the Israeli legislature, without establishing hard and fast rules about how it should be done. In any event, it is clear that "reservation" stands in complete contradiction with the essence of the government in Israel.

Elections to the Knesset are general, national, direct, equal, secret and based on proportional representation. This electoral system does not secure or guarantee *pro rata* representation for each group or for a certain area. Article 4 of "the Basic Law: the Knesset" prescribes the electoral system and it is a "prime clause," which can only be amended by a majority of all Knesset members.[22]

The Arabs of Israel participate in elections to the Knesset as citizens of equal rights. In contrast with the situation in most Arab countries, Arab women in Israel enjoy unrestricted voting rights.

Voting in elections was perceived for a long time by Arab countries as an expression of recognition of the existence of Israel. Therefore, in the past the Egyptian broadcasting station *Sawt Al-'Arab* tended to call upon Arabs in Israel to refrain from voting. This also applied to the PLO, but the scope of participation in elections among the Arab minority proved already then that this call did not get real response. Today, external activity for such a boycott is not discernible, however there are radical groups among Israel's Arabs, such as "Sons of the Village" and the "Progressive National Movement," who continue to boycott the elections. Their influence was felt mainly in a widespread boycott of elections to the tenth Knesset in 1981.[23]

In the first elections in 1949, Israeli Arabs were still in a state of shock, facing the new reality, but even then the percentage of their participation in elections reached 79.3 percent. In the following elections, the percentage of voters increased and reached 91 percent in 1955, but has since decreased. A sharp drop was felt in the elections to the eighth Knesset (1973) – from 80 percent to 75 percent, and afterwards, in the next Knesset (1977), to 69 percent.

Since the first Knesset, Arabs have been members in the Israeli Parliament. They were elected as representatives of Arab lists or within the framework of Israeli national parties who appointed Arab candidates in "secure seats."

The representation of Arabs in the Knesset is small compared to their percentage of the population, despite their active participation in elections. The main reason lies in the division of votes, which according to the present election system causes a loss of many votes, given to abortive parties, but, of course, refraining from voting is a significant factor.

Freedom of political organization is a founded principle in any democratic government. Within the framework of traditional Arab society, the extended family makes up a basic political unit.[24] The political party, based on the individual, is foreign to the traditional social structure. Accordingly, organizing into political parties is a sort of innovation, the product of the socioeconomic development since the establishment of the State, during the course of which social circles, founded on blood ties, were broken.

Nevertheless, the power of the political frameworks, which are based on family ties and/or the religious-communal link, are still strong. This factor is more strongly felt in the elections to the local council in Arab settlements. They are elected in free, secret and proportional representation elections by the residents in their area. In fact, they still reflect to a great degree the family or communal sections in the village. During the last decade, there has been a development of the Muslim movement based on religious radicalism.

The participation of Arabs in Jewish political parties was at first limited and was mainly expressed in the establishment of parties connected with them for the purpose of elections. Zionist parties, apart from Mapam, did not tend to accept Arabs among their ranks. The Labor Party opened its gates to Arab members in the early 1970s, followed by other Zionist movements. Rakah, the "New Communist List," is decisively supported by its Arab members. Its main activity is also concentrated in the Arab sector, and affairs pertaining to Israeli Arabs are paramount to its political struggle.

This applies both to the Progressive List for Peace, which originated in the elections to the eleventh Knesset in 1984, and the Democratic Arab Party, founded by 'Abd el-Wahhab Darawshah, and which first competed in the elections to the twelfth Knesset in 1988. Israeli Arabs enjoy freedom of political organization. At the same time, there is no doubt about the unique sensitivity pent up in this area, where tension flares up between hostile, radical Arab groups and the government authorities.

The case of the Al-Ard Movement reflects the predicament of the Israeli regime, which is pulled by two conflicting basic considerations that together form its very essence:

1. The nature of the democratic Israeli government, entitling its citizens to freedom, freedom of expression and the right to organize.
2. Preserving the integrity of Israel as a Jewish state *vis-à-vis* subversive extremist groups among the Israeli Arabs, who do not accept the existence of Israel.

The Al-Ard Movement, having been registered as a trading company following a ruling of the High Court of Justice against thre Registrar of companies, tried to become a political party. The Haifa District Commissioner refused to approve the association, as it was viewed as an organization aimed at undermining the very existence of Israel, while identifying with the hostile goals of the Arab national movement. The group's petition to the High Court of Justice against the Commissioner was denied.[25]

This ruling reflects the basic perception of Israeli Law regarding the boundaries of democracy in a difficult attempt at defining them. Undeniably, in the very delineation of the freedom to organize there lies a risk that under certain circumstances the government is liable to try and restrict, for the sake of securing its rule, or overstep those boundaries for its purposes, while violating the very essence of democracy.

Indeed, the Supreme Court judges did not ignore these possible ramifications of their ruling and stressed again and again the radical factors justifying the divergence from the principle of freedom to organize, while limiting the ruling to the narrow area in which it is essential in order to prevent the abuse of freedom in order to violate it. Many passages, stated in the ruling *a propos* these grounds, are therefore likely to actually serve as reinforcement of the right of political organization of the Arab minority in Israel. On the other hand, this ruling is a deterrent for extremist groups from further attempts to use the principle of political organization as a device for undermining the foundations of the State.

The growing integration of the Arab minority in Israel has placed a heavy obstacle in the way of illegal nationalistic organizing. The Al-Ard Movement tried to enjoy the protection of the law, as the chances of its operating underground were slight. Its leaders recognized the difficulty of expanding its ranks while operating against the law. They understood that the Arab public at large would not follow an underground movement, and that they should therefore create a legal framework suitable for their operations. After the judgment of the Supreme Court was given, the Al-Ard Movement was declared illegal by order of the Minister of Defense, by virtue of his authority pursuant to Defense (Emergency) Regulations.

The participation of the "Progressive List for Peace" (PLP) in the elections to the eleventh Knesset in 1984 again acutely stirred up the problem of freedom of political organization, in view of the concerns that this party, headed by Advocate Muhammad Mi'ari, is a reincarnation of the Al-Ard movement of which he was one of the founders. His activity several years previously reinforced these concerns, and the 1980 affidavit of Major General Avigdor (Yanush) Ben-Gal, Head of the Israeli Northern Command, was presented, *inter alia*, before the Central Elections Committee, clarifying reasons for issuing administrative restraining orders against Advocate Mi'ari for security reasons by virtue of Regulation 108 of the Defense (Emergency) Regulations.

It seems appropriate to present the main points included in that affidavit in order to illustrate the significance of the principal issue that was raised. And these are the grounds of Major General Ben-Gal in his words, as quoted by Chief Justice Meir Shamgar:

1. Shortly prior to issuing the order, and, more particularly, from the beginning of June [1980] and onward, there began, as assessed by competent security authorities . . . a severe deterioration in the security situation and in keeping public order in the Arab villages. It was determined at a certain stage that without adopting suitable measures, the situation could continue to deteriorate to the point of nationalistic unrest and extremely unruly agitation which could jeopardize the security of the State and actually disrupt public order and public peace . . .

2. The activity of the petitioner [Advocate Mi'ari]: Against the background of these events the petitioner himself acted: On June 3, 1980, the Committee of the Arab Council Heads in Israel was convened in the village of Rama in order to decide on measures in response to the assault on the mayors in Judea and Samaria [by Jewish extremists]. The petitioner was not summoned to the meeting, as he is not a head of a council and not even a member of a local council or a committee member. Notwithstanding, he . . . at his initiative, together with others, after a relatively moderate decision was passed, calling for only a strike of the council heads and for convening another assembly in Nazareth on June 5, 1980 [the anniversary of the Six Day War] the petitioner addressed those present and incited to hold a general strike that would disrupt daily life, as the situation in the street was ripe for this, and as demanded by the "grassroot organizations" in Nazareth and outside it with a view of promoting unity and reinforcing the Committee.

3. I saw this agitative and provocative activity of the petitioner's – which was maliciously intended to add fuel to the fire and

aggravate further the situation, which in any case was very explosive – in view of the petitioner's activity in the past, namely: (a) He is well known to the security forces for years as someone who acted to realize very radical goals, threatening the security and peace of the State of Israel; (b) From 1963 to 1973, he was already subject to restrictions pursuant to Regulations 109–110 due to his activity, including activity in the notorious Al-Ard Movement, which was prohibited due to its being subversive and negating the existence of the State; (c) The petitioner still maintains contacts with former activists of Al-Ard, including activists of terrorist organizations, and I don't believe that one can call these contacts purely "friendly," as the petitioner feigns in his affidavit of September 7, 1980; (d) The petitioner has also maintained contacts with various parties among the Arabs in the Administered Territories, for the express purposes of harming the State of Israel, its security and well-being, and for this reason the commanders of the Judea, Samaria and Gaza Strip regions prohibited him from entering their regions (pursuant to Regulation 112 in force also there). I firmly believe in this information, despite the fact that the petitioner has denied it; (e) I also maintain that the petitioner has been active, since March 30, 1976 (known as "Land Day," when a riot so severe was instigated that caused the use of firearms by the security forces and loss of life) in the organization of demonstrations, protests, strikes and provoking violence.

4. Under these circumstances, I reached the conclusion, in accordance with the reliable opinion of security authorities, that in order to prevent a further dangerous escalation of the situation and in order to restore calm, order and peace subject to my authority pursuant to Regulation 6 – several agitative persons, the petitioner being among them, must be restricted and supervision must be imposed on them. For this reason I have issued the order, forming the subject matter of the petition.

The Central Elections Committee decided to disqualify the list, and it appealed this decision before the Supreme Court, which saw fit to hear it together with the appeal of the Jewish ultra-nationalist Kach party against its disqualification. Thus, the appeals of the two extremist parties at the opposite ends of the political spectrum in Israel, were brought together in the same hearing. The ruling of the

Supreme Court in this case is considered the most comprehensive with regard to political organization since the establishment of the State and is known by its abbreviated name, "the Neiman Ruling."

The Supreme Court first had to distinguish the PLP from the Al-Ard movement, which had tried in 1965 to don a new official cloak, called the Arab Socialist List. As far as the facts were concerned, Chief Justice Meir Shamgar made it clear that "although the Socialist List was not exactly composed of the same individuals as the leadership of the Al-Ard Movement, yet it reflected that movement, which was declared illegal and the objects of which were defined by this court as illegitimate, since some of those heading it had also been "heads of Al-Ard": ten candidates were included in the Socialist List, among them five, i.e., half, who had been members of the illegal Al-Ard organization, which advocated the elimination of the State. In the case at bar, on the other hand, there is a list of 120 candidates, of whom only one – the person who heads it – belonged in the past to the Al-Ard Movement. The head of the party – Advocate Mi'ari – who is a former member of the Al-Ard organization, contended that he did not view the party as a continuance of the said illegal movement, and the diverse composition of the list of candidates was *prima facie* in order to support this thesis. He further explained in his appearance before the Elections Committee that he no longer represented the opinions of Al-Ard and that he had reservations about the Palestinian National Covenant of the PLO."

The Chief Justice emphasized that "the very denial of associating with the ideas of the previous organization does not necessarily serve as *juris et de jure* that this is indeed the case. Evidence could have come before the committee refuting the denial which point *prima facie* to the opposite conclusion."[26]

This last comment is important as a shield against pretentiousness, meaning that it is possible to "lift the curtain" and reveal the true face of a list, aiming at the destruction of the State, even if it does not openly reveal its goal.

The Court determined with regard to denying the right of PLP to compete in the elections that it was necessary to distinguish clearly between giving an administrative restraining order based upon the information given in Major General Ben-Gal's affidavit and the disqualification of a parliamentary list, since there were separate and different criteria for both actions.

The central question was whether the PLP might be disqualified due to the attempt of its members to establish political ties, with the object of meeting with a hostile organization, or a hostile country, while declaring to shake off the goals of the elimination of the State, which had served in the past as a basis for the Al-Ard members when they wished to compete in the elections; this is in view of the fact that the Public Prosecutor did not see the above-mentioned ties, which were known to them, as an offense and did not adopt any legal proceedings with regard thereto. This delineated the distinction between the Arab Socialist List of 1965 and the PLP of 1984, both on the level of the difference in the composition of the two parties and on the level of the ideological difference.

Now the Supreme Court approached the question whether the Central Elections Committee had the authority to impose further restrictions on the right to compete in elections to the Knesset, notwithstanding the fact that there was no explicit provision in the Basic Law: the Knesset or in any other law giving it such power.

In order to answer this key question, the Court extensively analyzed the status of a basic civil right, which is a constitutional principle and an essential part of the Israeli Law, while stressing that political rights are among "the most decisive and important" basic freedoms. Of these, the four most important ones are the right to vote, the right to be elected, the right to convene in a meeting or a demonstration, and the right to petition.[27]

Article 6 of the Basic Law: the Knesset defined the right to be elected on the basis of the principle of political equality.

Hence, restricting the right to be elected not only limits the rights of whoever wishes to be elected, but also the rights of the voters wishing to vote for a candidate of their choice, based on their right to equally enjoy with others what those with the right to vote are entitled to, pursuant to the provisions of the Elections Law. As far as the voter is concerned, restricting the right to be elected also indirectly limits the freedom of expression, since he is thereby denied the ability to join with others for the purpose of promoting his views and opinions, as the person nominated by him would have represented. Hence, extreme caution is required of the Court in examining the nature of the restrictions in order to emphasize that they are reasonable and non-discriminating.

This is the essence of a basic right, which has legal preference status, which is why each restriction of a basic right is contingent upon the existence of an express legislative foundation. Nonetheless, it is clear that the application of a basic right and its actual exercise are not absolute. "The use of a certain right by one person may, under given concrete circumstances, conflict with the legal right of another."

When can the exercise of a basic right be restricted? The answer lies in a summary of the ruling of Justice Shamgar, namely: "If it is probable that the exercise of a certain right will harm public security and public order, then in a concrete case the statutory authority, empowered for this purpose, may restrict the actual exercise of the right under the aforesaid circumstances." Hence, every restriction of a constitutional basic right must be supported by the following principles:

1. Probability of harm to public security or order.
2. A certain defined case in which the exercise of a right will indeed lead to said harm.
3. Express authorization of a constitutional authority to impose the said restriction.

In view of this perception, the Chief Justice drew the conclusion that the right of PLP to participate in the elections should not be restricted, since he was not convinced of the inherent probable risk, while afraid that the essence of the system of the Israeli government may be damaged by the bans and restrictions, which were an extreme tool and a sort of "last resort."

Justice Elon also reached the same conclusion, while emphasizing the right of self-defense, by virtue of the "natural law," against a parliamentary list wishing to eliminate the state, whereby there is no other recourse but to prevent this list from carrying out its scheme. This lack of choice has no basis in the rules of regular interpretation but it is based on a supreme order in Judaism: ". . . [H]e shall live by them [God's statutes] – and not die by them" (Leviticus, xviii, 5, Talmud-Yoma, 85 2(3)). And he adds: "This supreme order which exists by virtue of the natural law, may be presumed by the legislator who expects from the court and from any authority in the State to apply and implement it."[28]

Judge Aharon Barak agreed with the Chief Justice's ruling and determined that the "the *ratio decidendi*, which follows from Appeal 1/65 [the Arab Socialist List case] is limited also with regard to the refusal to approve a list which negates the very existence of the State and wishes to eliminate it."[29]

However, Judge Barak disagreed with the Appeal 1/65 precedent in the sense that, in his opinion, it was not sufficient that the platform of a list would contain the negation of the existence of the State in order not to approve participation of the list in the elections to the Knesset. He was also not of the opinion that the Elections Committee did not have the authority not to approve the participation in the elections of a list whose platform negated the existence of the state.

It is my opinion that the authority to veto exists both with regard to a platform negating the very existence of the state and with regard to a platform negating the democratic nature of the state, but the cause for exercising authority in these two cases must be that it is reasonably possible that the "threat" could be carried out in practice.

This principle of "reasonable possibility" is similar to "probability," and it may provide a dimension of flexibility in the exercise of authority, depending on the varying circumstances and in light of the extent of risk posed by such radical party, whose disqualification is being put to the test.

In summary, there is no doubt that the legal status of Israeli Arabs involves the impact of the focal problems of such a unique national minority, developing under such complex conditions. Light has been shed on this subject from the legal point of view, although it seems to me that the subject cannot be exhausted without trying to examine reality in everyday life, since constitutional principles are likely to become completely depleted of content in a society which is not ready to implement them. Articles of law and pompous declarations are not enough in order to achieve real equality for members of a national minority. It is imperative that a way be found to realize the equality in practice through real social integration.[30]

In the Israeli reality, and in view of Israel's unique security problems, it seemed that the Arab minority was destined to be alienated from the rest of Israeli society. Despite this internal contradiction, to which is added the social difference in all its intensity, the Arabs of Israel are gradually being integrated into the life of the country, although there is no uniform trend and most recently a certain regression has been observed. Radical groups on both sides feed the fire of social tension.

On this background, Israeli society faces a difficult challenge: to increase socioeconomic integration, to create awareness for mutual respect, and at the same time to promote the equality to which the Arab minority is entitled – but at the same time not to prejudice their right to be different. It is the right of the minority to preserve its uniqueness, to live out its social heritage and cultivate it, without violating the obligations toward the state in which it lives. Citizens of Israel, Jews and Arabs, must learn to recognize each other, each other's language, customs, social structure and national culture. By a special educational effort, they must break their children away from the legacy of hatred.

This is a massive task, which one cannot expect to be accomplished in a short time, but it is not impossible, and the first steps on the way to implementing it have already been taken.

6

Arabic-Language Press and Literature

Growth of the Arabic Press in Israel

Following the establishment of the State of Israel, the urgent need for an organ of expression for the Arab public in Israel was felt by a public shocked by the flight of its leaders and uncertain of its future due to the contradictory rumors being manufactured. Under these circumstances, the *Al-Yawm* newspaper, first published on September 28, 1948, was established, even before the fighting had ended. This was the first newspaper in the Arabic language in Israel. Jews managed the paper, but in a time of a difficult crisis, this was virtually a sole, reliable source of information for an Arab public thirsty for news of what was going on from a reliable medium.

Later on there reappeared communal newspapers and the mouth-pieces of the Communist Party in Arabic. In the renewed growth process of the Arab press, its "capital" was moved from Jaffa to Nazareth and to Haifa. Its reporters were mostly Christians, as in the period of the British Mandate.[1]

The Arab press in Israel developed rapidly, and as its standard of journalism improved, so controversies and moods found a fertile platform of expression. However, its total circulation is still small, since educated young Arabs generally prefer to read Hebrew newspapers, as they are more comprehensive, up-to-date and as they more accurately reflect both the trends of the Jewish public and the government policy. The old generation reads less and tends more to listen to the radio or to watch television. Nevertheless, the scope of circulation does not reflect the actual number of readers, since there is a widespread custom among the Arab public to pass on newspapers from one person to another.

An ever-growing group of young Arab journalists is springing up in Israel. They establish their professional standing gradually, while maintaining close contact with their Jewish colleagues. Arab journalists quite frequently also write in Hebrew newspapers and sometimes also serve as columnists, such as 'Atallah Mansur, a Christian journalist, who has been writing for many years for *Haaretz* newspaper, Quassem Ziyad in *Al Hamishmar*, Muhammad Khaliliya in the *Davar* newspaper and others. A large staff of gifted Arab journalists developed within the framework of the Voice of Israel radio in Arabic. Since the introduction of television in Israel, it has also served as a rich source for cultivating young Arab journalists, who train themselves to meet with the requirements of this medium. One of the more prominent personalities is the Druze reporter and producer, Rafiq Halabi, who has a reputation for being outspoken.

The Test of Free Expression

Since the establishment of the State of Israel there has been a complex conflict between the government and the Arab press attacking it, with fluctuations in the intensity of the confrontation, depending on the circumstances at the time and based on the "balance of power" between these two essentially different, unmatched parties. To a great degree, this struggle reflects the very fabric of the overall relations between the State and the Arabs of Israel living in its midst, while having an impact on it as well.

With this as a backdrop, friction arose from time to time with the military censor, and on more than one occasion the Minister of the Interior exercised his authority pursuant to Article 19(2)(a) of the Press Ordinance or even Regulation 94(e) of the 1945 Defense (Emergency) Regulations in ordering the discontinuation of the publication of a newspaper: shutting it down for a certain period, sometimes for several days and sometimes for several months.

The Minister of the Interior exercised his authority already in 1948, very shortly after taking the place of the High Commissioner pursuant to Article 19(2)(a) of the Mandatory Ordinance, following the termination of the British rule in Palestine. The order was exercised against the *Al-Ittihad* newspaper, which then began to be published as a nationalistic Arab weekly in the young country, the mouthpiece of the renewed Communist Party.[2]

The weekly reappeared after a short while, steering its way through a difficult reality. On May 15, 1953, censorship was again invoked due to an article published, following its Hebrew *Qol Haam* counterpart, opposing the "surrendering policy" of the Ben-Gurion government towards "its American masters":

> Further, its internal and external economic and political bankruptcy began to be revealed to the masses, who started to understand the abyss that this government is headed for, not just unemployment, poverty and famine, but also death in the service of Imperialism that is serving them as fodder for its war machine, whereas this is not the fate that the masses want, and they will prove their refusal. If Ben-Gurion and Abba Eban wish to fight and die in the service of their masters, let them go and fight alone. The people want bread, work, independence and peace and they will intensify their struggle to achieve these objects and prove to Ben-Gurion and his men that they will not let them speculate with their sons' blood in order to satisfy their masters.[3]

I have presented in full this part of the text, as a result of which the Minister of the Interior saw the entire article as "endangering public safety," also in order to illustrate the style of writing in those days, when both "sides" attributed enormous importance to every word.

The Minister of the Interior ordered that the *Al-Ittihad* newspaper be shut down for fifteen days, but its management did not accept the judgment and petitioned the Supreme Court, sitting as the High Court of Justice.

Justice Shimon Agranat, as he was then titled, examined the matter, considered the grounds, and agreed that the style was "caustic, emotional, even insulting." However, he emphasized that the decisive test is whether the publication is liable to pose a real threat in terms of *probability*, as opposed to *bare tendency*.[4] Absolute certainty regarding the development of the outcome which the legislator wished to prevent does not constitute a condition for exercising the authority, but on the other hand bare tendency is insufficient.

This concerns a criterion, which is a sort of "golden path" between the two other possibilities, i.e., this is what will probably happen due to the unlawful publication.[5]

The Public Prosecutor contended that the passage constituted a provocation to break the law by refusing to do one's duty of appearing for military service, but the court, despite the fact that it was willing to conclude that such a meaning was perhaps latent and even concurred with the Public Prosecutor that this would be the interpretation of the readers of the article, nonetheless posed the question: "In light of all the circumstances that existed at the time of the publication, did this indeed create a logical basis for the conclusion that – in view of the said meaning of the above-mentioned words – one of the dangerous results implied by the Public Prosecutor would be likely to occur?"

With a surgical knife, the Supreme court dissected the circumstances and adamantly determined at the end of the hearing that there was no probability that a danger would be created able to justify the exercise of the Minister of the Interior's authority to close down the paper.

The approach of the Supreme Court in this decisive ruling considerably narrowed the space of the "censor's scissors" in the following years. The judicial authority made it crystal clear, without leaving any room for doubt, that democracy is based on the system of public clarification and negotiations, on the

> process of clarifying the truth, so that the State would be able to put before it the wisest goal and be able to decide on the line of action likely to bring about the realization of this objective in the most efficient way. In order to clarify this truth, the principle of the right of freedom of expression serves as a medium and tool, since only by clarifying "all" the views and the free exchange of "all" the opinions, is such "truth" likely to become clear.[6]

Indeed in those days of "sparks and flames," the view of Justice Holmes, quoted in the following leading case, sounded a bit abstract:

> When people understand that time has pulled the ground from under many fighting beliefs, then they will also believe . . . that the good goal, which they aspire to achieve, would be more efficiently attained by the free trade of opinions – since the best test of truth is the power of the thought to be accepted by competing in the market, and the truth constitutes the only basis for realizing their aspirations in a sure way.[7]

The Supreme Court's judgment clarified the space and limits of freedom of expression; both the government and the *Al-Ittihad* newspaper assimilated the ruling that was issued before the Supreme Court. Subsequently the censor hardly interfered with the venomous charges regularly appearing in the newspaper, which regarded itself for many years as the sole national mouthpiece of the Israeli Arabs, in writing about injustice, mistreatment and discrimination. Government actions were always described in a negative light, its foreign affairs and defense policies were harshly condemned.

Egyptian officers who were taken prisoner in the Sinai Campaign in 1956 were astonished when reading editions of the *Al-Ittihad*. They could not believe that such a newspaper could indeed be published in Israel. Many accused it of "counterfeiting" the paper "for their sakes" in order to "convince" them that pure democracy, allowing full freedom of expression, indeed prevailed in Israel. Since then, these "counterfeit" editions continued to come out one after the other, lashing out at the Israeli government, criticizing those "collaborating" with it among the Arab dignitaries, but wary of new political streams liable to threaten the birthright of Communist Rakah. First in this series was the Al-Ard group, which also wanted a mouthpiece of its own, as the charges voiced by *Al-Ittihad* were too tame for its taste.

Al-Ard ignored the commandment of Article 4 of the Press Ordinance, in accordance with which the publishing of a newspaper warrants a license of the district commissioner.[8] They tried to circumvent this provision by inferring from the definition of the term "newspaper" that if it comes out on a one-time basis, it does not require a license. Their mouthpiece, full of threatening articles, was issued as a "one-time" paper again and again, while changing the name from time to time and making sure to use the name Al-Ard in different combinations. As a further "cautionary measure", another editor in charge was appointed for each new edition.

Beginning in October 1959, the Al-Ard movement published a weekly without a license for thirteen weeks until it was shut down by virtue of the authorities of the Press Ordinance. Subsequently there was less friction. But the 1980s saw a flourishing period for new Arab weeklies and monthlies, in the Galilee and Triangle, almost all of them connected to extremist political factions or at least to the PLO, as an umbrella organization. Some of them, according to their definition, were literary publications.

With the outbreak of the Intifadah, the censor's attitude became more rigorous; already on August 13, 1987, four months before the Intifadah's outbreak, the *Al-Jamahir* ("The Masses") newspaper had been closed down pursuant to Regulation 94e of the Defense

Regulations, as it was perceived as the mouthpiece of the "Popular Front for the Liberation of Palestine" (PFLP), whose leader, George Habash, had taken it under his patronage.

The weekly had been issued in Nazareth since 1985. Its editor, 'Afif Salam, had tended to write most of the articles himself, preaching Marxist principles and their *modus operandi* in the reality of the situation of Israel's Arabs.[9]

In anticipation of "Land Day" on March 30, 1988, when the winds of the Intifadah blew in from the Territories, Prime Minister Yitzhak Shamir, as Acting Minister of the Interior, decided to close the *Al-Ittihad* newspaper from the 25th to the 31st of that month, the day after the "Land Day" strike, as he was convinced that it was a factor inciting public riots along with the anticipated demonstrations.[10]

In the Triangle, *Al-Maydan* ("The Arena"), the mouthpiece of the "Sons of the Village" movement was shut down, and after that, in July 1990, an order was issued discontinuing the publication of the weekly, *Sawt al-Haqq wa-al-Hurriyyah*, which was published in Umm el-Fahm and viewed by the government as the mouthpiece of the Hamas.[11]

Taking an overall view, it seems that censorship did not frequently bare its teeth, although the confrontation undoubtedly became aggravated in recent years in view of the many journals bursting forth into the world, some of them resolved in their role as iconoclasts. When crossing the "red line," in the eyes of the censor, he used his scissors knowing full well that lying in wait for him would be a petition before the High Court of Justice and that the Supreme Court would scrutinize his considerations.[12]

The abundance of newspapers, weeklies, monthlies and journals being published by Israeli Arabs, in the Galilee and in the Triangle reflects the sense of freedom on this level. We shall look in detail at several of them, but for obvious reasons it is not possible in this chapter to cover the entire range.

The Major Newspapers

Al-Ittihad ("Unity")

Al-Ittihad is the mouthpiece of the Communist Party in Israel (known by its Hebrew acronym, "Rakah"). The first edition was published on the May 14, 1944, but the 1948 War cut off its continuity.

Its appearance was renewed ten years later, and today it is the mouthpiece of Rakah and the "Hadash" political front that it unites around it. For many years, the paper came out only twice a week, despite the fact that it was licensed as a daily paper, but this concession was not exercised until May 14, 1983.[13]

For a long time, Dr Emil Toma, the ideologist of Rakah, was its chief editor and he shaped it until his death in 1986, when it was inherited by the author Emil Habibi, and later by the poet Salem Jubran. The paper's editor today (1995) is Nazir Majalli. The paper's offices are located at the top of Elhariri Street in the Wadi Nisnas neighborhood of Haifa. Its chain of branches are spread throughout the country in Nazareth, Shefar'am, 'Arraba, Kafr Yassif, Jaffa, Umm el-Fahm, Tayyibeh, as well as in east Jerusalem.

The real control of this essential political tool is concentrated in the hands of the longstanding leader of the party, Tawfiq Tubi, who continues to determine the attitude of the paper, even after retiring from the Knesset in 1990. He holds the majority of the newspaper's shares and controls the financial mechanism, not without ever-increasing grumblings from various circles in Rakah itself.

Even today, there is no doubt of the influence of Communism in this newspaper, despite the collapse of the Kremlin, from which it always absorbed its doctrine. Its name still waves in bold red letters on its front page on top of which is the famous rallying cry of the International: "Proletarians of the World, Unite!" Yet, the paper's general attitude has become, during the last two or three years, somewhat less rigid and its fiery style has been modified to a great extent.

In its treatment of events, it used to be for many years a journal whose headlines reflect a constant attempt of condemning Israel in its presentation of news items. Incidents in Gaza would receive "preference" with a bigger, bolder headline than the murder of four Israelis in Eilat by terrorists.[14] Very prevalent are pictures of Israeli soldiers holding Arab detainees against the wall, their hands raised while their bodies are being searched, while policing the West Bank or the Gaza Strip. In one edition, the reader would focus on the picture of "the occupation forces arresting a young Palestinian in the square of the Church of Nativity in Bethlehem."[15] Proclamations of Yasser 'Arafat would be emphasized on the front page in a box with bold letters in two colors, along with a picture in which he is seen smiling, in contrast with the Israeli prime minister who is shown with a gaping mouth (as if trying to swallow the entire country).[16]

A meeting between the Soviet Foreign Minister and Yasser 'Arafat was depicted as if two gods had appeared under one headline, while the photographs of the two were prominent. A news item printed in bold black letters would tell of the decision of the contractors and farmers associations to lay-off 43,000 workers from the Territories. Another headline would announce in bold red letters: "Return to the Deportation Policy Will Pave the Way for 'Total Transfer.'"

Red and black used to be the colors of the newspaper, which was an odd bird in the landscape of the Israeli press, and even different from nationalistic Arab papers which were free from the fetters of prostration to Moscow. However, it has offered a rich variety of sections, its writers are experienced and know their work well.

First and foremost, the paper serves as an essential tool for the party. It is full of news items on the activity of the party's branches and cadres, accompanying the Knesset members of Rakah-led Hadash (Democratic Front for Peace and Equality) in their visits to the West Bank, the Gaza Strip and the Israeli Arab settlements. It is a mouthpiece for their speeches in the Parliament and national assemblies, a platform for seething articles against the Party's opponents, inside and outside, a mirror for strikes, demonstrations and protest assemblies. A one-day hunger strike of the Nazareth Municipality in protest of the ban on meetings with the PLO received a main headline at the top of the paper.[17]

No paper in the Arab sector glorifies "Land Day" every year to the extent that *Al-Ittihad* does, considering it not only a national day, but also an achievement of the Party, for Rakah regards itself as the "mother" of this historic demonstration.[18]

The abortive coup in the Soviet Union rocked the foundations of Rakah, which felt the support of the Kremlin being pulled from under it due to Gorbachev's *Perestroika* policy. His being suddenly ousted from the government immediately raised the hope that the good days would return, when the unreserved support of the Soviet Union for the Palestinian struggle was guaranteed. The editions of *Al-Ittihad* in those days at the end of August 1991 accurately reflected that mood. Pages of the paper were full of news *from there*; George Tubi who represented both the party and the newspaper in Moscow was quick in reassuring the well-being of the Israeli Arab students in the Soviet capital.[19] His brother, the veteran leader of the party, Tawfiq Tubi, published the position of

Rakah, using decisive language, saturated in the well-known style of the General Secretary:

> The recent incidents in the Soviet Union, the announcement of a state of emergency and the establishment of an Emergency Committee, came as a result of the severe economic, social and political crisis which the Soviet country and society face in view of the mistakes in carrying out *Perestroika* which have come to a dead end, and out of fear for economic collapse, hunger, civil war and the disintegration of the Soviet Socialist state.
>
> We emphasize the necessity of the Emergency Committee adopting measures to rescue the Soviet society from the economic abyss and for the sake of continuing the real democratic steps and leading Soviet society to a flourishing era.
>
> We are certain that the Soviet Union will continue to adopt a policy of peace, disarmament and preventing the holocaust of a world war, and will also continue its active participation in defending the issue of peace in the Middle East.
>
> The advocates of peace and progress consider it imperative for the sake of peace and human development to preserve the unity of the USSR and prevent its social disintegration, as well as the continued existence of the USSR and its socialist development.
>
> We object to intervention in the internal affairs of the USSR, as expressed in the declaration of the President of the United States George Bush and others, as well as any attempt to stir up internal strife and civil war in order to weaken and destroy the Soviet Socialist society.
>
> Our Communist Party stands together with the Soviet Communist Party in its struggle to preserve the principles of a socialist, human, developing society and guaranteeing the unity of the USSR and the existence of the Soviet state as a developing, modern and human socialist state which will participate in guaranteeing world peace and human progress.
>
> The political bureau of the Israeli Communist Party will follow the events in the USSR in the hope that it will overcome all its internal problems, and its participation vital to world peace and social progress will be assured.

Together with this formal notice, news items were highlighted on Israel's fear of an adverse affect on Jewish immigration, called "emigration," according to the terminology widely used by the Arab press. Photographs of Genady Yannaiyev, the new Soviet ruler, were prominently published. Tanks in the Soviet capital were depicted on the inside pages.[20]

But the next day, at the end of that stormy week, the picture of Gorbachev returned to the front page; the paper resumed its daily routine. Next to the President of the USSR, who was returned to his seat, appeared a picture of the heads of the Arab local councils in Israel, during a meeting in Jerusalem with Minister of the Interior Aryeh Der'i.[21]

The paper has a section for students – containing stories, pictures, proverbs, jokes, various news items and corners for expanding the national-ideological horizon, such as commemorating the 1948 Deir Yassin massacre.

It seems today that the paper is fighting for survival due to a shortage of ads and a drop in its distribution. In its festive edition on the anniversary of the 48th year of publication, the editorial board admitted that it was facing a financial crisis; it made an emotional address to increase the scope of annual or monthly subscribers, blaming the "oppressive government" for the paper's financial distress in preventing ads and its constant scheming against it.[22]

In an enormous ad, its editor in chief at that time, Salem Jubran, listed the newspaper's goals, while desperately admitting that it was at risk of shutting down. Under the heading: "There is no newspaper without financial backing," he unequivocally cautioned:

> It will be clearly said, without beating around the bush, that the continued daily publication of the newspaper is not something guaranteed. It obviously depends on the success of the subscription campaign and an expansion of the regular participants, in developing the daily sale in kiosks and by volunteer distributors, and also by cultivating the ads section.
>
> The financial difficulties of *Al-Ittihad* are always part of the crisis of our Party, and they are proof that the paper does not breathe from an external lung, financially or conceptually, but it breathes the soul of the people here, draws from the lung of the earth here.[23]

Along with *Al-Ittihad* as a daily paper, Rakah bears the task of publishing two longstanding journals that appeared in the first years following the establishment of the state: *Al-Jadid* ("The New"), a rich literary monthly, from whose hothouse sprung many writers, and *Al-Ghad* ("Tomorrow"), the youth mouthpiece of the Communist Party, which started out in July 1944 as a bi-monthly of the Association of Arab Intellectuals. During the time of the Mandate it also integrated supplements in English and Armenian.

In February 1952 it reappeared, at first without a license; afterwards, in October 1954, it was issued under a permit published by the Youth Alliance of the Israeli Communists, edited by Hanna Amin Abu Hanna.[24]

As-Sinarah ("Fishing Rod")

A bi-weekly journal published in Nazareth since 1982, *As-Sinarah* defines itself as "the most popular Arab journal in the country." Its editor, Lutfi Mash'ur, is a middle-aged intellectual, one of those close to Muhammad Mi'ari and who is well-connected to personalities from the Jewish public. He represents radical nationalist opinions speaking in a moderate voice.

The headlines of the journal frequently deal with political events; a photograph of Yasser 'Arafat is placed on the front page above the picture of armed Israeli soldiers pushing Arab girls; or a headline announcing the findings of a research study, pointing to the intention of 28 percent of the Christians in Haifa and 9 percent among the city's Moslem residents to emigrate.[25]

The news items are spiced with tendentious commentaries. Without hesitation, the journal ridicules the decision of a judge, who convicted young men cheering Saddam Hussein after the invasion of Kuwait, before the outbreak of the war. At the same time, it does not hesitate to publish the angry anti-PLO article of leftist Jewish MK Yossi Sarid, against the background of PLO's support for Saddam Hussein: "Let Them Look for Me."[26]

Underneath a bold headline, "Ariel Sharon Calls for the Settlement of Half the New Immigrants in the Galilee, the Triangle and the Negev (on Arab Lands)," is the publication of the enraged reactions of various Israeli Arab personalities, known for their nationalism, next to their picture. The newspaper devoted two full pages to an interview with Knesset Member and Herzliya Mayor Eli Landau under the heading: "I Have Called for a Dialogue with 'Arafat for Years, and If This Does Not Work Out, War Can Be Expected Today or Tomorrow."[27] Printed in another issue is an interview of the editor, Lutfi Mash'ur, with Nabil Sha'ath, Yasser 'Arafat's aide, in a meeting held in Granada, Spain.[28] Also Mansur Kardush, one of the former leaders of Al-Ard, was interviewed in *As-Sinarah*.[29]

It highlights news items on tension in the political relations between the State and the Druze community,[30] and it also underscored the strike of the heads of the Arab local councils who demonstrated opposite the Knesset.[31] It went on a campaign against the harsh treatment of Arab passengers at Ben-Gurion Airport,[32] and argued about the internal collapse of the Communist Party in Israel.[33] On the other hand, the poet Samih el-Qassem, one of the steadfast leaders of Rakah, received extensive coverage by the newspaper upon his return from his impression-packed visit to Iran.[34]

The journal has diverse sections: stories of personalities in the news, "Leaders and Favorites", sports, crosswords, poems, children's corner, readers' letters, many photographs, sometimes even of women in scant, not especially modest attire, in terms of tradition and religion.

The journal is run on a professional basis and to a high standard. It also meticulously draws from outside newspapers.[35] It seeks advertisements in Arabic and in Hebrew, in black-and-white and in color, among them advertisements of Zionist parties, such as an invitation of the Labor Party to a meeting of activists with Shimon Peres. Advertisements for the Labor Party (Alignment) on the eve of the elections to the 12th Knesset in 1988 kicked up a storm among the Jewish public when they were interpreted as support for the establishment of a Palestinian State. It was contended that they were worded differently by the paper's editorial board.

Amidst the political overflow, the paper is commercial in nature and noticeable is its constant struggle to keep afloat and cope with the tough competition that it faces on all sides.

Without a doubt it created an "advertising revolution" in the Israeli Arab press in succeeding to also capture huge ads of larger Israeli companies.

As-Sinarah initiates prize-winning competitions; it goes into the villages, collects everyday news, strives to establish close contact with the "heroes" of everyday events. For example, it once brought together in a striking picture a photograph of a lost baby returning to her home in the company of the paper's editorial board. It would publish on another page the story of a boy who was killed in a road accident by his home, and on another page a picture of a gigantic fish that was caught on the shore.[36] In contrast with other Arabic newspapers, *As-Sinarah* surveys events of a commercial nature, such as the opening of an enormous shopping mall, in which the editor himself is present at the festive opening.[37]

The paper's main competitor is undoubtedly *Al-Ittihad*, which is longstanding, haughty, and sees itself as a pioneer in the nationalist struggle. In contrast, *As-Sinarah* is much lighter, flexible, modern, although it also repeatedly reiterates its ideological concept. The papers struggle, clash and fight over the same public of readers. On the political level, *As-Sinarah* is considered close to the Progressive List for Peace, and therefore this is the platform from where its leaders shower criticism on Rakah.

Kull al-'Arab ("All the Arabs")

A relatively new journal that was edited by the late Muhammad Watd until his death in 1994, and later by Samih el-Qassem, it reflects their political image, and at the same time is rich in news items, photographs, both in color and in black-and-white. It also has sports, literature and film sections, as well as a great deal of information on local events. It has a marked trend of defending the popular classes, particularly in dealing with basic problems of unemployment, education, drop in the standard of living, etc. The writing is concise and capsulized. It strives to be well-rounded while choosing the news items. The journal has over 30 pages, coming out every Friday. It is now in its seventh year.

The journal adopts nationalist struggles, by devoting prominent headlines with pictures to them. It rallied to the support of the Israeli pacifist figure, Abie Nathan, during the period of his fast and published a petition, inviting its readers to sign it.[38]

At the onset of the struggle of the residents of Ramia neighborhood in the Bi'na village against the establishment of a new Jewish settlement of new immigrants from the former USSR on lands perceived by them as their own, *Kull al-'Arab* came out with a front-page headline framed in black: "Uprooting of Ramia Residents Is Part of the Plan to Judaize the Galilee"; next to the news item itself, which was strongly worded, waved the picture of an angry *fellah* with a *keffia* headgear, holding a watermelon from his field in his hand.[39]

Also the negotiations on the exchange of prisoners was presented in the light of the PLO position, while strongly criticizing the Israeli Government representative's disregard of the position of the Palestine Liberation Organization. It enthusiastically "reopened" the file of the Israeli Arab convicted murderers of the Haifa Jewish youth, Danny Katz. On another level, the paper encourages gifted students from the Arab sector.

The first editor, Muhammad Watd, continuously published long articles as part of his section named: "Free Opinion," in which he lashed out at the Israeli Government, expressed support of PLO positions, and determined that "the Zionist left has failed."[40] Ex-Communist Emil Habibi found a platform in the paper for his ideas.[41] Both of them now opposed Rakah, attacking it on the pages of *Kull al-'Arab*, sometimes also singling out prominent personalities within it. Muhammad Watd sharply criticized the article of poet Samih el-Qassem in the *Al-Ittihad* paper, receiving a strong reaction, which was published in *Kull al-'Arab* together with the cutting response of Watd. Samih el-Qassem addressed him derisively: "Take it easy, Muhammad," to which Watd responded: "Congratulations on the return of Samih el-Qassem to blind writing."[42]

The newspaper is full of commercial advertisements from a wide range of sources, from the Histadrut to construction companies, industrial enterprises and private people.

Sawt al-Haqq wa-al-Hurriyyah ("Voice of Truth and Liberty")

Sawt al-Haqq wa-al-Hurriyyah is a weekly which has defined itself as "a comprehensive Islamic newspaper." It stormed into the arena of the Arab sector on October 13, 1989, swept up in a gust of renewed religious belief, while setting itself against Zionism, against Israel and smacking of anti-semitic terminology. It was perceived as the mouthpiece of the Hamas, the Arabic acronym of "Islamic Resistance Movement." The map of Palestine is merged within the letters of the movement with the slogan: "From the Mediterranean to the River Jordan."[43] The paper was first published in the city Umm el-Fahm. Its owners, 'Ali Jabbarin and Sheikh Khaled Ahmad Muhanna, were already known in the past for their radical religious-nationalist views.[44]

In expressing the ideas of the Hamas, the paper glorified *jihad*, the Holy War for the liberation of Palestine, considered according to Article 15 of this movement's covenant as a personal duty, imposed on every Muslim.[45] The liberation of Palestine entails "the three circles" which according to the Hamas Covenant are the Palestinian, Arab and Muslim circles.[46] The paper expounded on the subject of struggle in accordance with the principles of Hamas, inflamed and incited, ignoring repeated warnings, until an order was issued to shut it down by virtue of Article 19(2)(a) of the Press Ordinance, despite the protests of its editors who claimed that its publications did not go beyond acceptable journalistic reporting and permissible commentary.

The paper competed with the Israeli-based Islamic Movement's monthly _As-Sirat_ ("The Straight Way"), although its distribution in kiosks was quite limited. It seems that the distribution of the paper was concentrated in the mosques during mass assemblies for prayer. On these occasions, the editions were enthusiastically purchased.[47]

After the paper was closed down pursuant to the order, its editor-in-chief, Sheikh Khaled Ahmad Muhanna, renewed its publication; it again comes out in Umm el-Fahm, is again a "comprehensive Islamic" paper, also called in its new garb by the same _Sawt al-Haqq wa-al-Hurriyyah_, while the continuity is also obvious in its contents, although apparently cautiously more moderate in view of its past experience.

Later Khaled Muhanna lost control of the paper and Hassan el-Khatib became its editor. The paper is now more closely tied to the Islamic Movement in Israel and the latter's former organ _As-Sirat_ has disappeared. There is no doubt about its religious–nationalist character, driven by its sense of mission, in the prayer borne on each page for the victory of Islam. An entire page will be devoted to a meeting with commanders of the Algerian "Islamic Salvation Front."

The paper attacks Israel. Following the destruction of a terrorist's home, it would place a headline "Villages Evicted of their Inhabitants to Be Occupied by New Immigrants," even showing a picture of the rubble and describing it in detail.[48]

The editions of the paper are small, containing about sixteen pages. The ads are mostly "local"; small employers in Umm el-Fahm, official advertisements of the municipality and of Islamic clubs.

The Outcry of Israeli Arab Literature

The Arab minority in Israel has built a vast corpus of literature that expresses its feelings, aspirations, and struggles with great force. This literature embraces the most extreme currents, including those who wish to wash away the reality of Israel, with which they cannot come to terms, and moderate writers who dare to express their wish for true integration in Israel. This complex literature, replete with contrasts, is a fascinating subject for comprehensive research. In the context of this work, however, we merely sketch its major trends.[49] It began with bitter, tragic poetry that articulated the trauma of 1948. The poet Ibrahim Tuqan foresaw the tragedy:[50] "A day will come, my Arab brother, of atrocities that shall turn your jet-black locks white." The Valley of Ibn 'Amer is the Arabic name of the Jezreel Valley, an area of extensive Jewish settlement from the 1920s onward. Tuqan also harshly condemns the elite, whose greed, corruption, and internal strife will bring calamity upon the people:

> The Arabs have sold your honor,
> O Valley of Ibn 'Amer.
> The children of the West are like the cubs of a lioness,
> While the children of the East are coiled around
> each other's necks.

After this fiery prophecy came to pass, the poet Tawfiq Mu'ammar, now standing on Israeli soil, cries out:

> The kings of Arabia are concerned for their thrones,
> The Arab rulers – for their seats and positions.[51]

In his collection of short stories, *Al-Mutasallil* ("The infiltrator"), he angrily declares: "The calamity of the Palestinian refugees was caused by the scandalous behavior and corruption of a handful of treacherous Arab leaders."[52]

However, in a subsequent collection of short stories, *Bit'hun*, he disregards the causes of the war, portraying the Israeli Arabs as the victims of an "Imperialist plot" as if they had never attacked the Jewish inhabitants at all. Another poet construes the results of the war as the return of one people and the exile and dispossession of the other, the revitalization of one and the devastation of the other, admission and expulsion, a joy that is sorrow:

> We wept when the others burst into song
> And took the road toward heaven . . .
> We wail and send up prayers,
> While they rejoice sevenfold . . .

> The years of wandering in Sinai were forty,
> and the others returned.
> And then we departed
> when the others came back.[53]

A vestige of the Palestinian people remains in its homeland, its ground pulled from under its feet in both senses, shrouded in a sense of isolation but with glimmers of hope, and this minority raises its prayers on high in its poetry, forcibly disembodied, its soul convulsing, its only son is a poet from a small village in Wadi 'Ara who studies Hebrew, assimilates the victorious nation's poetry, translates Bialik, the Jewish national poet, into his mother tongue, and defines himself as follows in his poem "To the Cloud":[54]

> I am the soil. Withhold not the rain from me.
> I am all that remains of it.
> Therefore, I have planted trees in my forehead.
> I have dedicated my poems to vineyards, wheat and roses
> So that you may identify me.
> Bring me rain.

The political theme dominates all strata of Israeli Arab literary endeavor, reflecting the tension between the two rival camps – the nationalist-extremist versus the moderate, more acquiescent – and the intermediate shades of the spectrum of attitudes toward Israel. A lavish set of symbols helps the "warrior poets" express their animosity toward Israel, their hope to overtake it, and their longing for a day of vengeance.

In this context, the "executioner" evidently denotes the Israeli regime, and the poet addresses him in the following terms:

> Here I will stay, in the stone house, in the shack built of branches of trees, or in one of the caves of my land . . . Take note, executioner! Here I will stay. I will eat rye for bread, I will eat leaves off the trees, and you, O executioner, shall die of your hatred![55]

Tawfiq Zayyad, Rakah's strongman in Nazareth and mayor of the town between 1975 and his death in an automobile accident in 1994, penned a short story replete with symbols in which Israel is depicted as a "little hornet" that serves the "last Sam" (evidently the United States), with "red bears" (the Soviet Union) standing guard across the way. In another poet's work "the birds that will return" are the refugees who will return, and the poet exclaims: "I am the budding branch that will remain here, defy the roar of the storm, and embrace the birds that will return despite the calamities!"[56]

"Dawn" represents victory over Israel; "night" is the current political reality. Therefore:

> O brothers! The night is taking its last breath in the beloved
>   homeland, and
> over the mountains of death, a nightingale bursts into song.
> O those who have lost the way!
> Behold, I see a ray of dawn's light . . .
> Behold, I hear the thunder of the waves; I hear the songs of
>   those returning.[57]
> Sindbad is returning, and with him the precious treasure![58]

The poet Samih el-Qassem vows to "take revenge," and there is
no need to specify who will take revenge on whom. He calls his
poem "La wa-la" (No, no) and he instills hope in his readers:

> . . . It was an odious yesterday that trampled us underfoot
>   contemptuously . . .
> We swore that our root would not wither.
> We swore that our blood would not remain unavenged.[59]

For Samih el-Qassem, Israel evidently represents the latest meta-
morphosis of *Qaraqush*, the depostic tyrant Prince Qaraqush bin
'Abdallah al-Asadi, who ruled in Acre until it was conquered by
Saladin. This oppressive ruler was chosen intentionally to symbolize
Israel because he had been defeated by Saladin, who liberated the
entire country from the Crusaders; the architects of the Palestinian
nationalist ideology wish to portray Israel as a modern Crusader
state and therefore similarly fated.[60]

Mahmud Dasuqi, an ultranationalist poet, states in a poem recited
at a rally in his home village of Tayyibeh: "Lift your voice on high;
do not fear! Pour out your blood, because blood is the glory of liberation." This is the poetry of revolt, anger, and a call for vengeance.
The "liberation" is the destruction of Israel, for its very existence
"shackles" the poet. Such motives are found mainly in poetry, but
they also surface in short stories and novels, where the principle of
presenting matters in "black and white" generally prevails. Many
poems of resistance emphasize the proud identity of the Palestinian
vis-à-vis the anonymous "ruler" against whom caustic comments are
lobbed:

> Write it down:
> I am an Arab! And my I.D. number is 50,000.
> I have eight children
> And the ninth will be born next summer.

> Now why should that upset you?!
> Write it down:
> I am an Arab!
> You stole my father's vineyards
> And the land I used to till . . .

The poem concludes with the following warning:

> I do not hate people,
> And I do not damage other people's property.
> But if I feel hunger,
> I shall eat my oppressor's flesh.
> Beware! beware of my hunger,
> And the rage that burns within me.[61]

Twenty years later, the poet Munib Makhul, a member of the Sons of the Village, wrote:

> If I cannot have my own identity,
> Nor base the future of my liberty in my free homeland,
> Then every peace is worthless,
> And every agreement is nothing but ink on paper.[62]

The Six Day War is the Palestinians' "second calamity," called the *Naksah* to distinguish it from the *Nakbah*, the 1948 disaster. The 1967 war initially sowed confusion in the Israeli Arab literary field. The defeats inflicted on the Arab countries' armies led again to a temporary silence; the thunder of artillery silenced the muses. Before long, however, Arabic creativity resumed on all fronts. The renewed encounter with compatriots in the West Bank and Gaza, the new horizons, the open bridges, and the experience of change left their mark on poetry, short stories, and novels; a corresponding general awakening took place in the plastic and theatrical arts.

In Emil Habibi's short story, *Al-Kharazah az-Zarqa' wa-'Awdat Jubaynah* ("The Blue Pearl and Jubaynah's Return"), a daughter returns to an eastern Galilee village to reunite with her aged mother after a twenty-year separation. The crippled mother is cured, the village spring, previously dry, again provides water, and "at last the almond trees blossomed." In another short story by the author-politician, an elderly teacher climbs into the white blossoms of the trees when he returns to the landscape of his homeland.

In the six short stories that make up the collection, a woman peddler of rags (*Umm ar-Rababikah*) attempts to glimpse the house that was once hers, like other bewildered figures on whom the years have left a deep imprint:

> Silently they scan our alleys and contemplate the balconies and windows. Some knock on doors and ask for permission to enter in order to steal a glance. They ask for a drink of water and then slip silently away. The houses they entered were their homes.[63]

Hajjah Umm Hassanein also trudges wearily to her city, Haifa, in a short story by Najib Sawsan, looking for her brother. However, he has already died; thorns and thistles are growing on his grave.[64]

Emil Habibi yearns for the reunification of the two segments of the Palestinian people. Nabil 'Awda, in contrast, protests that the true encounter will not take place as long as Zionism reigns in the country. True to his beliefs, IDF soldiers prevent a family reunion in his story *Liqa Ba'da 'Ishrin 'Aman* ("Encounter After Twenty Years"). They bombard the family home, leaving only a baby in the shattered building, a symbol of hope for the Palestinian national resurrection.[65]

Arabic fiction is also replete with descriptions of the horrors of war, the second cycle of exile and dispersion. "The smile has committed suicide," cries a refugee of this period in 'Isam Khuri's story *Al-Qadiya* (The problem):

> We lived between tin walls and roofs, prey to the sun and cold, a life without a homeland, susceptible to moods that carry a charge of hatred previously unknown.[66]

The Druze writer Muhammad Nafa' of Beit Jann, a member of the twelfth Knesset, describes "heaps of corpses" and points an accusing finger at the child-killing soldiers of the Israel Defence Forces, and then emerges from this *de profundis* to resuscitation after death, a motive that recurs in most stories written in the aftermath of the Six Day War.[67]

From the 1980s on, the writers are increasingly inclined to identify with the "voice of Palestine," the Palestinian voice that supersedes Arabism, as Jamal Qa'war demonstrates in his poem, "The Four Colors," i.e., those of the PLO flag:

> My Palestinian voice is but
> A call of truth heard from a podium;
> My Palestinian voice is but

The heart's song for total victory.
My Palestinian voice is but
A book written in blood.[68]

The Palestinian national struggle is a central theme for the poets Jamal Qa'war, Fawzi 'Abdallah, Shafiq Habib, Suleiman Daghash, and Na'im 'Areidi, and the dramas of playwrights Salim el-Khuri and Salim Makhul.

Writers in exile also occupy important positions in this genre. Examples are the poet Mahmud Darwish, who wrote for the Communist Party until he left the country in 1971, the writer Tawfiq Fayyad, who emigrated to Egypt, and the poet Fawzi el-Asmar.[69]

Creative artists from the ranks of Rakah also focused on the Palestinian issue, but frequently from a Marxist angle. The most outstanding writers among them are the Druze poet Samih el-Qassam, Tawfiq Zayyad, Salim Jubran, Emil Habibi, Muhammad 'Ali Taha, and Hanna Ibrahim.[70]

During the late 1980s and early 1990s, a new theme became prominent in Israeli Arab writings: the Intifadah. Mahmud Darwish's poem, "Transients with Transient Words," in which he called upon Israelis to leave Palestine, caused a furor among Jewish intellectuals when it was released because the poet, although in exile when he shot these arrows across Israel's prow, was still considered an Israeli Arab. His poem was published in the Haifa monthly *Al-Ghad*, which also printed Samih al-Qasem's "Letter to Occupiers Who Do Not Read." He presented this opus to his readers on glossy paper with photos of the "Glorious Uprising" in the background.[71]

Israeli Arab creative writing maintains only the weakest of relations with modern Hebrew literature but draws heavily on cultural sources in Arab countries. While the language factor is undoubtedly the main reason for this, it also reflects the difficulties that the two peoples' creative artists face in their attempts at cultural interaction. A cultural atmosphere within which Jewish and Arab writers would enjoy mutual enrichment has not yet been created in Israel. But the beginnings of such a process, through joint discussion of various issues and formation of social contacts between writers of both communities, are already observable.

Interest in each other's literary produce increased as a result of the translation work that has been carried out in Israel for more than thirty years. One fascinating project in this field took place in the mid-1960s, to be renewed sporadically later, in which works by

Jewish and Arab writers appeared together – each in both languages – in an anthology called *Encounter*.

Recently we have witnessed a maturing of Arabic literature: works by Arab writers in Israel have become more delicate and rich; they carry a nationalistic gospel while being influenced by world literature. Arabic literary writing in Israel is on the verge of a new era.

Conclusion: Israel's Arabs in the Peace Process

_____

With the approach of elections to the fourteenth Knesset in 1996, signs have been increasing of an impending groundswell in the Arab sector that could very well throw the general Israeli political picture into disarray. The first incident was the appearance in late 1994 of a book by Mahmud 'Abbas ("Abu Mazen"), a PLO leader who had represented his organization at the negotiations which led to the Oslo agreement in the summer of 1993.

Publication in the book of minutes of meetings held in 1992, prior to the Israeli elections, between Sa'id Kan'aan, a PLO activist from Nablus, and Ephraim Sneh, formerly director of the Civil Administration in Judea and Samaria, and later Minister of Health in the Rabin government, caused an uproar. The minutes leave the strong impression that the Labor Party, then in opposition, asked the Palestine Liberation Organization, among other things, to call upon Israel's Arabs to support left-wing parties in the upcoming elections against the right-wing bloc, and thus secure the formation of a Labor government instead of the existing Likud one. The book contained quotations pointing to Labor–PLO collusion, the aim of which was to slow down the Washington negotiations between the PLO-backed Palestinian delegation and the Likud government, in order to affect Jewish votes as well; the entire story, though, was dismissed out of hand by all of its protagonists, including – strangely enough – Abu Mazen himself.

The furor abated somewhat, but this rather odd episode raised a question of grave consequences: does the PLO have the power, under certain circumstances – such as the present electoral tie between Labor and the Likud – to decide the outcome of Israeli elections by diverting Arab votes in the direction suitable to itself?

The very fact of this possibility, should it actually be realized, would constitute a challenge to the foundations of Israeli sovereignty. After all, if it were possible for an outside party, to say nothing of one which contains elements hostile to Israel, to determine what the Israeli government should be composed of, the result would be a dependence which conflicted directly with Israel's very essence as a Jewish state. Israel would find itself in a situation where, despite recurring victories in all past wars, it would lose its elementary right, namely that only its citizens choose its government, without pressure or instructions from any outside political body.

This analysis seems so extreme that many will say it is merely theoretical, and not realisic. Does the PLO have an arm working inside Israel as a Trojan horse, to function as the deciding factor between two compelling, and perpetually deadlocked, blocs, and thus choose Israel's prime minister?

An examination of political reality proves that this particular scenario, one that is so palpably odd, is not really so groundless. But in order to get to the bottom of this issue, one must understand the processes at work among Israeli Arabs as constituting a condition composed of opposites, leading to results which cannot be foreseen.

The Arabs of Israel, at the approach of the twenty-first century, are light-years away from their situation at the end of the 1948 War of Independence. No longer are they "the Arabs who stayed," little better than traitors in the eyes both of their Palestinian brethren who fled in droves during that war, and of Arab rulers; neither are they seen as a "fifth column" by the Jewish majority. They do not live today in two worlds without belonging to either, as in the pained lament of the late poet Rashed Hussein.

In some ways, perhaps they aspire to belong to both worlds, being proud Palestinian Arabs and citizens of Israel with equal rights at the same time. As such, they pay single-minded heed to the voices of their brethren outside Israel. They want to help in the establishment of a Palestinian state, and are even willing to serve as spokesmen within Israel for the yearnings of their people, but not at any price. They are not willing to be engaged in dangerous underground activities that would sacrifice the gains they have made thus far, although they are sensitive to the political currents raging about them and are ready to prove their national allegiance. They are not, however, willing to flout the law, even if they sometimes operate in the gray area on its fringes.

They will not automatically answer any call of the PLO, Hamas or the Islamic Jihad. Their own existential considerations will serve as a necessary "filter" of the various expectations entertained of them. So long as their positions do not create a head-on collision with the Jewish majority, they will contrive ways of "eating the sheep and leaving it whole"; their own good, as they see it, will be what dictates their actions.

In the past, the PLO failed to create a single, unified Arab political block that would garner a majority of Israeli Arab votes in Knesset elections. At times, it even prevailed upon competing Arab lists to sign agreements providing for the sharing of excess votes. When the Intifadah broke out, the PLO Executive Committee held a secret session which focused on whether Israel's Arabs should join it, with tangible acts; after a violent debate, it answered in the negative. The deciding consideration was the PLO's realization that if it called upon Israel's Arabs to engage in violent acts, it would not be heeded; Israel's Arabs would not endanger themselves, either individually or as a public, with sober views that knows how to find a way for itself between the hammer and the anvil.

When they vote for the Knesset, they are above all Palestinian Arabs, and as such will support political forces that seek compromise. They will lend their full electoral support to the Left, either by directly supporting the Labor Party or Meretz (a fusion in 1992 of the Citizens' Rights List, Mapam, and Shinui) or by creating a parliamentary "obstructionist bloc" composed of Arab parties that can prevent the formation of a Likud-led government. Such a voting position is the key to considerable power.

Yet it beehoves one to stress that the votes of Arab Israelis do not constitute the pivot of balance between two rival blocs, neither of which can manage to attain a decisive advantage over its rival. This is because of limitations placed upon Arab support for the Right, whose positions, at least to the extent that relations with the Palestinians are concerned, do not leave an opening for representatives of the Israeli Arabs sector to support it in forming a government.

The above must be seen as a basic consideration in any analysis of possible scenarios concerning the future influence of Arab voters on the composition of the government and on the choice of its head. This will remain the case as long as Arab voters do not remain oblivious to the political positions of the Right regarding an improvement in the status of Israel's Arabs, an increase in allocations for their welfare, the development of their villages, and narrowing of social gaps, as measures on the road to equality.

There is no doubt that the Right is prepared to make far-reaching concessions regarding equality for the Arab minority. However, it will have difficulty changing its fundamental attitudes regarding the basic demands of the PLO or taking any step which might help prepare the ground for a Palestinian state.

Should limitations upon Arab Knesset members regarding support for a right-wing government undergo significant change, the result would be a considerable increase in the importance of Arab votes. For the time being, though, such a development seems unrealistic.

In other words, both the Likud and the political forces active in the Arab sector currently operate under severe, self-imposed limits on their room for maneuver. Lacking even the slightest basis for a partnership, they are both limiting their chances for enhancing their power, despite the fact that it would confer considerable advantages on both sides. It is worth noting that on the municipal level, the "mutual taboo" has already been lifted. Indeed, agreements between Arab local authority heads and the Likud leadership have already been forged, yielding benefits to both sides.

However, thus far the chasm between the Right bloc and Israel's Arab sector remains unbridged. All trends of opinion among that sector remain unalterably opposed to the Likud's political outlook, and they cannot even threaten to support it if the demands they make in their everyday struggle for equality are not met by a Labor coalition.

It is clear that a conflict exists between the necessity for Isareli Arabs to support the Oslo process and their full utilization of their electoral strength. As the 1996 campaign approaches, the Israeli Arabs' "obstructionist bloc" in the Knesset has become an "obstructed bloc"; they have no choice but to make an alliance with one side of the political equation. Israel's Arabs have thrown their full weight behind the peace agreement. There can be no doubt that without their wholehearted backing for the Rabin-Peres government, the historic turning in the Arab-Israeli conflict toward mutual recognition between the State of Israel and the Palestine Liberation Organization could not have been created. That turning point, within the framework of the "Gaza and Jericho First" agreement signed in Oslo at the end of 1993, had been reached at the end of a long and secret negotiating process. In that respect, they have realized the yearnings of generations to become a "bridge to peace."

What Israel's Arabs have received for this support has consisted mainly of the fundamentally changed relationship between the State and themselves. Their country is no longer at war with their nation. The winds of peace are blowing between the two peoples, peoples torn by a century of such animosity that it sems as if the Oslo agreement has attained the unattainable.

The millennium has yet to arrive, though. Both sides realize that the process is not irreversible, given the intensity of the opposition it has aroused, both among Palestinian extremists and many in Israel, who see the agreement as a danger to the very survival of the Jewish state. Those conducting the negotiations on both sides realize perfectly well that the process is in its early stages and must overcome serious hurdles: Hamas and Islamic Jihad terrorism, which lies in wait at every corner, threatens to drench in blood each sprout of progress achieved after wearying deliberations conducted with stubborn persistence between leaders conducting the process, who are themselves vilified as traitors by their internal opponents – as painfully emphasized in the assassination of Prime Minister Yitzhak Rabin on November 4, 1995.

In this complex state of affairs, Israel's Arabs realize the time has not yet come to demand the full price of their support from a government endeavoring to maintain power with an exceedingly slender majority and constantly threatened with collapse. Although, since the signing of the Oslo agreement, the scope of government allocations to Arab villages has increased, reaching a record NIS 1.1 billion (around $370 million) in 1995. A sharp perception of discrimination remains in the Arab sector. Huge outlays are required for infrastructure development, as well as for education, which now enjoys prominence among Israel's Arabs over all other considerations.

While the entire spectrum of the Israeli-Arab political leadership is insistent about increasing allocations significantly, expanding sources of employment in the Arab sector, encouraging industry, releasing assets owned by the Muslim *waqf*, and granting recognition to villages whose inhabitants had been displaced during the 1948 War of Independence, among many other demands, it also realizes that elementary political wisdom calls for restraint. In the words of one Arab Labor Party Knesset member, Deputy Minister of Health Nawwaf Masalha, "We have much power, but it is actually a double-edged sword. We could bring the government down, but it could crash on our heads and we would be crushed with it."

It appears that this attitude and recognition has, on several occasions, prevented the government from falling during crises between itself and the "obstructionist bloc." However, not all members of the bloc bear that feeling to the same extent. Dr Ahmad Tibi, advisor to Yasser 'Arafat, complained not long ago, "We're not a suspicious object, nor are we deserters, nor immigrants from Australia. It is incumbent upon us to make full use of our political leverage to attain our goals."

The rivalry between competing forces in the Arab sector will intensify as the election approaches, with each trying to prove its own preferability by attacking the government, as a means of obtaining additional benefits for its voters. One cannot dismiss out of hand that toward the end of the Knesset's term, one of the Arab parties will demonstrate its power by withdrawing support for the government, thus bringing the election date forward.

The pattern of support for the Oslo agreement created during the thirteenth Knesset will not necessarily prevail in the years after 1996. The reasons for this are due to the frustration felt by the "obstructionist bloc," disappointment with the Palestinian Authority, and lack of tangible results from the process in general.

Matters are becoming increasingly difficult for the Arab leadership which supports the peace process because of the enhanced strength of Hamas and Islamic Jihad in the Gaza Strip and West Bank. This is not merely because of terrorism, which engenders reactions from Jewish hotheads who conflate Israeli Arabs with terrorist organizations, as if they were parts of one whole, but because the Islamic Movement threatens secular political forces; while the Islamic Movement in Israel is not connected to fanatical Muslim groups in the Territories, it does indirectly derive inspiration from them, as both it and they are offspring of the Muslim Brotherhood.

The Islamic Movement is by necessity the enemy of the Communist Party, and of the Democratic Arab Party, as well. The DAP, with its purely Muslim leadership, is highly suspicious of the Islamists, especially at a time when its position has been politically weakened.

The Islamic Movement sees itself as the alternative to all secular political forces in the Arab sector, contending that "Islam is the answer." It makes no attempt to hide its aim: to arrest the process by which Israeli Arabs have been integrating into the life of the State, or the process of *Asralah*, Israelization. The movement's preachers point angrily to the infiltration of Hebrew words into everyday Arabic usage.

The Islamic Movement, like Hamas, is basically opposed to the peace process, negates Israel as a political entity, and even nurtures enmity toward Judaism, as part of the eternal struggle of Islam, although its leaders are very careful not to present these positions openly, as a precaution against legal measures. Its activists visit the abandoned mosque in Hittin, site of the victory of the Muslim hero Saladin over the Crusaders. This extremist Muslim movement sees a parallel to the current situation in Israel; they are certain that, like the Crusaders, Israel will also vanish from the face of the earth.

The Islamic Movement is in no hurry. It does not preach terrorist actions or a bloody war. Victory need not come only through the battlefield, but rather by bringing about social and economic crises. One can engender a *jihad*, a holy war, by other means as well. Taking control of significant centers of power, prinicipally in local government, and constructing a far-reaching economic base will, they believe, achieve the same aim, but by a "quiet revolution."

It is not even clear if the movement will decide to contend in the Knesset elections. It is gripped by an internal dispute, with extremist elements stating that participation in elections to the Israeli Knesset is tantamount to recognition of the secular Zionist state, which they will not tolerate. This trend in the movement is led by the mayor of Umm el-Fahm, Sheikh Raid Salah Mahajna, a graduate of the Islamic College in Hebron. He is supported by the movement's leader in the Galilee, Sheikh Kamal Khatib. They are opposed by the movement's leader, Sheikh 'Abdallah Nimr Darwish of Kafr Qassem, who has shown more flexibility; he is loath to forgo the political power expected to accrue from a sweeping victory at the polls.

A compromise may be found whereby the Islamic Movement will not appear on the ballot in its own name; instead, it would establish a new political body dependent on it, and would then call upon the masses of its believers to vote for that body. The names of candidates to head the list are constantly being bandied about, ranging from Dr Ahmad Tibi, whose star has faded somewhat, to Dr Majed el-Hajj, a young, vigorous man who is also fluent in Hebrew and is a charismatic university lecturer.

In the meantime, the movement is acting carefully. For the time being, it emphasizes historical events which evoke the glory of Islam. It does not even have a political manifesto, the composition of which would probably underscore the similarity between itself and Hamas, something it wants to downplay at this stage, for fear of putting the Jewish majority and the Israeli authorities on their guard. Those leaders who do think of running for the Knesset do not dismiss out of hand the possibility of their being blocked by a government that has been following their movement's progress with concern. After all, Hamas is also a realization of the Muslim Brotherhood ideology, which suddenly shed its scholarly cloak and became a terrorist organization.

In any event, the Islamic Movement has patience; it is spreading a net of cells in the Arab sector, each cell being called a family (*usrah*). Its activities combine propaganda (*da'wah*) with the establishment of an infrastructure for an Islamic society (*takwin*). Its publishing organ, *Sawt al-Haqq wa-al-Hurriyyah*, aims poisoned arrows at the Jewish state, but makes sure to do so in a way that does not expose its editors to criminal prosecution. The movement is laying its foundations in nursery schools, making its long-term investment in two- and three-year-old toddlers. Its motto is education. It is building its political strength through football teams, day-care centers, mosques, and charitable associations. In this way, it erects an "iron wall" against anything which clashes with its world view. With this enormous infrastructure, the Islamic Movement may very soon prove itself the sworn enemy of the peace process and the most potent force among Israel's Arabs which threatens general support for it.

At the same time, another political current is being crystallized which wants to change Israeli Arab reality as part of the Jewish state. It is being formed from the Sons of the Village movement and remnants of the Progressive List for Peace, under the leadership of Muhammad Mi'ari, and intellectual circles led by Dr 'Azmi Bishara and Dr Sa'id Zeidani, two Israeli Arabs who lecture at Bir Zeit University in the West Bank. They call for the dissolution of Israel as a Jewish state, repeal of the 1948 Law of Return, which applies to the Jews of the Diaspora, and creation of Palestinian Arab autonomy. They claim that in order for Israel to live in peace, it must first achieve peace with its Arab citizens. Among other things, it calls for a "reopening of the 1948 files," in other words: the return of masses of Arab refugees who fled the State in that year and want to return, the right to rebuild the Arab villages destroyed, and the release of absentees' land.

This camp also wants to have a secular Arab front coalesce around itself, as it takes advantage of the political void engendered by the decline of the Israeli Communist Party and the Democratic Arab Party. It is opposed to both the trend toward integration, called Israelization (*Asralah*) and the turn toward religion as embodied by the Islamic Movement. It seeks to create an alternative to both paths. This current is opposed to PLO rule, attacking both Arafat and Israel in the same breath. It is connected to the PLO oppositionist groups, the PFLP and the PDFLP.

During the course of the peace process, disillusionment has set in among Israeli Arabs with the PLO, whose position has weakened. The greatest achievement of Hamas, the breaking of the political monopoly of the Palestine Liberation Organization, has permeated into the Arab sector of Israel.

Israel's Arabs are aware of their relatively advantaged socioeconomic standards, compared to those of the inhabitants of the areas where the Palestinian Authority rules. That is also the background for the increasing trend among men in the Territories, particularly those who live near the "Green Line," to marry Israeli Arab women. In vain do public figures in the Territories denounce these marriages of convenience, which have become increasingly prevalent since the Oslo agreement.

These factors, even though they tend to undermine PLO influence, strengthen the trend toward integration into the life of the country and away from separation. Israeli Arabs are also apprehensive about a rise of the Right; hence, the desire remains to help with the peace process, including the establishment of a Palestinian state with east Jerusalem as its capital. And to this end it is probable that Israel's Arabs will support the PLO against Israel in the forthcoming steps of negotiations as a political lobby striving for enhanced influence.

Leading Israeli Arab political figures also have become involved in attempts to mediate between the PLO and Hamas, under the backdrop of a threatened civil war in Gaza. Israeli Arab leaders worked well on the "peace council," and reaped tangible success. Most noticeable among those active in it were Dr Ahmad Tibi and Islamic Movement leader Sheikh 'Abdallah Nimr Darwish. In April 1995, in the midst of a serious crisis in Gaza between the two camps, they received a hasty summons. This phenomenon is in its infancy and indicates an effort on the part of Israel's Arabs to have some influence over what happens inside the Palestinian Authority, without losing their separate status. It is a unique development which Dr Majed el-Hajj has defined as an outgrowth of "double marginality" in respect of both Israel and the inhabitants of the Territories. It is a somewhat improved version of the lack of belonging to either world.

Israel's Arabs now comprise the third largest Palestinian community, after those of the Territories and Jordan. Like the Palestinians in Jordan, those in Israel form a unique society; they gain in strength as they integrate into the country of their residence, albeit that there are major differences in the conditions under which these two Palestinian entities are developing.

The rate of natural increase among Israel's Arabs is high. Demographic forecasts based on natural population dynamics indicate that minority members will comprise over 22 percent of the population in the year 2000, and will reach the levels of 1.5 million in 2010 and 1.8 million in 2020.

Arab villages are expanding, and as they do so, the distance between them and Jewish settlements decreases, creating friction. Demography and geography are working in tandem, yet at the same time, integrationist tendencies are strengthening. Since the Gulf War, there has been an 80 percent decrease in the rate of participation by Israeli Arabs in violent activities. Estimates are that 60 percent, perhaps even 70 percent, of Israel's Arabs support the Oslo agreement and seek a practical solution. Those who seek separation are a small minority; it is the Islamic Movement which constitutes the principal threat to the integrationist trend. This movement is still a riddle; at the time of writing, late 1995, it is still not possible to discern its long-term objectives. Who will gain the upper hand: the extremist, fanatical trend under Sheikh Raid Salah Mahajna in the Triangle and Sheikh Kamal Khatib in the Galilee, or Sheikh 'Abdallah Nimr Darwish, a pragmatic, realistic man for whom a practical outlook is more important than the written law? Darwish rejected the dictate of the Muslim Brotherhood with the dictum, "No one knows the pathways of Mecca as well as its sons." In other words, Israel's Arabs must find their own way according to the circumstances under which they live, and not "bang their heads against the wall"; integration is an irreproachable necessity, as long as it does not involve abrogation of basic values.

The attempt to pressure Israel into accepting the principle of "Right of Return" for millions of Palestinians abroad also brings with it tremendous changes. The more progress that is made in the peace process, the more pressing this question is going to become. The potential threat to *all* who live within the Israeli and Palestinian jurisdictions is tremendous, and would jeopardize the still-fragile peace process.

The peace process will blunt various tensions, but it will also sharpen the yearning for equality and strengthen demands for autonomy. The State of Israel will have to grapple with this complex problem and future generations will have to attempt to reconcile the conflicting aspirations of a democratic Jewish country interacting with a Palestinian Arab minority which has the traits of a majority.

Notes

1 In the Midst of Change

1. Maryam Mar'i, "The New Class," *Politika*, vol. 21 (July 1988), p. 33 (Hebrew).
2. The armistice line between Israel and its neighbors prior to the Six Day War in 1967.
3. The "Little Triangle" is the name of an area in the central part of Israel stretching along its pre-1967 eastern border, from the edge of the Jezreel Valley in the north to the outskirts of Tel Aviv in the south. It is mostly populated by Arabs.
4. Herut was the right-wing opposition party established by the late Menahem Begin in 1949. It later became the core of today's Likud.
5. *New Outlook* (Israel), December 1961, p. 35.
6. The General Syndicate (*Histadrut*) of Workers in Israel. The Histadrut is an association of almost all the labor unions in Israel. Founded in 1920, the Histadrut is one of the major political bodies in Israel.
7. A day of strikes and demonstrations by Israeli Arabs, and now also residents of the Territories, held annually on March 30; first held in 1976 in protest over the appropriation of land in Arab villages by the Israeli government.
8. A Hebrew acronym for the Israeli Communist Party, since 1965.
9. The High Court of Justice adjudicates petitions filed by citizens against government institutions.
10. It should be noted that Arab radicals in Israel still hold to the idea of a Palestinian state that would include Israel as well, disregarding the PLO's recognition of Israel in the Oslo agreement of 1993.
11. The *waqf* is the Muslim charitable endowment, a traditional Islamic institution in charge of property donated by individuals to support religious and social needs. Control over the *Waqf* property accords considerable political power to the religious establishment, and was wielded during the British Mandate over Palestine by the Palestinian religious-political leader, Hajj Amin el-Husseini. In Israel, as in Muslim countries, the government administers most of the *Waqf* property.
12. "Peace Day" – a day to mark the solidarity of Israeli Arabs with the Intifadah.

13. Organized groups in the territories affiliated with various organizations for enforcing the discipline of strikes during the Intifadah and for attacking individuals who are suspected of collaboration with Israel's organizations.

14. Hadash – a Hebrew acronym for a mainly Arab parliamentary alliance led by Rakah, the Democratic Front for Peace and Equality.

15. The leadership of the Intifadah in the territories; a coalition of representatives of various Palestinian organizations.

16. I was part of the Israeli delegation at this Tunis meeting and I heard Halabi's harsh criticism of this Israeli view. I could not convince him that one cannot burn the candle at both ends. Ultimately he did not participate in the deliberations, which were conveyed to him by microphone into an adjoining hall.

17. I had occasion to hear Rustum Bastuni, a Haifa engineer, tell about events there in the spring of 1948. He was a student at the Technion technical college at the time. While his family were packing their things in anticipation of the fall of the city to the Jewish forces, a group from among his Jewish fellow-students knocked on his door late at night. They tried to dissuade him from leaving, promising that no harm would come to him if he stayed. He let himself be persuaded and did not leave with his family. At that time, he could not have anticipated that a year later he would be elected a member of the first Israeli Knesset. Later, he was greatly disappointed with the slow pace of integration of Arabs in Israeli life. He found no place in Israeli society, and emigrated. See his article in *Hamizrah Hehadash* (The New Orient), vol. 15 (1965), pp. 1–6 (Hebrew).

18. *Haaretz*, April 30, 1958.

19. The debate and vote took place in February 1963 and one Druze, one Christian Arab, and one Muslim supported the government, despite the contrary pressure to which the Muslim MK was subject (*Maariv*, February 20, 1963). See also Jacob M. Landau, *The Arabs in Israel: A Political Study* (London, Oxford University Press, 1969), pp. 32–8.

20. Mapai – the Hebrew acronym for Eretz-Yisrael Workers' Party, the core of today's Labor Party.

21. See Ori Stendel and Emmanuel Hareuveni, *The Minorities in Israel* (Tel Aviv, 1973), p. 68 (Hebrew).

22. The letter is dated June 6, 1960. It is preserved in the Israeli State Archives. The emphasis on "you" is in the original.

23. Ori Stendel and Emmanuel Hareuveni, *The Minorities in Israel*, ibid.

24. The author can testify to this method from personal experience.

25. There is no intention of giving a full account of the policies in question. In 1971, the author – then on the staff of the Advisor – drafted a comprehensive position paper. It was first discussed in the top political forum of the ruling party alliance and afterwards in the cabinet. It was approved, after some changes had been introduced. Government policy on the Israeli Arabs is fully discussed in a book by two journalists on the staff of *Haaretz*, Uzi Benziman and 'Atallah Mansur, *Subtenants: The Arabs of Israel – Their Status and the Policy towards Them* (Jerusalem, 1992) (Hebrew).

26. See Ori Stendel: "Obstructing the Implementation of Government Policy," *Haaretz*, September 17, 1976. The article cites erroneous data used in a "situation assessment" by Yisrael Koenig, the administrator in charge of the Northern District, as well as unfounded recommendations based on them.
27. At that time, there was a vehement debate about whether the post of Advisor on Arab Affairs was needed at all. See Ori Stendel: "The Israeli Arabs in the Vortex of Contradictory Trends," *Seqirah Hodshit*, August 1985, p. 28 (Hebrew).

2 Arab Society in Israel

1. Uziel Schmelz, "Demographic Development of the Arab Countries in Our Region," Part II, *Hamizrah Hehadash*, vol. 23 (1973), p. 22 (Hebrew).
2. Gabriel Baer, *Arabs of the Middle East* (Tel Aviv, 1973), pp. 13–14 (Hebrew).
3. Gad Gilbar, "Demography and Politics in the Middle East," *Seqirah Hodshit* no. 5 (1988), pp. 25–6 (Hebrew).
4. The reasons for "inflating" population size are both economic and political. See Gilbar, "Demography and Politics in the Middle East," p. 26.
5. Baer, *Arabs of the Middle East*, pp. 21–3.
6. The estimate of the non-Jewish population at the end of 1948 within Israel's current frontiers, including the Little Triangle, which was annexed later, but excluding eastern Jerusalem, was reconstructed according to 1961 census data. See Seventh Census Publications, Table 1, pp. 3–4. At the end of the Mandate period, there were 800,000 Arab and Druze in the area, including nomadic Bedouin in the south. Cf. Eliyahu Ben-Amram, "The Arab Population in Israel: Demographic Description," *Hamizrah Hehadash*, vol. 15 (1965), p. 7. See also Ori Stendel, "The Minorities in Israel," *Israel Economist* (Jerusalem, 1973), pp. 10–13.
7. The estimate is based on *Statistical Abstract of Israel, 1994*, Table 2.1, p. 43, and assumes that Jewish immigration from the former Soviet Union and Ethiopia closed the gap in natural increase by 0.3 percentage points. Without this mass immigration, Arabs would surely account for more than 19 percent of the population of Israel. Not including the Arab population of Jerusalem, the minority population within the "Green Line" is approximately 863,000.
8. The average annual increase between 1957 and 1965 was 3.1 percent in Iraq and 3.3 percent in Jordan. See Schmelz, "Demographic Development of the Arab Countries in Our Region," pp. 31, 46.
9. See Baer, *Arabs of the Middle East*, pp. 24–5. Cf. Schmelz, "Demographic Development of the Arab Countries in Our Region," p. 55. See also Schmelz, "Natural Movement," pp. 11–12. See also Layish, *Changes in Arab Society in Israel* (Jerusalem, Bureau of the Advisor on Arab Affairs, 1966), pp. 1–6 (Hebrew). Compare this with the situation in the West Bank under Jordanian rule, when eastward migration of

men caused a "demographic vacuum," created a shortage of young men, and forced many young women to remain husbandless after missing their opportunity. Ori Stendel, "The Arab Population in Judea and Samaria," *Seqirah Hodshit*, August 1988, pp. 6–7 (Hebrew).

10. See *Statistical Abstract of Israel, 1994*, Table 3.1, p. 116. In 1945, the number of live births among Muslim residents of Palestine soared to 54,200. Yaakov Shimoni, *Arabs of Eretz Yisrael* (Tel Aviv, 1947), p. 416 (Hebrew).

11. Shimoni, ibid., p. 416.

12. *Statistical Abstract of Israel, 1994*, Table 3.1, p. 117.

13. *Statistical Abstract of Israel, 1994*, Table 3.25, p. 150. Life expectancy is 72.4 years for men and 75.5 for women.

15. See *Statistical Abstract of Israel, 1990*, Table 2.1, p. 38; *Statistical Abstract of Israel, 1994*, Table 2.1, p. 43; and Uziel Schmelz, "Natural Movement and Population Growth," in Aharon Layish (ed.), *Arabs in Israel* (Jerusalem: Magnes, 1981), p. 40 (Hebrew).

15. Adherents of monotheistic religions, Jews and Christians, were known as *ahl al-kitab* (people of the Book) or *ahl adh-dhimmah* (protected non-Muslim subjects). Muslim countries allowed them to practice their faith but did not consider them fully empowered citizens. Apart from several brief periods of time, Islam was not imposed upon them. Therefore, not only was their assimilation inhibited, but the foundation for preserving the religious group in the Middle East as a social unit was laid. See Baer, *Arabs of the Middle East*, p. 88. See also Haim Zeev Hirschberg, "Jews in Muslim Countries," in Hava Lazarus-Yaffe (ed.), *Chapters in the History of the Arabs and Islam* (Tel Aviv, Reshafim, 1967), pp. 262–315.

16. Law no. 462 of 1955, dated September 24, 1955.

17. Baer, *Arabs of the Middle East*, pp. 90–1.

18. Mandatory Government data, 1922 census: Palestine, Department of Statistics, *Statistical Abstract of Palestine*, 1944–45, p. 17.

19. See Ben-Amram, "The Arab Population in Israel," p. 7. According to the 1931 census, Arabs accounted for 83 percent of the population of Palestine.

20. The estimate is for March 31, 1947.

21. This estimate also includes nomadic Negev Bedouin. See Ben-Amram, "The Arab Population in Israel," p. 7.

22. See Uziel Schmelz, "The Demographic Structure of Arabs and Druze in Israel," *Hamizrah Hehadash*, vol. 28, p. 245, Table 1.

23. See Ori Stendel, "Changes in the Arab Population of Jerusalem," in Yehoshua Prawer and Ora Ahimeir (eds), *Twenty Years in Jerusalem* (Jerusalem, Ministry of Defense and the Jerusalem Institute of Israel Studies, 1988), p. 112 (Hebrew).

24. For a comprehensive analysis, see Zvi Eisenbach, "Changes in the Fertility of Muslim Women in Israel in Recent Years," *Hamizrah Hehadash*, vol. 32 (1989), pp. 80–1 (Hebrew).

25. Michel 'Aflaq, of Christian (Greek Orthodox) origin, sought in nationalism a solution to his personal problem as a member of a religious minority amid a Muslim majority. This explains his ardent aspiration

to define the essence of the national group on a totally secular basis; practically speaking, the Arab national movement rejected his view. When 'Aflaq began to disseminate his philosophy on the composition of the Arab nation, it was rumored that he had converted to Islam. Members of Anton Sa'ada's Syrian Party would chide 'Aflaq: "Your slogan is 'One Arab Nation with One Eternal Mission'; one Arab nation, very well. But what is the eternal mission, if not Islam? – which has nothing to do with you, Christian that you are!" In this context, see Yitzhak Oron, "The Arab Socialist Revival Party: Its History and Ideas," *Hamizrah Hehadash*, vol. 9 (1959), pp. 244–61.

26. The data refer to early 1995 and are based on the author's estimate. The Christian cross-section is based on data from the 1983 Population and Housing Census, no. 7, p. 31. It is not improbable that since that census, the numerical ratio between the Christian denominations has changed slightly because of differences in the rates of natural increase and/or emigration, but the differences are presumably not significant.

27. More than 10 percent of the Christians are not Arabs; they are of non-Arab European or Asian-African origin and include monks and clergy, Armenians, Ethiopian Copts, and Christian spouses of Jews.

28. For the causes and stages of this process, see detailed analysis in Amihud Yisraeli, "The Occupational Revolution in the Minority Sector in Israel," *Hamizrah Hehadash*, vol. 26 (1976), pp. 232–9. See also Henry Rosenfeld, *They Were Peasants: Studies in the Social Development of the Arab Village in Israel* (Tel Aviv, 1964), pp. 47–54, 155–87 (Hebrew).

29. From a lecture by Dr Gideon Kressel at a workshop, the first of its kind, on December 29, 1991, at the Sheraton Hotel in Herzliya, sponsored by the Advertisers Association, on "Advertising and Sales Promotion in Arab Society in Israel and the Occupied Territories." See Yitzhak Reiter (ed.), *Review of the Events in the Arab Sector in Israel* (Jerusalem, Bureau of the Advisor on Arab Affairs – Office of the Prime Minister), no. 11, p. 12 (Hebrew).

30. From a lecture by Eli Ashkenazi, chief executive officer of the Israeli-Arab Bank, given at the same workshop, ibid.

31. Naim Areidi, *I Returned to the Village* (Tel Aviv, Am Oved, 1986), pp. 7–8 (Hebrew). The poet, a Druze born in the Galilee village of Meghar, writes in Hebrew and specializes in the works of Uri Zvi Greenberg, on whom he wrote his doctoral dissertation at Bar-Ilan University. See his article "Between My Two Cultures," *Mifgash* (Encounter), Hebrew-Arabic forum for creative writing, no. 2(6) (summer 1985), pp. 10–11 (Hebrew).

32. Consider, for example, the blood dispute between clans in Nahf as a result of an ancient dispute. *As-Sinara*, December 7, 1990 (Arabic).

33. A commission of inquiry appointed by the Minister of the Interior and the police in May of that year, chaired by attorney Amnon Goldenberg, reached the unequivocal conclusion that the attack had been planned and carried out with firearms evidently procured from

the security forces in which inhabitants of Julis served. For the detailed conclusions, see *Review of the Events in the Arab Sector in Israel* 11 (December 1981), pp. 14–16 (Hebrew).

34. Dr Subhi Abu Ghosh, "Integration of the Clan into a Local Council in an Arab Village," in Ori Stendel (ed.), *Arab Society in Israel* (Jerusalem, Office of the Prime Minister, 1963) (Hebrew).

35. Cf. the decline of the position of *mukhtar* in Egypt, in Baer, *Arabs of the Middle East*, pp. 183–5.

36. Elie Rekhess, *The Arab Village in Israel: A New Political-Nationalist Focal Point* (Tel Aviv, 1985), pp. 3–5 (Hebrew).

37. The list of guest lecturers included Ruth Dayan and the late Moshe Sneh, Major-General (Res.) Haim Laskov, and the director-general of the Education Ministry. Such "debating society" institutions are lacking in Arab localities today.

38. Qawuqji initially stationed his headquarters in the "Big Triangle" (the Nablus-Tulkarm-Jenin area), whence he purported to spread his control over the entire country. He even set up a broadcasting station there, run by the Syrian journalist Nasser ed-Din, and a "supreme court" under 'Abdallah et-Tamer. Nazareth was second in status at this time. Its prestige rose following the shattering defeat of the "Army of Salvation" in the April 1948 hostilities at Mishmar ha-Emeq. A month later, Qawuqji left the country to regroup; upon his return, he made Nazareth his "capital." See Ori Stendel, *Nazareth Past and Present* (Jerusalem, 1966), pp. 17–25.

39. See George Salameh, "The Bazaar," *Kardom*, February 19, 1982, pp. 98–100. Salameh lists at least fourteen markets and describes them in detail (Hebrew).

40. On the *harat* in Middle Eastern cities, see Baer, *Arabs of the Middle East*, pp. 214–15.

41. See *Haaretz*, July 25, 1991.

42. Yosef Algazi, "Under the Extinguished Lamps," *Haaretz*, July 7, 1991.

43. See Zvi Eisenbach, "Fertility of Muslim Women," *Hamizrah Hehadash*, vol. 32 (1989), p. 91, based on data from the 1983 population and housing census, Table 43.

44. Estimate based on *Statistical Abstract of Israel, 1994*, Table 2.7, p. 53, and Table 2.14, pp. 62–3.

45. Zeev Zivan, "Relations between the Jewish Community and the Negev Bedouin: The Interface and its Influence on Shaping the Settled Frontier in the 1940s and 1950s" (MA dissertation, December, 1990). From an abstract delivered at a workshop at Giv'at Haviva in August, 1991, pp. 4–6 (Hebrew).

46. The census of Negev Bedouin was not completed until 1952. In this context, see the remark by Rustum Bastuni in his article "Arab Society in Israel," *Hamizrah Hehadash*, 15 (1965), p. 2 (Hebrew).

47. In their formative period, the Bedouin were divided into two main groups: descendants of *Qahtan* or southern Arabs (*Shamar*), and descendants of *Ma'ad* ('*Aneiza*). Although these family trees are fictitious, they are extremely important in the Bedouin consciousness.

See Baer, *Arabs of the Middle East*, p. 141. See also J. Ginat, *The Bedouin* (Jerusalem, 1966), p. 3 (Hebrew).

48. Emmanuel Marx, *Bedouin Society in the Negev* (Tel Aviv, 1974), p. 59 (Hebrew).

49. Ginat, *The Bedouin*, pp. 25–7. Cf. Baer, *Arabs of the Middle East*, p. 141; Shimoni, *Arabs of Eretz Yisrael*, pp. 135–6; 'Aref el-'Aref, *History of Beersheba and Its Tribes* (Tel Aviv, 1933), pp. 14–20; and Marx, *Bedouin Society in the Negev*, p. 58 (all in Hebrew).

50. This factor is of decisive importance in Bedouin settlements throughout the Middle East; see Baer, *Arabs of the Middle East*, pp. 145–9.

51. For land prices in these towns, see *Haaretz*, November 29, 1990. For government policy on the Bedouin settlements in the Negev, see Arnon Medzini, *The Spread of Bedouin Settlement in the Galilee as a Product of Spontaneous Settlement and Deliberate Government Policy* (Haifa, Haifa University Monogeography Series, 1984), pp. 19–25 (Hebrew). Rahat was established in 1973. This time, having learned from the errors in planning Tel Sheva, the entire concept was revised. In this town, peasant families settled in 36 socially autonomous neighborhoods. Afterwards (in 1977), the outline plan for Tel Sheva, too, was revised on the basis of clan-specific neighborhoods separated by topographical features.

52. See *Statistical Abstract of Israel, 1990*, Table 2.14, p. 63. Cf. *Statistical Abstract of Israel, 1994*, Table 2.12, p. 68.

53. See Moshe Stavsky, *The Arab Village* (Tel Aviv, 1946), pp. 87–9 (Hebrew). On changes in women's clothing from one generation to the next and on relations between girls, their mothers, and their surroundings in this respect, see Joseph Ginat, *Women in Muslim Rural Society* (New Brunswick, New Jersey, 1982), p. 19.

54. See Eisenbach, "Fertility of Muslim Women," p. 81. Cf. *Statistical Abstract of Israel, 1990*, Table 3.17, p. 132. The total fertility rate in 1989 was 4.68 for Muslim women, 4.0 for Druze women, and 2.65 for Christian women. Most young men who marry by the age of 30 express interest in family planning and cite three or four children as a desirable goal. The most common means of contraception are the IUD, the rhythm method, and *coitus interruptus*. See Ginat, pp. 156, 157.

55. Sometimes she faces cruel disappointment, as when Umm Nimr (mother of Nimr) discovered that her son was not up to the task – i.e. impotent (*marbut*, literally "tied"). "At that juncture, the father intervened and took his son to a doctor in Tulkarm, evidently to no avail. The family members then consulted a seer, for the danger facing the family was exceedingly grave: if the bridegroom could not prove his manhood, the bride's parents would take her back. Since Nimr's sister had married his bride's brother as part of an exchange marriage (*badl*), the latter marriage, too, would be annulled. Worse still, the sister was no longer a virgin. Her situation would be dire, not through any fault of her own, of course, but such were the rules of *badl*. When Nimr finally managed to prove his potency on the ninth evening, sighs of relief resounded from an entire family," and from the readers of Ginat's book, who had come to like the young

Nimr very much. Joseph Ginat, *Women in Muslim Rural Society*, pp. 128–9.

56. Ibid., pp. 157–9.
57. According to the minutes of the hearing on January 17, 1990, in Nazareth District Court, criminal file 234/89.
58. The defendant suffers from serious bronchial problems and life-threatening asthma attacks. See also Moshe Reinfeld, "She Was Forbidden to Love Him," *Haaretz*, July 30, 1991. See Gabi Zohar, "Three Relatives of the Arab Girl whose Body Was Found near Gan Shmuel Arrested," *Haaretz*, October 24, 1991, *Maariv*, October 24, 1991.
59. For the attitude of the Quran toward the spousal relationship, consult *Surat an-Nisa*, particularly v. 38, *Al-Quran*.
60. See Ginat, *Women in Muslim Rural Society*, pp. 177–85, 223–4.
61. *Maariv*, September 4, 1991. Cf. Arye Dayan, "Her Father, Her Brother, Her Husband," *Haaretz* weekend supplement, September 13, 1991, pp. 4–7. Dayan talks of Arab feminists, called "prostitutes" in Islamic circles, whom many women call for assistance in their struggle against family-honor killings or forced marriages and divorces. Voice of Israel News, November 4, 1991, described the demonstration by the women members of this organization opposite the Ramle police station. See also Rana Nashashibi, "The Veil Has Not Yet Been Lifted," *Haaretz* Rosh Hashana supplement (September 1991), p. 41. Even on this internal Arab issue, "Zionism" is blamed for being "interested in keeping the Arabs backward." See "The Background of Family Honor," *Kull al-'Arab* (Nazareth), September 13, 1991 (Arabic).
62. Eisenbach, *Hamizrah Hehadash*, 32 (1989), p. 82. Progress in this field has evidently been very slow. The second stage of the population and housing census, conducted in 1961 using a 20 percent sample, showed that only 12 percent of Arab women aged 14 and above worked outside the home. The rate for those dwelling in towns was 16 percent. Ori Stendel, *Minorities in Israel* (Jerusalem, 1972), p. 75 (Hebrew).
63. Former Supreme Court Justice Prof. Moshe Zilberg analyzes this statute in *Personal Status in Israel* (Jerusalem, 1961), pp. 398–433. Cf. Layish's socio-legal study on various issues toward which he displays a thorough, original approach. Aharon Layish, *Women and Islamic Law in a Non-Muslim State* (New York–Toronto, John Wiley and Sons; Jerusalem, Israel Universities Press, 1975), pp. 4, 41, 81, 83, 86, 133–4, 145, 151, 187, 191, 195, 246–7, 256, 257, 263–4, 268–9, 307–11, 329–30.
64. Shimoni, *Arabs of Eretz Yisrael*, p. 180.
65. For the factors that led to this characteristic situation, see G. Baer, *Arabs of the Middle East*, pp. 41–2 (Hebrew).
66. The in-depth discussion in Ginat's book refutes the conventional wisdom that young men always seek the hand of *bint 'amm* – a paternal cousin – by force of custom. Ginat shows that both the young groom and his father, acting on his behalf, rarely prefer this model, although it is occasionally imposed upon them for various reasons

(*Women in Muslim Rural Society*, pp. 126–32). See also the introduction by Emmanuel Marx, p. xiii. For an analysis of the concept of *bint 'amm*, see p. 118.

67. Layish, *Women and Islamic Law*, pp. 109–10.
68. Ginat, *Women in Muslim Rural Society*, pp. 107–8; cf. ibid., pp. 78–82.
69. Ginat, *Women in Muslim Rural Society*, p. 212, fn. 64.
70. Alois Musil, *The Manners and Customs of the Rwala Bedouin* (New York, American Geographic Society – Oriental Explorations and Studies, no. 6, 1928), p. 235. See also Henry Rosenfeld, "Change, Barriers to Change and Contradictions in the Arab Village Family," *American Anthropologist*, 70 (December 1968). See also Ginat, *Women in Muslim Rural Society*, pp. 176, 210, fn. 27.
71. Ginat, p. 221.
72. See the discussion on women as property owners in Ginat, *Women in Muslim Rural Society*, pp. 172–6, and also p. 210, fn. 29, on women in Tayyibeh who were also recorded as the owners of their dwellings.
73. Layish, *Women and Islamic Law*, p. 98.
74. Ginat, *Women in Muslim Rural Society*, pp. 160, 222.
75. Ginat, *Women in Muslim Rural Sciety*, pp. 203–7.
76. See Layish, *Women and Islamic Law*, pp. 78–85, for a detailed analysis of the decline of polygamy and the attitude of *qadis* toward attempts to perpetuate it.
77. Layish, *Women and Islamic Law*, p. 12, fn. 46.
78. Layish, *Women and Islamic Law*, pp. 125–212. For a summary of changes in the status of Muslim women in Israeli legislation, see Blanche Kamma, *The Status of the Arab Woman in Israel* (Jerusalem, Office of the Prime Minister – Bureau of the Advisor on Arab Affairs, 1984), pp. 11–24 (Hebrew).
79. Ori Stendel, "The Status of the Arab Woman in Israel at the Dawn of 1976," *Bitahon Sotziali*, 9–10 (December 1975), pp. 142–3 (Hebrew).
80. Layish, *Women and Islamic Law*, pp. 22–5. See *Haaretz*, July 14, 1970, and Stendel, "The Status of the Arab Woman," ibid., p. 143, note 7.
81. For a fascinating analysis of this custom among urbanizing Arabs in Ramle and Lydda, see Gideon M. Kressel, "The Dowry: A Reconsideration," *Hamizrah Hehadash*, vol. 26 (1976), pp. 203–31.
82. See Ginat, *Women in Muslim Rural Society*, introduction, p. xvi.
83. From "Three Polls among Israeli Arabs: 1. The Arab Young Generation and its Attitude toward Religion," *Hamizrah Hehadash*, vol. 15 (1965), p. 86, column 2. In 1991, a young man from 'Usfiya who had chained his wife to the window grille of his bathroom declared: "I did not know it was against the law to chain a woman up" (*Haaretz*, September 20, 1991).
84. *Yedioth Ahronoth*, December 23, 1965; cf. "Near the Shelter," *Haaretz*, February 7, 1966.
85. *Hamizrah Hehadash*, vol. 15 (1965), p. 5.
86. Rana Nashashibi, *Haaretz* Rosh Hashana supplement (September 1991), p. 41.
87. See Yoram Ben-Porat, *The Arab Labor Force in Israel* (Jerusalem, The Morris Falk Institute for Economic Studies in Israel, 1966).

88. See *Statistical Abstract of Israel, 1990*, Table 22.10, p. 612. Cf. Ben-Porat, *The Arab Labor Force*, p. 18. He refers to the situation as it was during the 1961 Population and Housing Census. The *Statistical Abstract of Israel, 1994*, does not have up-to-date figures.

89. Eli Rekhess, "The Intellectuals," in Aharon Layish (ed.), *The Arabs in Israel: Continuity and Change* (Jerusalem, 1981), p. 185 (Hebrew).

90. *Kol Hair*, December 18, 1987 (Hebrew). Hadash is the Hebrew acronym of the Communist-led Democratic Front for Peace and Equality. The Progressive Nationalist Movement (PNM) is a radical nationalist group which, unlike the Arab Communists, does not recognize Israel's right to exist.

91. *Statistical Abstract of Israel, 1990*, Table 22.43, p. 648.

92. Cf. Rekhess, "The Intellectuals," pp. 181–3.

93. For example, I studied the list of graduates of the School of Social Work at the Hebrew University of Jerusalem. The number of minority graduates during the period 1961–84 was 40 out of 550 – a relatively high 7.2 percent. A closer look, however, showed that many had been forced to choose this topic. The Arab enrollment at this school was high in view of the ratio between the sexes among their Jewish counterparts. See The Hebrew University, School of Social Work, *Survey of Graduates, 1961–1984* (Jerusalem, May 1985), pp. 1–67. See also an interview with a graduate of the Hebrew University in social sciences, born in 1965, who is working in his profession. Yitzhak Pollack and Muhammad Mahamid, *Charcoal Stigma: The World of Young Arabs in Israel* (Givat Haviva, Institute of Arab Studies, 1989), pp. 15–21 (Hebrew).

94. To gauge the trends of thought that prevail in this group (university students and graduates), see interviews with them, ibid., pp. 1–61.

95. Muhammad Mi'ari, "The Problem of Identity among Arab Intellectuals in Israel," in Alouph Hareven (ed.), *One of Every Six Israelis* (Jerusalem, The Van Leer Institute, 1981), pp. 172–3 (Hebrew). See also articles by Lutfi Mash'ur, the editor of *As-Sinarah*: "Palestinian, Arab, Israeli," *Haaretz*, October 26, 1990.

96. Fawzi el-Asmar, *To Be an Arab in Israel* (Jerusalem, 1975), p. 6.

3 The Political Arena

1. The process commenced with the revolt of 1936–39. The *mufti*, Hajj Amin el-Husseini, fled. Other leaders were exiled. During World War II, the traditional Arab leadership in Palestine was torn between rival factions, without any ability to form meaningful rule. In November 1945, outside mediation brought into being a revitalized Higher Arab Committee, but that body did not actually constitute a unified leadership, and internal contention continued unabated. The Arab League deepened its hold over the internal politics of Palestinian Arabs.

2. Yehoshua Palmon, the first to hold the post of Advisor to the Prime Minister on Arab Affairs, describes the circumstances of Israeli Arabs at the end of the war thus: "In the three areas, the population was left without food, without police, without law courts, without an

educational system . . . " He goes on to relate about the political abyss in the Galilee: "Without *mukhtar*s, without communal leaders, without religious leaders, without any leadership of any kind." *Haaretz*, February 4, 1966.

3. For the reciprocal impact of religion on family relationships, see Henri Rosenfeld, *They Were Peasants* p. 77.

4. See a description relevant of the socio-political structure of the large Galilee village of Rama, where the Greek Orthodox Dar Hanna clan faced the Catholic Nakhleh clan. Shimon Shamir, "Changes in the Village Leadership of ar-Rama," *Hamizrah Hehadash*, vol. 11 (1961), pp. 241–57 (Hebrew).

5. See the research paper by Henry Rosenfeld, "Changes in the Social Structure of the Arab Village of Tayyibeh," *Mibifnim*, April 1956. Compare with the paper by Shimon Shamir on the changes in the village leadership of Rama, ibid., pp. 242–4.

6. In the past, importance was attached to the number of men in a clan, as a measure of its power in times of violent confrontation. At that time, clans were very frequently drawn into bloody brawls. Under Israel's democracy, women were also "counted"; for the first time in the history of local Arab society, women were granted an equal voice with men at times of genuine decision-making, such as elections to the Knesset, local government or municipalities.

7. *Mapam* – Hebrew acronym for the left-wing United Workers Party.

8. *Rafi* – Hebrew acronym for the short-lived Israel Workers List, which, under Ben-Gurion, split from Mapai in 1965 and later reunited with it.

9. George Hakim was born in Tanta, Egypt, in 1908 and served as a school principal in Cairo. He settled in Palestine in 1943, having advanced in the ecclesiastic hierarchy. He was in Lebanon during the 1948 war. Since the late 1960s, he has been Patriarch of the entire Greek Catholic community in the Middle East, residing in Damascus.

10. See, for example, *Nida ash-Sha'b* of November 3, 1947 (Arabic). The last Arab Communist mission to Hajj Amin el-Husseini was comprised of National Liberation League leaders Emil Toma, Fuad Nassar, Rushdy Shahin, and Muhammad Nasser. The delegation publicly announced that its visit was a manifestation of its devotion to the leader and of their members' readiness to "sacrifice themselves." Shortly after this solemn assertion, the picture changed due to Soviet policy.

11. Fuad Nassar, for example, headed an Arab gang during the 1936 riots, but in 1948, loyally toeing the Soviet line, he propagandized in Egyptian-occupied territory for the withdrawal of Arab troops from Palestine. The Egyptians arrested him and incarcerated him at Abu Aguila in Sinai, whence he managed to escape to Jordan, only to be arrested by the authorities there in December 1951. Nassar served as the secretary of the Jordanian Communist Party after the war. Other leaders made their way to Lebanon. For details on the development of Arab Communist organizations in Palestine under the British Mandate, see G. Z. Yisraeli, *History of the Communist Party in Israel* (Tel Aviv, Am Oved, 1953) (Hebrew).

12. Among the liberated prisoners was 'Awda el-Ash'hab, one of the old-time Arab Communists of Palestine. In 1948, he distributed leaflets in Hebron urging the Arab armies that had invaded Palestine to leave the country. He was subsequently arrested by the Egyptians and incarcerated at Abu Aguila. (His brother, Na'im el-Ash'hab, stayed on the other side of the "Green Line" and succeeded Fuad Nassar as the leader of the Jordanian Communist Party after Nassar was incarcerated in Jordan.) Subsequently, 'Awda el-Ash'hab became a senior staff member at the print shop of the Communist journal *Al-Ittihad* in Haifa. Other men liberated at this time were 'Ali 'Ashur, an important Maki activist and veteran deputy editor of *Al-Ittihad*, and Salim el-Qassam, a dynamic functionary who, after the establishment of the state, became secretary-general of the Communist Workers' Congress in Nazareth.

13. All three are deceased. Yanni died in 1962, followed by Jabur Jabur. The last of the trio, Elias Ni'matallah Kusa, died in Haifa on June 21, 1971. These three exemplars of the old generation zealously espoused the Arab ultranationalist line. Although the world of the Communist Party was alien to them, they viewed it as an ally in their struggle against Israel.

14. See Ilan Greilshammer, "The New Communist List and the Twelfth Knesset Elections," in Jacob M. Landau (ed.), *The Arab Sector and the Knesset Elections* (Jerusalem, The Jerusalem Institute of Israel Studies, Publication no. 35, 1988), p. 54 (Hebrew).

15. All four had belonged to the National Liberation League. Emil Habibi, Bulus Farah, and Emil Toma laid the foundations of this organization in 1944. They cooperated in various areas until they parted ways on the Soviet Union's attitude toward partition and the establishment of a Jewish state in Palestine. Until then, they were known for their extensive propaganda activities.

16. Emil Habibi, a native of Haifa and a member of the Protestant community whose family originally came from Shefar'am, a teacher by profession, was second in command to "Moussa," the leader of the PCP. He was the author of the historic leaflet that, by strongly condemning the behavior of the PCP's Jewish members, rendered the party's 1943 schism unbridgeable. Subsequently he abandoned his leader by helping to set up the League, and rose to the leadership of the People's Club, an organization of leftist intellectuals. His pseudonym, "Juhaynah," was the name of one of his two daughters. At the end of his political career, he clashed with the Rakah leadership that came into being in the 1980s and became an oppositionist until he and his supporters were effectively deposed after the twelfth Knesset elections. For a memoir of his childhood, see his autobiographical article "Like a Wound," *Politika* 21 (July 1988), pp. 6–9 (Hebrew).

17. See Danny Rubinstein's excellent article, "Rakah's Cross," *Davar* weekly supplement, October 10, 1969.

18. *Al-Ittihad*, July 5, 1991, based on Yosef Algazi's article "Rear-Guard Action Waged with Linguistic Gems," *Haaretz*, August 16, 1991 (Hebrew).

19. He adds: "Imagine what that group of regimes, which couldn't breathe without its American lungs, is capable of stitching together for our Palestinian people." Ibid., p. 4b.
20. For the most part, this was the old Haifa group that also included leaders from Nazareth. The first to lose their sway were leaders from Jaffa who had formerly held senior positions in Communist organizations.
21. Ori Stendel, "Rakah Attempts to Occupy Key Position in the Arab Street," *Haaretz*, March 31, 1976. The article was written *before* "Land Day" and published after it.
22. 'Atallah Mansur, "After the Rule of the Notables," *Haaretz*, February 11, 1984 (Hebrew). The chairman of the committee, Shefar'am mayor Ibrahim Nimr Hussein, explained how this seemingly municipal committee branched into politics in the following simple terms: "We cannot ignore political problems. The very air we breathe is saturated with politics." Ibrahim Nimr Hussein drafted the committee's principles together with Tawfiq Zayyad; Ahmad Abu 'Isba, chairman of the Jat local council; and Nimr Murqus, chairman of the Kafr Yassif local council.
23. *Al-Ittihad*, April 27, 1984.
24. See Zeev Schiff and Ehud Yaari, *Intifadah* (New York, Touchstone, 1990), p. 173.
25. See article by Yosef Algazi, a former Communist, which subjects Rakah to pungent criticism for its paralysis: "Leadership under Pressure," *Haaretz*, May 18, 1990 (Hebrew). Algazi writes, *inter alia*: "The almost ritualistic use of rhetorical devices and codified concepts sometimes ending in '-ism' has created an artificial language that is but one manifestation of divorce from reality."
26. Danny Rubinstein, *Haaretz*, October 3, 1990, p. 7b. The party leadership were now embroiled in an open crisis. *Al-Ittihad* began publishing a series of articles on this subject by Meir Wilner, who explains in sorrow: "The events in the East are saddening, but we have to focus on our existential problems here" (*Al-Ittihad*, October 21, 1991). Cf. Dr Majed el-Hamza's article on the changes in the Soviet Union; note the photo of Karl Marx embedded in the article (*Al-Ittihad*, October 12, 1991).
27. Danny Rubinstein, *Haaretz*, October 2, 1990. Rubinstein shares this conclusion: "Paradoxically, Rakah is nearing the end of its path as the party of the Arab Israeli establishment after all of its rivals have adopted its outlook: the struggle for equality and peace. Now, without Eastern European backing and without the stipends, the question is: who will succeed Rakah?" On the fierce internecine clashes within Rakah, see *As-Sinarah*, March 8, 1991. The subheadings of the article reflect the abruptness of the downfall as seen by the correspondent: *"The party is in steady decline: Al-Ittihad from the frying pan into the fire; Ibrahim Malek's resignation from the Central Committee; the editor of Al-Ittihad entertaining new ambitions; serious conflict between Tawfiq Tubi and Tawfiq Zayyad."* Evidently the paper, which did not disguise its PLP sympathies, had declared war to the death against Rakah. Its

editor, Lutfi Mash'ur, a product of Rakah, went so far as to accuse the party of treason. Reviewing the political development of Israeli Arabs, he railed: "They forbade us to deal with the basic question of shaping our identity. Thus, for example, [the authorities] sanctioned the activities of only one party, Maki-Rakah, a binational party with a markedly Israeli orientation. Many of us, some in retrospect, believe that Rakah fulfilled a very important function of 'state' in softening up the masses and absorbing their fury, whereas it had once been a haven for national and nationalist outlooks seeking shelter and refuge" (*Haaretz*, October 26, 1990).

28. An earlier abortive attempt to set up an Arab extremist political body had been made by the attorney Elias Kusa and the Muslim political activist Taher Fahum before the third Knesset elections. In November 1954, a leaflet was distributed among Israeli Arabs at their initiative calling for the formation of an "Israeli Arab bloc" against "the government's policies of persecution." Some time later, the bloc turned into a party that concentrated on distributing leaflets and sending letters of protest to the media. This party never managed to expand beyond the confines of a small circle of middle-aged, middle-class nationalist notables. They lacked political organizational tools and did not perform with alacrity. Across the divide was Maki, which opposed the consolidation of a rival organization. The party disbanded after the elections, leaving its activists with no alternative but to become an "auxiliary external branch" of the Communist Party.

29. The following unvarnished remarks by Sabri Jiryis, a graduate of the faculty of law at the Hebrew University and one of the young leaders of the Al-Ard group, are instructive: "I obtained in Jerusalem an opportunity to study. My political views matured, acquired clarity and, little by little, solidified." Quoted by 'Atallah Mansur, "A Young Arab Extremist Describes the Problem," *Haaretz*, December 12, 1965.

30. On July 10, 1959, before Al-Ard was founded, Emil Habibi alluded to this in his column in *Al-Ittihad*: "A handful of comrades who joined us in the Popular Front are attacking us behind our backs. This cannot go on . . . " A few days later, the full extent of the rift became evident. Mansur Kardush, a major activist in Al-Ard, emphasized that the schism was the result of the Nasser-Qassem conflict.

31. High Court of Justice, 241/60, Kardush *vs.* Registrar of Companies, *Judgments* 15, p. 1151 (Hebrew).

32. Supplementary hearing 16/61, Registrar of Companies *vs.* Kardush, *Judgments* 16, 1209 on p. 1223. See also *Haaretz*, June 27, 1962 (Hebrew).

33. In July 1964, Al-Ard sent a detailed memorandum to UN Secretary-General U Thant, venomously defaming the government of Israel. Copies of the memo were sent to foreign embassies and well-known newspapers abroad.

34. Formerly a judge in Haifa District Court.

35. He served as director-general of the Ministry of Justice and as a lecturer at the Hebrew University of Jerusalem, and subsequently as president of the National Labor Court.

36. Elections Appeal 1/65, Yaakov Yerador *vs*. Chairman of the Central Elections Committee for the Sixth Knesset, *Judgments* 19(3), p. 365.

37. Elections Appeal 1/65, ibid., p. 387. However, Justice Shimon Agranat emphasized that he did not negate the right of any of the candidates to be elected *personally* or to run as a candidate on another list.

38. For the continued operations of Al-Ard activists outside Israel, see chapter 4: "The PLO Discovers the Israeli Arabs." For a summary of the movement's history by one of its leaders, Habib Qahwaji, see his book *The Full Story of the Al-Ard Movement* (Jerusalem, 1978) (Arabic). Qahwaji elaborates on the origins of the movement, recalls his young adulthood in the early 1950s as a Greek Catholic teacher in the Orthodox School in Haifa, and describes the nationalist writers' circles that coalesced at the time.

39. 'Atallah Mansur, "Al-Ard Old-Timers Set Up a New Organization with the Same Principles," *Haaretz*, January 10, 1991.

40. For material on the movement's birth pangs, see Zahi Iskandar, "Sons of the Village: A View Ahead in Anger," *Lamerhav*, January 6, 1979 (Hebrew).

41. A manifesto distributed by the Sons of the Village in Nahf was published in the newspaper *Maariv*, on May 21, 1976.

42. Elie Rekhess, *The Arab Village in Israel: A New Political-Nationalist Focal Point* (Tel Aviv, Tel Aviv University, The Moshe Dayan Center, 1985), p. 12 (Hebrew).

43. See remarks by Muhammad Keywan in an interview with Pamela Smith, *Journal of Palestine Studies*, vol. 8, no. 1 (Autumn 1978), pp. 161–71. See also Elie Rekhess, "Arabs in Israel and the Arabs of the Territories," *Hamizrah Hehadash*, vol. 32 (1989), p. 175.

44. *Review of the Events in the Arab Sector in Israel*, no. 8, p. 4 (Hebrew).

45. See *Maariv*, January 24, 1983, *Review*, 16, p. 19; *Review*, 19, pp. 11–12 (Hebrew).

46. *Review*, 11, p. 1; *Review*, 12, p. 1 (Hebrew).

47. This doctrine found expression in an article by the lawyer 'Abd el-Fattah, "The Role and Position of the Palestinian Masses from Within toward the Intifadah," *Ar-Rayah*, August 18, 1988 (Arabic). See Elie Rekhess, "Arabs in Israel and the Arabs of the Territories," p. 187, in which he also notes the article of Suleiman Abu Irshid on the subject, *Ar-Rayah*, August 26, 1988.

48. See the weekly *Al-'Awdah* (The Return), which was published in East Jerusalem and supported Fatah, issue of October 29, 1983 (Arabic).

49. *Al-'Awdah*, October 29, 1983 (Arabic).

50. See Ori Stendel, "Voting Trends for the Tenth Knesset among Israeli Arabs," *Hamizrah Hehadash*, vol. 30 (1981), booklets 1–4, pp. 138–48 (Hebrew).

51. *Review*, 33–34, p. 27.

52. In Sakhnin, the nationalist list was disqualified, and in 'Arraba, it withdrew. In Umm el-Fahm, Sons of the Village won one seat, while the breakaway Al-Ansar list won one; in Tayyibeh, the An-Nahdah group obtained one seat; in Ma'ilya the Ma'ilya al-Ghad movement obtained two seats; in Daburiyya, Sons of the Village obtained one

seat and in Kabul, the PNM won two seats; in Tira, the Sons of Tira won one seat. *Review*, 33–34, p. 8, comments 1–2.

53. See *Al-Ittihad* April 23, 1984, and the letter sent by Al-Ansar to the editor of the newspaper, in which they explain their reservations to the Progressive List for Peace, ibid., May 31, 1984.

54. See Institute of Arab Studies, *Survey of Israeli Arabs* (Givat Haviva, May 1990), p. 11 (Hebrew).

55. Muhammad Mi'ari was third on the Socialist List, which had been disqualified by the Central Election Committee in 1965. He was a member of the Preparatory Committee charged, in April 1984, with preparing a common platform for extremist nationalist elements, in accordance with an initiative by the Nazareth Progressive movement, which was founded in 1982 and joined forces in 1984 with the Jewish leftist group "Alternativa" to create the PLP. See *Review*, 16, May 1982, pp. 15–19; *Review*, 19, August 1982, pp. 19–24; *Review*, 35, 36, December 1983–May 1984, p. 106; *Review*, 39–40, April–May 1984, pp. 8–9 (Hebrew). On the birth of the PLP, see *Al-Anba*, May 9, 1984, and also *At-Tadamun* May 25, 1984 (Arabic). See also Ori Stendel, "The Location of the Progressive List for Peace," *Haaretz*, July 1, 1984 (Hebrew). The article, written before the Knesset elections, around the time of the PLP's initial appearance, foresaw the results of the election, and beyond them, the future relations between that party and the Communist Party.

56. See Elie Rekhess, "Arabs in Israel and the Arabs of the Territories," *Hamizrah Hehadash*, vol. 32 (1989), p. 182.

57. For a detailed explanation of the reasons, see Ori Stendel, "The Right of Israeli Arabs to Be Different: Legal Aspects," *Hamizrah Hehadash*, vol. 32 (1989), pp. 202–3. For the text of the notice sent to the PLP leadership giving the reasons on the basis of which the minister of defense considered declaring the PLP an illegal organization, under Amendment 84 (1)(b) of the Defense (Emergency) Regulations, 1945, see *Review*, 39–40, pp. 8–9.

58. For the full legal details of this case, see chapter 5 below.

59. Stendel in "The Right of Israeli Arabs to Be Different," p. 205.

60. In an interview with the East Jerusalem paper *Al-'Awdah*, Mi'ari stated emphatically, "The PLP is painting the history and geography of the Galilee, the Triangle, and the Negev in four colors [i.e. the colors of the Palestinian flag] . . . and is imparting a genuine Palestinian coloration to the Arab public." *Review*, 43–44, p. 1.

61. See the joint announcement of these organizations in the December 28, 1982 issue of *Al-Ittihad* following a meeting in Moscow, as well as an interview with Suleiman en-Najjab, of the Palestine Communist party leadership, in *Zo Haderekh*, May 29, 1985 (Hebrew).

62. *Al-Fajr*, March 4, 1985 (Arabic).

63. Rekhess, "Arabs in Israel," *Hamizrah Hehadash*, vol. 32 (1989), pp. 182–3.

64. *Haaretz*, July 22, 1990 (Hebrew).

65. Reiter, Yitzhak, "The Democratic Arab Party and Its Place in the Orientation of Israeli Arabs," in Jacob M. Landau (ed.), *The Arab*

Sector in Israel and the 1988 Knesset Elections (Jerusalem, 1989), p. 75 (Hebrew).

66. *Haaretz,* September 11, 1990; *Yedioth Ahronoth,* September 11, 1990 (Hebrew).

67. See *Election Appeal* 1/88, p. 11, paragraph 8; also Stendel in "The Right of Israeli Arabs to Be Different," p. 205 (Hebrew).

68. Majed el-Hajj, "Elections Among Arabs under the Shadow of the Intifadah: Propaganda and Results," Jacob M. Landau (ed.), *The Arab Sector in Israel and the 1988 Knesset Elections,* p. 38 (Hebrew).

69. *Haaretz,* August 14, 1988.

70. *Sada al-Jalil,* September 23, 1988 (Arabic).

71. The Democratic Arab Party won 27,012 votes, or over 4000 votes over the minimum vote of 1 percent of those cast to gain entry into the Knesset; this was roughly twice the vote represented by a single Knesset seat. Had the DAP and PLP signed an agreement for transfer of excess votes, two seats would have been "saved."

72. Avraham Diskin, "Statistical Perspectives of Voting in the Arab Sector" in Jacob M. Landau, *The Arab Sector in Israel and the 1988 Knesset Elections,* the table on p. 28 (Hebrew).

73. *Hadha al-Usbu',* August 9, 1990 (Arabic).

74. *Sumud* is a highly significant concept meaning standing together under pressure, without breaking, without surrendering. This is the challenge confronting the inhabitants of the Territories captured in the Six Day War, including East Jerusalem. See Ori Stendel, "Changes in the Arab Population in Jerusalem," in Yehoshua Prawer and Ora Ahimeir (eds), *Twenty Years in Jerusalem* (Jerusalem, Jerusalem Institute of Israel Studies, 1988), p. 104 (Hebrew).

75. *Al-Ittihad,* August 19, 1990 (Arabic).

76. *Yedioth Ahronoth,* January 24, 1988; *Haaretz,* January 24, 1988; *Hadashot,* January 29, 1988. The founding convention was held on April 9, 1988 with the participation of a delegation from the Territories. Muhammad Khaliliya, "800 Arab Sector Leaders Establish a New Arab Party: the Democratic Arab Party," *Davar,* April 10, 1988 (all in Hebrew).

77. The last futile attempt to establish an independent Arab party was undertaken by the Bedouin Nuri el-'Uqbi. He set up the Arab Citizens' Movement, which ran for the tenth Knesset elections in 1981 and won only limited support. In 1982, MK Muhammad Watd of Mapam once again raised the idea after his colleagues had been angered by a series of actions and statements, which culminated in his attempt to organize protest absences from the festivities organized on the occasion of the thirty-third anniversary of the Knesset, which coincided with the centenary of Zionist Jewish settlement in Ottoman Palestine. See *Review,* 13, p. 16. See also article by journalist Qassem Ziyad, "An Arab Party: Yes or No?", *Al Hamishmar,* February 25, 1982 (Hebrew).

78. See 'Atallah Mansur, "Congestion in the Arab Street," *Haaretz,* October 27, 1988 (Hebrew). The first of the Christian candidates got the ninth slate and was followed by the first Druze candidate. Yitzhak Reiter, "The Democratic Arab Party and its place in the orientation of Israeli

Arabs," in Jacob M. Landau (ed.), *The Arab Sector in Israel and the 1988 Knesset Elections*, p. 65, note 13 on p. 79 (Hebrew).

79. "And What Will Happen after the Elections?", *Ad-Diyar* (the DAP organ), November 4, 1988, and also *Shu'un Filastiniyyah* (Palestinian Affairs), no. 187, October 1988, p. 97, analysis by the PLO's research center (Arabic).

80. DAP platform, pp. 5, 7.

81. 'Atallah Mansur, "Darawshah Steals the Show," *Haaretz*, November 29, 1988 (Hebrew).

82. "Success of the Party of Arabism [is] a Victory for our Palestinian People," the headline of DAP's paper, *Ad-Diyar*, November 4, 1988 (Arabic).

83. 'Atallah Mansur, "The PLP Has Forfeited Two Worlds," *Haaretz*, November 6, 1988 (Hebrew).

84. A list of the party's candidates appears in the DAP platform, pp. 12–13.

85. Reiter, "The DAP and Its Place" in *The Arab Sector in Israel and the 1988 Knesset Elections*, p. 68.

86. Reiter, "The DAP and Its Place," p. 69, and note 44 on p. 1.

87. Faiz 'Abbas, "Darawshah: 'We Are The True Victors'," *Hadashot*, November 2, 1988 (Hebrew). Cf. his pre-election forecast: "A Quarter of a Million Voters May Send 14 Deputies to the Next Knesset." 'Abd el-Wahhab Darawshah, "Unprecedented Weight," *Politika*, 21 (July 1988), pp. 22–3 (Hebrew).

88. *Yedioth Ahronoth*, August 17, 1990 (Hebrew).

89. Ibrahim Malek and Sarah Ossetzki, *Initial Reactions of Israeli Arabs to Iraq's Invasion of Kuwait* (Giv'at Haviva, Institute of Arab Studies, August 19, 1990), p. 5 (Hebrew).

90. Ibid., p. 5.

91. The party had decided by late September 1991, before the thirteenth Knesset elections, to explore the possibility of setting up a single Arab list. On September 25, 1991, a negotiation committee was established headed by attorney 'Abd er-Rauf Mawasi of the Fureidis local council, the party's deputy chairman. The initiative was approved by "Abu Hatem," Ibrahim Nimr Hussein, chairman of the Monitoring Committee, but nothing came of it. *Davar*, September 26, 1991.

92. See Thomas Mayer, "Young Muslims in Israel," *Hamizrah Hehadash*, vol. 32 (1989), pp. 10–11 (Hebrew).

93. See, for example, 'Abdallah Nimr Darwish, *Toward Islam* (Nablus, 1975) or 'Abdallah Nimr Darwish, *O Muslims* (Tulkarm – his first missive, published on June 11, 1976) – both in Arabic.

94. Thomas Mayer, "Young Muslims in Israel," p. 4 (Hebrew); Thomas Mayer, "The Islamic Opposition in Syria 1961–1982," *Orient*, vol. 24 (1983), pp. 589–609 (English); 'Abdallah 'Umar, *The Islamic Struggle in Syria* (Los Angeles, 1983).

95. *Davar*, September 26, 1991.

96. Avner Regev, *Arabs of Israel: Political Issues* (Jerusalem, 1989) Appendix B, pp. 33–5 (Hebrew).

97. *Al Hamishmar*, June 10, 1981 (Hebrew). Hanna Muweis had been a

Hadash member of the ninth Knesset, while serving as chairman of the Committee. Tawfiq Zayyad joined the Committee in 1976, upon his election as mayor of Nazareth.

98. *As-Sinarah*, August 23, 1991 (Arabic).
99. As'ad 'Azaiza Jamal, head of the Daburiyya municipal council, dared oppose a general strike on "Land Day," 1990, but remained in a minority. In 1991, the majority adopted his view that local assemblies were sufficient.
100. Concerning internal controversy within the Committee, see 'Atallah Mansur, "Making a Way Through to Local Government," *Haaretz*, June 5, 1989.
101. Regev, *Arabs of Israel*, p. 14 (Hebrew).
102. Ibrahim Malek and Sarah Ossetzki, *Initial Reactions of Arabs in Israel to Iraq's Invasion of Kuwait* (Givat Haviva, Institute of Arab Studies, August 19, 1990) (Hebrew).
103. Out of 2,897,000 eligible voters in the 1988 election, 347,000 were minority members, or 12 percent of the total, compared to 18.5 percent of the population. Compare *Statistical Abstract of Israel, 1990*, table 2.1, p. 38. See also Uziel Schmeltz, "The Natural Movement and Population Growth," in Aharon Layish (ed.), *The Arabs in Israel: Continuity and Change* (Jerusalem, 1981), p. 35. See also Avraham Diskin, *Elections to the Twelfth Knesset* (Jerusalem, Jerusalem Institute of Israel Studies, 1990), p. 60 (all in Hebrew).
104. *Statistical Abstract of Israel, 1990*, table 2.22, pp. 80–1. The median age for Druze is 18.6, while among Christians it is 25.8.
105. Actually, it comes to at least 90 percent, as at least 10 percent of eligible Jewish voters have emigrated. Diskin, *Elections to the Twelfth Knesset*, p. 7.
106. The highest non-participation rate was in 1981, when only 69 percent of eligible Arabs voted. See Ori Stendel, "Voting Trends for the Tenth Knesset Among Israeli Arabs," *Hamizrah Hehadash*, vol. 30 (1981), pp. 117–20 (Hebrew).
107. Diskin, *Elections to the Twelfth Knesset*, pp. 61–2 (Hebrew).
108. *Kull al-'Arab*, September 13, 1991 (Arabic).
109. See short newspaper article by Uriel Linn, MK, "All Because of a Measly Half Percent," *Yedioth Ahronoth*, October 17, 1991 (Hebrew).

4 Relations with Arabs Abroad

1. See Ori Stendel, *A Comparative Description of Israeli Arab Settlements and Settlements in Judea and Samaria (the "West Bank")* (Jerusaiem, The Prime Minister's Office, January 1968) (Hebrew). Cf. Sami Mar'i, "Higher Education in Three Divided Arab Villages" in *Hamizrah Hehadash*, vol. 26 (1976), pp. 27–36. This research, sponsored by the Ford Foundation, compared the "half" villages Barta'a, Beit Safafa and both Baqa el-Gharbiyya and Baqa esh-Sharqiyya, even though the latter is a village in its own right.
2. Son of Hassan bek Shukri, former mayor of Haifa. He was prominent among the Arab dignitaries after the 1948 war, maintaining his high

position by running the local *waqf* property skilfully. The delegation consisted of twenty-one dignitaries, including Muhammad Hubeishi, the *Qadi* of Acre (*Haaretz*, February 17, 1977).

3. She recounted her tragedy to the researcher, Dr Gideon M. Kressel, when she was pregnant. See his article "The Dowry: A Re-examination" in *Hamizrah Hehadash*, vol. 26 (1976), pp. 215–16.

4. Appeared as an article in 1981 in Alouph Hareven (ed.), *One of Every Six Israelis* (Jerusalem, Van Leer Institute, 1981), pp. 44–5 (Hebrew).

5. Referring apparently to a story by A. B. Yehoshua: "An Arab and a small girl are approaching the house . . . The Arab turns out to be old and mute. His tongue was cut off in the war. By them or by us. Does it matter? Who knows what were the last words that stuck in his throat?" A. B. Yehoshua, *Until the Winter of 1974* (Tel Aviv, 1975) (Hebrew).

6. Ghassan Kanafani, *Resistance Literature in Occupied Palestine 1948–1966*, (Beirut, 1966) (Arabic). See also Gideon Shiloh, "The Attitude of Literary Criticism in Arab Countries to Arabic 'Resistance Literature' in Israel," *Hamizrah Hehadash*, vol. 24 (1974), pp. 47–8 (Hebrew).

7. See the words of the poet Rashed Hussein upon his return from a conference of the non-aligned countries at Belgrade, *New Outlook*, December 1961, p. 35. Cf. Gideon Shiloh, *Israeli Arabs in the Eyes of the Arab States and the PLO* (Jerusalem, Magnes Press, 1981), pp. 11–19, 60–9 (Hebrew).

8. It is worth noting that prior to the 1967 War not a single Israeli Arab joined a terrorist cell, though some did join groups engaged in intelligence gathering; see *Haaretz*, October 30, 1968, reporting data given to the Knesset by the then Defense Minister Moshe Dayan (Hebrew); see also *Al-Ittihad*, October 1, 1968 (Arabic) and *Haaretz*, November 27, 1969. See also Shemuel Segev, "Ideological Motives of Israeli Arabs in Joining Terrorist Organizations," *Maariv*, November 27, 1968. Compare Shemuel Toledano's statement to *Maariv*, November 28, 1968 and his "Israeli Arabs: Achievements and Dilemmas," *Seqirah Hodshit*, January 1973, p. 9 (Hebrew).

9. See Professor Yehoshafat Harkabi's collection of papers: *The Resolutions of the Palestinian National Assemblies* (Jerusalem, 1975), p. 160 (Hebrew). Cf. Muhammad 'Abd er-Rahman, "The Arabs in Israel: New Directions in Identification with the Struggle of the Palestinian People," *Shu'un Filastiniyyah* (Palestinian Affairs) no. 112, March 1982, p. 41 (Arabic). See also Shiloh, *Israeli Arabs*, pp. 75–8.

10. According to a survey conducted in August 1989 by the Jerusalem Institute for Applied Social Research, 97 percent of the Israeli Arabs questioned supported the establishment of a Palestinian state alongside the State of Israel; 95 percent regarded the PLO as the legitimate representative of the Palestinians, expressing hope that Israel would recognize it and negotiate with it. *Yedioth Ahronoth*, August 25, 1989.

11. Salman Natur, "Trying to Think Aloud" in *Politika*, no. 21 (July 1988), p. 4 (Hebrew). The war in Lebanon preoccupied Natur, who wrote about the Israeli armor in Beirut and its environs in his book *Writer of*

Fury. Mahmud Darwish wrote a foreword for it, and passages from it were translated into Hebrew and printed in *Mifgash*, 2(6), pp. 77–82.

12. See *Review*, 20–21, pp. 4–5 (Hebrew).
13. *Intifadah* may be approximately translated as "awakening" or "rousing oneself." For an analysis of the term, see Zeev Schiff and Ehud Yaari, *Intifadah* (Jerusalem/Tel Aviv, 1990), p. 21 (Hebrew).
14. Ibid., pp. 205–6.
15. *Hadashot*, March 7, 1988 (Hebrew).
16. *Survey of Israeli Arabs*, 3 (May 1990), p. 13 (Hebrew).
17. *Haaretz*, February 21, 1988. See also Ran Kislev, "In the Vise of Dual Loyalty," ibid., March 18, 1988, and Elie Rekhess, "Arabs in Israel," *Hamizrah Hehadash*, vol. 32 (1989), pp. 187–8.
18. See resolutions of the founding session of the Monitoring Committee at Shefar'am on March 10, 1990 in support of the Intifadah, according to *Survey of Israeli Arabs* no. 3, pp. 13, 21 (Hebrew).
19. *Al-Ittihad*, April 11, 1990.
20. *Zo Haderekh*, December 23, 1987 (Hebrew). On January 23, 1988, a rally of identification with the Intifadah was held at Nazareth. A Palestinian transmitter operating from southern Syria which had started broadcasting some time earlier called over and over again on "all Palestinian residents" to take part in the protest demonstration. At the rally – replete with fiery speeches – MK 'Abd el-Wahhab Darawshah announced his resignation from the Labor Party. *Haaretz*, January 24, 1988.
21. *Yedioth Ahronoth*, July 11, 1988; *Haaretz*, September 9, 1991; *Yedioth Ahronoth*, October 14, 1988. Despite the overall decrease in Intifadah activities, some individual Israeli Arabs continued setting fires in forests and orchards, often enough to prove that the "nationalist spark" had not gone out; *Hadashot*, October 4, 1991 (Hebrew).
22. Some members of the Monitoring Committee claimed that they had not known beforehand of the proposed date for the proclamation of the "State of Palestine." Tawfiq Zayyad asserted that the proclamation should be greeted with rejoicing, not with a strike; *Al-Ittihad*, November 13, 1988.
23. Elie Rekhess, "Arabs in Israel," *Hamizrah Hehadash* 32 (1989), p. 188; see also Darawshah's interview with *Koteret Rashit* of January 27, 1988 (Hebrew).
24. *Davar*, February 19, 1990; *Yedioth Ahronoth*, February 26, 1990; *Haaretz*, February 27, 1990 (Hebrew).
25. Israeli Police, *Annual Report* (Jerusalem, July 1989), p. 15 (Hebrew).
26. See, for example, a petition against the commander of the Ketziot detention camp concerning contacts with detainees there, High Court of Justice, 593/82, *Judgments* 37(3), p. 365. Prominent among the said lawyers were Felicia Langer and Leah Tsemel. See Tom Segev, "Felicia Langer as a Story," a review of her autobiography *In My Own Way*. The review appeared in *Haaretz*, September 6, 1991.
27. I remember an Israeli Arab lawyer whose car headlights were blown out while he was pleading in a court in the West Bank. He needed a special affidavit describing the occurrence in order to get compensa-

tion for "damage due to hostile action."

28. Yizhar Beer, "Everyone Covets His Share in the Loot," *Haaretz*, July 9, 1990.

29. Ibid., Cf. Ron Ben-Yishai's article, "Attrition Gets Institutionalized" *Yedioth Ahronoth*, May 18, 1990. His conclusion is that the Palestinians do not "move up to the next form." Despite their efforts and those of the PLO leadership urging them on, they remain at the level of the "single stone."

30. For an analysis of the attitude of Israeli Arabs, see As'ad Ghanem and Sarah Ossetzki-Lazar, "Green Line, Red Lines: The Israeli Arabs Facing the Intifadah" in *Survey of Israeli Arabs* no. 3 (Giv'at Haviva, Institute of Arab Studies, May 1990), p. 2 ff. The authors hold that the Intifadah turned the "Green Line" into a red line across which the violence should not be allowed to spread. In support of their view, they cite the Monitoring Committee which stated that "the Israeli Arabs will not keep still, but at the same time we want to continue being citizens of the State of Israel and have no intention of joining a civil disobedience campaign" (*Maariv*, January 14, 1988). According to a poll carried out by Prof. Sammi Smooha of Haifa University it appears that there has been an increase among the number of people questioned who point to the Israeli dimension in their definition of their own identity. Their percentage rose from 65.1 in 1985 to 67.9 percent in March 1988. For the poll, 1,200 people were questioned. The above data are from As'ad Ghanem, ibid., p. 7 (all in Hebrew).

31. Ibid., pp. 8, 20.

32. Ibid., pp. 10, 20. Also *Davar*, April 2, 1990; *Al Hamishmar*, April 2, 1990 (Hebrew).

33. *Hetz* (quarterly on education and philosophy), July 1989, p. 2; *Haaretz*, May 24, 1989 (Hebrew).

34. Public lecture by Dr Majed el-Hajj at the Hebrew University in Jerusalem, *Haaretz*, July 25, 1989. Similarly, Jum'a Qassasi, mayor of the Bedouin town of Rahat, a member of the Islamic Movement, following the uprooting of olive trees at Laqiyya by the Israel Lands Administration; Israeli TV, May 8, 1990. Dr 'Aziz Haydar of the Truman Institute is of the opinion that "the Israeli Arabs strive for recognition as a national minority, that is, for a revision of the relations between them and the state." He added that he could not tell whether they would join the Intifadah, yet it was clear that "their patience is running out and a catastrophe is at hand." *Haaretz*, May 9, 1990, *Al Hamishmar*, May 13, 1990.

35. The vehement public discussion about what name to use is in itself a subject worthy of research. The historian would pose the question why a similar discussion did not take place among the Jewish population about what to call the events of 1936–39. Was it the change in the balance of power which influenced the Jewish public's present readiness to concede this "minor" point?

36. See concluding statement of a protest meeting against racism, held at a Nazareth theatre on April 23, 1990. Jews and Arabs participated in the meeting, including Knesset members from various parties,

men of religion, local authority representatives, and trade-union functionaries; As'ad Ghanem in "Green Lines, Red Lines," *Survey of Israeli Arabs* no. 3, p. 7. (For the full text in Hebrew and Arabic, see ibid., p. 22.)

37. On the support of Palestinian Arabs for the Axis powers during World War II, see Shimoni, *Arabs of Eretz Yisrael*, pp. 315–17.
38. For example, *Ash-Sha'b*, August 12, 1990, and the east Jerusalem press in general from the date of the invasion onward.
39. See Sarah Ossetzki-Lazar and As'ad Ghanem, "The Arabs in Israel under the Shadow of the Gulf War," *Survey of Israeli Arabs no. 6* (Giv'at Haviva, May 1991), p. 3 (Hebrew).
40. *As-Sirat*, August 17, 1990. Also, *As-Sirat*, January 11, 1991 (Arabic).
41. *Yedioth Ahronoth*, August 17, 1990.
42. *Hadha al-Usbu'*, August 9, 1990 (Arabic).
43. *As-Sinarah*, February 1, 1991. Cf. *As-Sirat*, January 25, 1991, February 15, 1991, February 22, 1991 (Arabic).
44. *Yedioth Ahronoth*, supplement, February 1, 1991.
45. Israeli Radio interview cited in *Survey of Israeli Arabs* no. 6, p. 6. (My emphasis – O.S.).
46. *Maariv*, January 18, 1991.
47. *Davar*, February 7, 1991; *Haaretz*, December 28, 1990.
48. *Yedioth Ahronoth*, February 24, 1991, carried a photograph of the "relative" gloating and holding a picture of the Iraqi minister, saying: "Suddenly, everybody shakes my hand."
49. *Haaretz*, February 6, 1991.
50. *Maariv*, January 31, 1991.
51. *Maariv*, February 4, 1991. See an advertisement in *Haaretz* December 14, 1990, reading: "*Ahlan wasahlan* [welcome]! Our house is open."
52. See claims put forward at a meeting of Arab Local Council Heads (part of a Center for Local Government meeting) at Herzliya on February 5, 1991; *Haaretz*, February 6, 1991, also *Haaretz*, January 8, 1991, carrying a statement by the Defense Minister on the distribution of gas masks in the Arab sector.
53. *Al-Ittihad*, February 4, 1991; see also *As-Sinarah*, December 7, 1990 (Arabic).
54. *Kan'aan*, no. 3 (July 1991), p. 72 (Arabic). Palestinian nationalists attach particular importance to this issue in view of Dr Uri Milstein's book, which states that the Deir Yassin massacre is pure fiction (*Haaretz*, September 6, 1991). See also Tom Segev, "Deir Yassin, 'Abdallah, Democracy" *Haaretz*, September 20, 1991; also Yerah Tal, "There Was No Massacre There" *Haaretz*, September 8, 1991 (all in Hebrew). Alongside the revival efforts by nationalist Arab intellectuals, there is a prominent renewed interest among Jewish scholars as well in the case of the Kafr Qassem massacre of 1956. See, for instance, the weekend supplement of *Hadashot*, October 25, 1991, from p. 6 on.
55. On these heroic figures see Danni Rubinstein, "The Gallery of Palestinian Martyrs," *Haaretz*, December 25, 1990 (Hebrew).
56. Shimoni, *Arabs of Eretz Yisrael*, pp. 96, 102, 237–8, 311, 317.
57. Danni Rubinstein, *Haaretz*, December 25, 1990.

58. *Review*, no. 3, p. 33.
59. 'Ali Salameh was the son of gang commander Hassan Salameh, who was killed in the war of 1948.
60. The police prepare for such events with the utmost alertness. The Supreme Court, having accepted the argument that a demonstration close to Fatah Day was liable in all probability to cause disturbances, prohibited a women's demonstration "for peace in critical times" shortly before the Gulf War (*Haaretz*, December 28, 1990).

5 Minority Rights under Israeli Law

1. HCJ 10/48 Ziv *vs.* Executive Commissioner of the Municipal District *et al.*, *Judgments* 1, 85, p. 89. On the subject in general see Ori Stendel: "The Right of Israel's Arabs to Be Different: Legal Aspects," *Hamizrah Hehadash*, vol. 32 (1989), pp. 192–207 (Hebrew).
2. HCJ 73/53, 87/53 *Qol Haam* Ltd.; *Al-Ittihad vs.* Minister of the Interior, *Judgments* 7–871, p. 884. The principle of freedom of expression is examined in this petition, based on the concept that the democratic process expresses *"the choice of the Nation's shared goals and the ways of realizing them, by way of clarification and verbal debates, i.e. by open clarification of problems presently on the State's agenda and a free exchange of opinions on them."* Ibid., p. 876, opposite the letter "G" (Hebrew). This ruling made the order *nisi* decisive and overruled the order to close down the two newspapers. This has since become a cornerstone in adjudication. With regard to the censorship, the guiding precedent is HCJ 680/88, Schnitzer et al. *vs.* the Chief Military Censor and the Minister of Defense, *Judgments* 42(4), 617. See chapter on Arab Press.
3. On the legal significance of the Declaration of Independence, before the legislation of the Judicial Foundations Law, and on its status following that legislation, see the ruling of Justice Menahem Elon: Appeal 23/84, *Judgments* 39(2), 225, p. 293 opposite the letters A.B. See also Amnon Rubinstein, *Constitutional Law of the State of Israel* (Tel Aviv, 1967), pp. 7–10 (Hebrew).
4. "From the Point of View of an Israeli Arab," *Herut*, February 13, 1964 (Hebrew). In 1991 a lively public debate was held on the issue of the recruitment of minorities into the IDF and the integration of Israeli Arabs within the framework of a National Service. This debate was opened with the decision of Minister David Magen to re-examine the national service of minorities in the IDF on a voluntary basis. The subject was covered by the newspapers just prior to the outbreak of the Gulf War. See Ori Stendel, "National Service for Israeli Arabs: Should There Be a Law?", *The Jerusalem Post*, January 11, 1991, p. 8. Compare: Moshe Sharon, "National Service for Arabs Can't Work," *The Jerusalem Post*, January 6, 1991, p. 4, and Danni Rubinstein, "No to National Service," *Haaretz*, January 10, 1991. Yerah Tal, "Talk of the Day with 'Izz ed-Din 'Ammash, Chairman of the Jisr ez-Zarqa Local Council, member of Ratz: 'The Druze Are Discriminated Against Despite their Military Service'," *Haaretz*, December 26, 1990.
5. *Haaretz*, December 26, 1990. On the demonstration of members of the

"Druze Initiative Committee" against mandatory recruitment into the IDF, see *Haaretz*, December 31, 1990.

6. Article 51 of the Law, 5710 [1950], p. 159. See Ori Stendel, "Basic Perception of the Minorities in the State in Israeli Law" in Alouph Hareven (ed.), *Living Together* (Jerusalem, Van Leer Institute – working paper, September, 1982), pp. 32–47 (Hebrew).
7. *Judgments* 19(3), pp. 365, 386.
8. *Laws* 930 (March 13, 1979), p. 77; cf. Government of Palestine, *Official Gazette* 1945, Addition 2, p. 855.
9. *Laws* 37, 5710 [1950], p. 86.
10. Article 1(b) of the Law. Eretz Yisrael – "Land of Israel" is the Jewish traditional name in Hebrew of the land called Palestine internationally until 1948; therefore, the name (Palestine) has been added in the English translation of the law.
11. For a full analysis of the Absentees' Property Law, 1950 see Aharon Litkovski's article: "The Present Absentees in Israel," *Hamizrah Hehadash*, vol. 10 (1960), pp. 186–8. The article deals with the problem of the present absentees and the absentees' property, as well as the Acquisition of Land Law (Confirmation of Deeds and Compensation), 1953, ibid., pp. 189–92 (Hebrew).
12. Absentee Property Law (Amendment no. 3) (Release of Consecration Properties and the Use Therein), 1965, *Laws* 445, 5725 [1965], p. 58.
13. On the legal status of the *waqf* properties, see Aharon Layish, "The Muslim *Waqf* in Israel," *Hamizrah Hehadash*, vol. 15 (1965), pp. 38–56.
14. *Laws*, 330, 5721 [1961], p. 118.
15. See Amnon Rubinstein, *Constitutional Law*, note 3, p. 86. On the topic in general, see Aharon Layish: "The Religious Jurisdiction of the Muslims in Israel," *Hamizrah Hehadash*, vol. 13, (1963), pp. 19–37.
16. *Judgments* 32(2), p. 800, Muhammad Sa'id Burkan versus the Minister of Finance, the Company for the Restoration & Development of the Jewish Quarter in the Old City in Jerusalem Ltd. and the Minister of Housing.
17. Ibid., p. 808, para. 6, opposite the letters D, E (author's emphases).
18. Ibid., p. 805, opposite the letter G.
19. Ibid., p. 802, opposite the letter A.
20. Ibid., p. 805, opposite the letter B.
21. Ibid., p. 807, opposite the letter C.
22. *Laws* 244, 5718 [1958], p. 69.
23. Ori Stendel, "Voting Trends to the Tenth Knesset Among Israeli Arabs," *Hamizrah Hehadash*, vol. 30 (1981), pp. 141–2.
24. See Gabriel Baer, *Arabs of the Middle East*, pp. 74–86 (Hebrew).
25. HCJ 64/253, Jiryis *vs.* the Haifa District Commissioner, *Judgments* 18 (4), 673.
26. Appeal 2/84, 3, Neiman *vs.* Chairman of the Central Elections Committee to the Eleventh Knesset; Avneri *vs.* Chairman of the Central Elections Committee to the Eleventh Knesset, *Judgments* 39 (2), 225 on p. 248; opposite the letters A–C (Hebrew).
27. Ibid., p. 262, opposite the letters C–E.
28. Ibid., p. 241 (opposite the letters C–D).

29. Ibid., p. 304 (opposite the letter E).
30. See Ori Stendel, "The Arabs of Israel: Between Hammer and Anvil," *Israel Yearbook on Human Rights*, vol. 20 (1991), pp. 287–308.

6 Arabic-Language Press and Literature

1. Christians were ahead of Muslims in all cultural areas throughout the Middle East due to the high level of education which they enjoyed and their extensive ties with Western countries. Shabetai Shevitz, *The Arab Press in Israel* (Jerusalem, 1964), pp. 8–9 (Hebrew).
2. See the English text of Clause 19(2)(a), HCJ 73/53, 87/53, *Judgments* 7(2) 871, pp. 873–4.
3. HCJ, ibid., p. 875, opposite the letters C–D.
4. See detailed grammatical analysis, ibid., p. 887, opposite letters A–C.
5. Ibid., p. 887, opposite the letter E.
6. Ibid., p. 877, opposite the letter D.
7. Ibid., p. 877 opposite letters E–F.
8. The conditions required for obtaining a license are prescribed in Article 5 of the Ordinance; they include, *inter alia*, requirements regarding the personal qualifications of the editor, such as age, at least a high-school education, absence of legal deficiency and a clean criminal record. Press Ordinance, Palestine Laws, Chapter 116.
9. See the article by Yaron Zelig, "Closing a Newspaper," *Hotam*, September 4, 1987, p. 8.
10. Qassem Ziyad, "Rakah Mouthpiece *Al-Ittihad* Was Closed until March 31," *Al Hamishmar*, March 25, 1988, pp. 1, 4. Compare Elie Rekhess, "The Closing of *Al-Ittihad*: Change of Policy?" *Otot*, no. 25 (May 1988). The Arabic journal *Al-Mithaq* has been previously closed in Jerusalem. The Hebrew journal, *Derekh Hanitzotz*, whose editors were Jews, was shut down for an unlimited period.
11. See the history of the newspaper below, as part of this chapter. See also the article by Qassem Ziyad, "The Silent Voice of Freedom," *Al Hamishmar*, July 12, 1990, p. 9.
12. For an exhaustive discussion on the authority of the military censor to disqualify an article by virtue of the Defense (Emergency) Regulations, 1945, see Judgment Shnitzer, HCJ 680/88, *Judgments* 42(4), 617.
13. On the first steps of the newspaper in Israel, see Shevitz, *The Arab Press in Israel*, pp. 15–19.
14. *Al-Ittihad*, November 26, 1990.
15. *Al-Ittihad*, December 18, 1990.
16. Compare the two photographs; *Al-Ittihad*, August 27, 1991 and June 20, 1991.
17. *Al-Ittihad*, May 26, 1991.
18. See *Al-Ittihad*, on the days covering the 30th of March since the first "Land Day" in 1976, mainly 1982, 1988 and 1991.
19. *Al-Ittihad*, August 20, 1991. The statement of the Secretary General also appeared in this edition.
20. *Al-Ittihad*, August 21, 1991.
21. *Al-Ittihad*, August 22, 1991.

22. *Al-Ittihad*, December 19, 1990.
23. *Al-Ittihad*, May 26, 1991. The paper began to appear in a reduced format, while cutting down the spread of articles. See for example, *Al-Ittihad* October 12, 1991 and October 21, 1991.
24. Shevitz, *The Arab Press in Israel*, p. 27. See there details on other Arabic journals that no longer appear: *Al-Mirsad*, a weekly of Mapam's Arab division, *Al-Fajr*, a literary monthly of Mapam, *Al-'Amal*, a mouthpiece of the Labor Party and others. Ibid., pp. 28–9.
25. *As-Sinarah*, December 7, 1990. Issue 406, dedicated to a review of three years of the Intifadah.
26. *As-Sinarah*, August, 14, 1990. *Haaretz*, August 17, 1990; *As-Sinarah*, August 10, 1990. For an article in response see Ori Stendel, "Reconciliation or Escalation," *Haaretz*, August 27, 1990. Yossi Sarid is a welcome guest in the newspaper. See, for example, his impressions following his meeting in prison with PLO activists Redwan Abu 'Ayyash and Ziyad Abu Zayyad: "Meeting in Prison," *As-Sinarah*, December 14, 1990.
27. *As-Sinarah*, August 14, 1990.
28. *As-Sinarah*, May 3, 1991; the picture of the editor with the advisor appears on the first page. His perception of the PLO as "a representative and leader of our people, not ours" was presented in a forceful article, reflecting his personal political conviction. Lutfi Mash'ur, "Palestinian, Arab, Israeli," *Haaretz*, October 26, 1990.
29. *As-Sinarah*, September 13, 1991.
30. Advocate Yusuf Qabalan, "A Visit of Shamir with Sheikh Tarif [the Druze leader] Will Not Solve Our Problems," *As-Sinarah*, May 10, 1991.
31. *As-Sinarah*, August 23, 1991.
32. *As-Sinarah*, September 13, 1991. The editor, Lutfi Mash'ur, was handling this matter personally.
33. *As-Sinarah*, March 8, 1991, p. 14.
34. *As-Sinarah*, May 24, 1991, p. 14. Today, as he has become editor of the rival newspaper *Kull al-'Arab*, a constant war is waged against him on the pages of *As-Sinarah*.
35. See, for example, a caricature from the *Washington Post*, following Iraq's invasion of Kuwait; a picture of the border between the two countries, while breaking up the letters of the name of the country Kuwait into two: *Ku Wait*, meaning: Caution!, *As-Sinarah*, December 7, 1990, p. 32.
36. *As-Sinarah*, May 10, 1991.
37. *As-Sinarah*, March 15, 1991.
38. *Kull al-'Arab*, May 24, 1991, p. 2.
39. *Kull al-'Arab*, August 16, 1991.
40. Muhammad Watd, formerly a "permanent" Knesset Member on the left-wing Zionist Mapam list, left its ranks during the Intifadah, moved over to Rakah, but did not find space for his activity there.
41. Emil Habibi, who for many years was one of the philosophers of Rakah and a Knesset Member on its behalf, withdrew from the party following the elections to the twelfth Knesset. He continues his extensive

writing as an author and journalist. See *Kull al-'Arab*, August 16, 1991.

42. Ibid., p. 10, on facing columns, *Kull al-'Arab*, "hosting" Samih el-Qassem, "treating him" with a publication of his picture. Later, however, Samih became chief editor of *Kull al-'Arab* and everything has, of course, changed.

43. "Hamas" is a profound concept, which means burning religious fire, stormy-combatant fervor. The movement sees itself as an inseparable part of the Muslim Brotherhood, which was founded in Ismailia, Egypt in 1928 by the "Chief Guide," Hassan el-Bana. Today Hamas activists see themselves as the military arm of the movement in the territories of Palestine. Their goal is to form a large Islamic state through social reform. Its leader, Sheikh Ahmad Yassin, was arrested in 1989, together with 200 Hamas activists in Gaza.

44. Sheikh Khaled Muhanna, born in 1958, studied in the Islamic College in Hebron between 1976 and 1979, together with Sheikh Raid Salah Abu Shakra and Sheikh Hashem 'Abd er-Rahman; the three are leaders of the "Young Muslims" in Umm el-Fahm. Thomas Mayer, "Young Muslims in Israel," *Hamizrah Hehadash*, vol. 32 (1989), pp. 11–12.

45. *Fard 'Ayn*, the duty of every individual, as opposed to the Muslim orthodox view of *jihad* as *"Fard Kifayah,"* i.e. a duty, which, if fulfilled by a sufficient number of believers, is not required by others.

46. Article 14 of the Covenant, as opposed to the three Palestinian circles in the PLO doctrine, which are the circles of the inhabitants of the West Bank and the Gaza Strip, the Arab citizens of Israel, and the Palestinians dispersed throughout the world.

47. *Haaretz*, July 9, 1990. See also the article by Qassem Ziyad, "The Silent Voice of Freedom," *Al Hamishmar*, July 12, 1990, p. 9.

48. *Sawt al-Haqq wa-al-Hurriyyah*, September 6, 1991, pp. 1, 15.

49. For a comprehensive analysis, see Avraham Yinon, "Arabic Literature in Israel," *Hamizrah Hehadash*, vol. 15 (1965), pp. 57–84 (Hebrew). Cf. George Qanaze's exhaustive study, "Ideological Fundamentals in Arabic Literature in Israel," *Hamizrah Hehadash*, vol. 32 (1989), pp. 129–38 (Hebrew). On the roots of Israeli Arab literary endeavors, see Matti Peled, "Palestinian Poetry during the Mandate Period," *Moznayim*, October–November 1983 (Hebrew).

50. See Salman Masalha, "People within Words," *Politika*, no. 21 (July 1988), p. 44 (Hebrew).

51. Tawfiq Mu'ammar, *Memoirs of a Refugee*, p. 59 (Hebrew). His book describes the battle of Haifa in the spring of 1948.

52. Tawfiq Mu'ammar, *The Infiltrator* (Nazareth, 1957), pp. 9–11 (Arabic).

53. Samih el-Qassem, from *Songs of the Roads* (Nazareth, circa 1965). "The others" are, of course, the Jews, who are establishing their state on the ruins of Palestine. For a view of the displacement of the refugees, see Qanaze', "Ideological Fundamentals in Arabic Literature in Israel," pp. 129–30.

54. Rashed Hussein, from "I Am the Earth: Withhold Not Your Rain From Me" (Arabic), in Masalha, "People within Words," p. 45.

55. From the poem "Here Will I Stay" by Salem Jubran, ex-editor of

Al-Ittihad and formerly a leader of the Communist Party. Another nationalist author, Faraj Nur Salman, calls his book *The Innocents and the Executioners*. His Arab compatriots are the innocents; Israel's leaders are the executioners.

56. From the poem "We are the Root that Still Lives" by Naif Saleh Salim, published in *Al-Ittihad*, October 8, 1965 (Arabic).
57. I.e., the refugees.
58. From "Sindbad's Journey" by Hail 'Asaqla, published in *Al-Ittihad*, January 21, 1966 (Arabic).
59. Published in the journal *Hadha al-'Alam*, May 5, 1966. In another poem, "Witness of Death" (Arabic) he repeats his oath: "Tomorrow, I swear . . . the night shall not be a long dark night! . . . "
60. Qanaze', "Ideological Fundamentals in Arabic Literature in Israel," pp. 135–6. To gauge Samih el-Qassem's credo in later years, including the Khomeinistic spirit that it acquired after his return from a visit to Iran, see interview with him in *As-Sinarah*, May 24, 1991 (Arabic).
61. Mahmud Darwish, *The Olive Leaves* (Haifa, 1961), pp. 5–10 (Arabic). The poet emigrated from Israel and gradually made his way to the top of the PLO's information apparatus in Beirut until he became the "Minister of Cultural Affairs." He resigned from the Palestine National Council in September 1991 over the fateful decision to attend the peace conference, and later condemned the Oslo agreement of 1993.
62. Munib Makhul, "Voice of Palestine," in *The Sown Ones* (Acre, 1980), p. 120 (Arabic).
63. Emil Habibi, *The Six-Day Sextet*. The collection was published in 1970, three years after the war. See Mahmud 'Abbasi, "Motives and Symbols in Arabic Literature after the Six Day War," *Mifgash*, 2(6), summer 1985, p. 33 (Hebrew).
64. *Al-Anba*, September 24, 1971 (Arabic).
65. *Al-Jadid*, March 1968 (Arabic).
66. *Al-Jadid*, July–August 1972 (Arabic).
67. Mahmud 'Abbasi, *Mifgash*, p. 34 (Hebrew).
68. Jamal Qa'war in the anthology *September* (Nazareth, 1985), p. 93 (Arabic).
69. See George Qanaze, "Ideological Fundamentals in Arabic Literature in Israel," p. 132. Fawzi el-Asmar recounted his own story in his book *To Be an Arab in Israel*, published by Yisrael Shahak, Jerusalem, 1975 (Hebrew).
70. Explicit exhortations to adopt Marxism are expressed by Hanna Ibrahim in *A Voice from the Void* (Acre, 1981), pp. 23–37 and 43–7; by Tawfiq Zayyad in his poems "Communists" and "To the Workers of Moscow," in the anthology *I Support You* (Haifa, 1969); and by Salem Jubran in the anthology *Comrades of the Sun* (Nazareth, 1975), pp. 23–7 (all in Arabic). Emil Habibi can no longer be considered a Rakah author, but his literary growth certainly coincided with his tenure as a Rakah leader.
71. *Al-Ghad* ("Tomorrow"), March 1987. For harsh criticism of these two poems, see Masalha, "People within Words," p. 50.

Bibliography

BOOKS

Hebrew

'Aref, 'Aref el-, *History of Beersheba and its Tribes* (Tel Aviv, 1933).

'Areidi, Na'im, *Poems* (Tel Aviv, Am Oved, 1986).

Asmar, Fawzi el-, *To Be an Arab in Israel* (Jerusalem, 1975).

Baer, Gabriel, *Arabs of the Middle East* (Tel Aviv, 1973).

Ben-Porat, Yoram, *The Arab Labor Force in Israel* (Jerusalem, 1966).

Benziman, Uzi and Mansur, 'Atallah, *Subtenants: The Arabs of Israel – Their Status and the Policy towards Them* (Jerusalem, 1992).

Diskin, Avraham, *Elections to the Twelfth Knesset* (Jerusalem, 1990).

Ginat, Joseph, *The Bedouin* (Jerusalem, 1966).

Harari, Yehiel (ed.), *Elections in the Arab Sector, 1977* (Givat Haviva, 1978).

Hareven, Alouph (ed.), *One of Every Six Israelis* (Jerusalem, 1981).

Harkabi, Yehoshafat (comp.), *The Resolutions of the Palestinian National Assemblies* (Jerusalem, 1975).

Kamma, Blanche, *The Status of the Arab Woman in Israel* (Jerusalem, 1984).

Layish, Aharon, *Changes in the Arab Society in Israel* (Jerusalem, 1966).

Malek, Ibrahim and Ossetzki, Sarah, *Initial Reactions of Israeli Arabs to Iraq's Invasion of Kuwait* (Giv'at Haviva, Institute of Arab Studies, August 1990).

Marx, Emmanuel, *Bedouin Society in the Negev* (Tel Aviv, 1974).

Medzini, Arnon, *The Spread of Bedouin Settlement in the Galilee as a Product of Spontaneous Settlement and Deliberate Government Policy* (Haifa, Haifa University Mongeography Series, 1984).

Pollack, Yitzhak and Mahamid, Muhammad, *Charcoal Stigma: The World of Young Arabs in Israel* (Giv'at Haviva, Institute of Arab Studies, 1989).

Regev, Avner, *Arabs of Israel: Political Issues* (Jerusalem, 1989).

Rekhess, Elie, *The Arab Village in Israel: A New Political-Nationalist Focal Point* (Tel Aviv, 1985).

Rosenfeld, Henry, *They Were Peasants: Studies in the Social Development of the Arab Village in Israel* (Tel Aviv, 1964).

Rubinstein, Amnon, *Constitutional Law in the State of Israel* (Tel Aviv, 1967).

Schiff, Zeev and Yaari, Ehud, *Intifadah* (Jerusalem-Tel Aviv, 1990).
Shevitz, Shabetai, *The Arab Press in Israel* (Jerusalem, 1964).
Shiloh, Gideon, *Israeli Arabs in the Eyes of the Arab States and the PLO* (Jerusalem, 1981).
Shimoni, Yaakov, *Arabs of Eretz Yisrael* (Tel Aviv, 1947).
Stavski, Moshe, *The Arab Village* (Tel Aviv, 1946).
Stendel, Ori, *A Comparative Description of Israeli Arab Settlements and Settlements in Judea and Samaria (the "West Bank")* (Jerusalem, 1968).
——, *Minorities in Israel* (Jerusalem, 1972).
—— and Hareuveni, Emmanuel, *The Minorities in Israel* (Tel Aviv, 1972).
Yehoshua, A. B., *Until the Winter of 1974* (Tel Aviv, 1975).
Yisraeli, G. Z., *History of the Communist Party in Israel* (Tel Aviv, Am Oved, 1953).
Zilberg, Moshe, *Personal Status in Israel* (Jerusalem, 1961).

Arabic

Darwish, 'Abdallah Nimr, *O Muslims* (Tulkarm, 1976).
——, *Toward Islam* (Nablus, 1975).
Darwish, Mahmud, *The Olive Leaves* (Haifa, 1961).
Ibrahim, Hanna, *A Voice from the Void* (Acre, 1981).
Jubran, Salem, *Comrades of the Sun* (Nazareth, 1975).
Kanafani, Ghassan, *Resistance Literature in Occupied Palestine* (Beirut, 1966).
Makhul, Munib, *The Sown Ones* (Acre, 1980).
Mu'ammar, Tawfiq, *Memoirs of a Refugee* (Nazareth, [1958]).
——, *The Infiltrator* (Nazareth, 1957).
Qahwaji, Habib, *The Full Story of the Al-Ard Movement* (Jerusalem, 1978).
Qassem, Samih el-, *Songs of the Roads* (Nazareth [1965]).
Qa'war, Jamal, *September* (Nazareth, 1985).
Al-Qur'an
Salman, Faraj Nur, *The Innocent Ones and the Executioners* (Acre, 1960).
Zayyad, Tawfiq, *I Support You* (Haifa, 1969).

English

Ginat, Joseph, *Women in Muslim Rural Society* (New Brunswick, NJ, 1982).
Landau, Jacob M., *The Arabs in Israel: A Political Study* (London, Oxford University Press, 1969).
Layish, Aharon, *Women and Islamic Law in a Non-Muslim State* (New York-Toronto, John Wiley and Sons; Jerusalem, Israel Universities Press, 1975).
Musil, Alois, *The Manners and Customs of the Rwala Bedouin* (New York, 1928).
Schiff, Zeev and Yaari, Ehud, *Intifadah* (New York, Touchstone, 1990).
Umar, Abdallah, *The Islamic Struggle in Syria* (Los Angeles, 1983).

ARTICLES

Hebrew

'Abbas, Faiz, "Darawsha: 'We Are the True Victors'," *Hadashot*, November 2, 1988.

'Abbasi, Mahmud, "Motives and Symbols in Arabic Literature after the Six Day War," *Mifgash*, 2(6) (Summer 1985).

Abu Ghosh, Subhi, "Integration of the Clan into a Local Council in an Arab Village," in Ori Stendel (ed.), *Arab Society in Israel* (Jerusalem, 1963).

Algazi, Yosef, "Leadership under Pressure," *Haaretz*, May 18, 1990.

——, "Rear-Guard Action Waged with Linguistic Gems," *Haaretz*, August 16, 1991.

——, "Under the Extinguished Lamps," *Haaretz*, July 7, 1991.

'Areidi, Na'im, "Between My Two Cultures," *Mifgash*, 2(6) (Summer 1985).

Bastuni, Rustum, "Arab Society in Israel," *Hamizrah Hehadash*, vol. 15 (1965).

Beer, Yizhar, "Everyone Covets His Share in the Loot," *Haaretz*, July 9, 1990.

Ben Amram, Eliyahu, "The Arab Population in Israel: Demographic Description," *Hamizrah Hehadash*, vol. 15 (1965).

Ben Yishai, Ron, "Attrition Gets Institutionalized," *Yedioth Ahronoth*, May 18, 1990.

Darawshah, 'Abd el-Wahhab, "Unprecedented Weight," *Politika*, no. 21 (July 1988).

Dayan, Arye, "Her Father, Her Brother, Her Husband," *Haaretz weekly supplement*, September 13, 1991, pp. 4–7.

Diskin, Avraham, "Statistical Perspectives of Voting in the Arab Sector," in Jacob M. Landau (ed.), *The Arab Sector in Israel and the 1988 Knesset Elections* (Jerusalem, 1989).

Eisenbach, Zvi, "Changes in the Fertility of Muslim Women in Israel in Recent Years," *Hamizrah Hehadash*, vol. 32 (1988–89).

Ghanem, As'ad and Ossetzki-Lazar, Sarah, "Green Line, Red Lines: The Israeli Arabs Facing the Intifadah," *Survey of Israeli Arabs* no. 3 (May 1990).

Gilbar, Gad, "Demography and Politics in the Middle East," *Seqirah Hodshit* no. 5 (1988).

Greilshammer, Ilan, "The New Communist List and the Twelfth Knesset Elections," in Jacob M. Landau (ed.), *The Arab Sector and the Knesset Elections* (Jerusalem, 1988).

Habibi, Emil, "Like a Wound," *Politika*, 21 (July 1988).

Hajj, Majed el-, "Elections among Arabs under the Shadow of the Intifadah: Propaganda and Results," in Jacob M. Landau (ed.), *The Arab Sector in Israel and the 1988 Knesset Elections* (Jerusalem 1989).

Hirschberg, Haim Zeev, "Jews in Muslim Countries," in Hava Lazarus-Yaffe (ed.), *Chapters in the History of the Arabs and Islam* (Tel Aviv, 1967), pp. 262–315.

Iskandar, Zahi, "Sons of the Village: A View Ahead in Anger," *Lamerhav*, January 6, 1979.

Khaliliya, Muhammad, "800 Arab Sector Leaders Establish a New Arab Party – the Democratic Arab Party," *Davar*, April 10, 1988.

Kislev, Ran, "In the Vise of Dual Loyalty," *Haaretz*, March 18, 1988.

Kressel, Gide'on M., "The Dowry: A Reconsideration," *Hamizrah Hehadash*, vol. 26 (1976), pp. 203–31.

Layish, Aharon, "The Religious Jurisdiction of the Muslims in Israel," *Hamizrah Hehadash*, vol. 13 (1963), pp. 19–37.

Linn, Uriel, "All because of a Measly Half Percent," *Yedioth Ahronoth*, October 17, 1991.

Litkovski, Aharon, "The Present-Absentees in Israel," *Hamizrah Hehadash*, vol. 10 (1960).

Mansur, 'Atallah, "A Young Arab Extremist Describes the Problem," *Haaretz*, December 12, 1965.

——, "After the Rule of the Notables," *Haaretz*, February 11, 1984.

——, "Al-Ard Old-Timers Set Up a New Organization with the Same Principles," *Haaretz*, January 10, 1991.

——, "Congestion in the Arab Street," *Haaretz*, October 27, 1988.

——, "Darawshah Steals the Show," *Haaretz*, November 29, 1988.

——, "Making a Way Through to Local Government," *Haaretz*, June 5, 1989.

——, "The PLP Has Forfeited Two Worlds," *Haaretz*, November 6, 1988.

Mar'i, Maryam, "The New Class," *Politika*, no. 21 (July 1988).

Mar'i, Sami, "Higher Education in Three Divided Arab Villages," *Hamizrah Hehadash*, vol. 26 (1976), pp. 27–36.

Masalha, Salman, "People within Words," *Politika*, no. 21 (July 1988).

Mash'ur, Lutfi, "Palestinian, Arab, Israeli," *Haaretz*, October 26, 1990.

Mayer, Thomas, "Young Muslims in Israel," *Hamizrah Hehadash*, vol. 32 (1989).

Mi'ari, Muhammad, "The Problem of Identity among Arab Intellectuals in Israel," in Alouph Hareven (ed.), *One of Every Six Israelis* (Jerusalem, 1981).

Nashashibi, Rana, "The Veil Has Not Yet Been Lifted," *Haaretz* Rosh Hashana supplement (September 1991).

Natur, Salman, "Trying to Think Aloud," *Politika*, no. 21 (June 1988).

Naur, Salman, "Writer of Fury," *Mifgash*, 2(6), pp. 77–82.

Oron, Yitzhak, "The Arab Socialist Revival Party: Its History and Ideas," *Hamizrah Hehadash*, vol. 9 (1959), pp. 241–61.

Ossetzki-Lazar, Sarah and Ghanem, As'ad, "The Arabs in Israel under the Shadow of the Gulf War," *Survey of Israeli Arabs* no. 6 (May 1991).

Peled, Matti, "Palestinian Poetry during the Mandate Period," *Moznayim*, October–November 1983.

Qanaze', George, "Ideological Fundamentals in Arabic Literature in Israel," *Hamizrah Hehadash*, vol. 32 (1989), pp. 129–38.

Reinfeld, Moshe, "She Was Forbidden to Love Him," *Haaretz*, July 30, 1991.

Reiter, Yitzhak, "The Democratic Arab Party and Its Place in the Orientation of Israeli Arabs," in Jacob M. Landau (ed.), *The Arab Sector in Israel and the 1988 Knesset Elections* (Jerusalem, 1989).

Rekhess, Elie, "Arabs in Israel and the Arabs of the Territories," *Hamizrah Hehadash*, vol. 32 (1989).

——, "The Closing of *Al-Ittihad*: Change of Policy?" *Otot*, no. 25 (May 1988).

——, "The Intellectuals," in Aharon Layish (ed.), *The Arabs in Israel: Continuity and Change* (Jerusalem, 1981).

Rosenfeld, Henry, "Changes in the Social Structure of the Arab Village of Tayyibeh," *Mibifnim*, April 1956.

Rubinstein, Danny, "No to National Service," *Haaretz*, January 10, 1991.

——, "Rakah's Cross," *Davar* weekly supplement, October 10, 1969.

——, "The Gallery of Palestinian Martyrs," *Haaretz*, December 25, 1990.

Salameh, George, "The Bazaar," *Kardom*, February 1982.

Schmelz, Uziel, "Demographic Development of the Arab Countries in Our Region," pt. 2, *Hamizrah Hehadash*, vol. 23 (1973).

——, "Natural Movement and Population Growth," in Aharon Layish (ed.), *Arabs in Israel* (Jerusalem, 1981).

——, "The Demographic Structure of Arabs and Druze in Israel," *Hamizrah Hehadash*, vol. 28 (1980).

Segev, Shemuel, "Ideological Motives of Israeli Arabs in Joining Terrorist Organizations," *Maariv*, November 27, 1968.

Segev, Tom, "Deir Yassin, 'Abdallah, Democracy," *Haaretz*, September 20, 1991.

——, "Felicia Langer as a Story," *Haaretz*, September 6, 1991.

Shamir, Shimon, "Changes in the Village Leadership of ar-Rama," *Hamizrah Hehadash*, vol. 11 (1961), pp. 241–57.

Shiloh, Gideon, "The Attitude of Literary Criticism in the Arab Countries to Arabic 'Resistance Literature' in Israel," *Hamizrah Hehadash*, vol. 24 (1974).

Stendel, Ori, "Arab Population in Judea and Samaria," *Seqirah Hodshit*, August 1988.

——, "Basic Perception of the Minorities in the State in Israeli Law," in Alouph Hareven (ed.), *Living Together* (Jerusalem, Van Leer Institute – Working Paper, September 1982).

——, "Changes in the Arab Population of Jerusalem," in Yehoshua Prawer and Ora Ahimeir (eds), *Twenty Years in Jerusalem* (Jerusalem, 1988).

——, "Obstructing the Implementation of Government Policy," *Haaretz*, September 17, 1976.

——, "Rakah's Attempts to Occupy Key Positions in the Arab Street," *Haaretz*, March 31, 1976.

——, "Reconciliation or Escalation," *Haaretz*, August 27, 1990.

——, "The Israeli Arabs in the Vortex of Contradictory Trends," *Seqirah Hodshit*, August 1985.

——, "The Location of the Progressive List for Peace," *Haaretz*, July 1, 1984.

——, "The Right of Israeli Arabs to Be Different: Legal Aspects," *Hamizrah Hehadash*, vol. 32 (1989).

——, "The Status of the Arab Woman in Israel at the Dawn of 1976," *Bitahon Sotziali* 9–10 (December 1975).

——, "Voting Trends for the Tenth Knesset among Israeli Arabs," *Hamizrah Hehadash*, vol. 30 (1981).

Tal, Yerah, "Talk of the Day with 'Izz ed-Din 'Ammash, Chairman of the Jisr ez-Zarqa local council, Member of Ratz," *Haaretz*, December 26, 1990.

——, "There Was No Massacre There," *Haaretz*, September 8, 1991.

"Three Polls among Israeli Arabs: 1. The Arab Young Generation and Its Attitude toward Religion," *Hamizrah Hehadash*, vol. 15 (1965).

Toledano, Shemuel, "Israeli Arabs: Achievements and Dilemmas," *Seqirah Hodshit*, January 1973.

Yinon, Avraham, "Arabic Literature in Israel," *Hamizrah Hehadash*, vol. 15 (1965), pp. 57–84.

Yisraeli, Amihud, "The Occupational Revolution in the Minority Sector in Israel," *Hamizrah Hehadash*, vol. 26 (1976), pp. 232–9.

Zelig, Yaron, "Closing a Newspaper," *Hotam*, September 4, 1987.

Zivan, Zeev, "Relations between the Jewish Community and the Negev Bedouin: The Interface and Its Influence on Shaping the Settled Frontier in the 1940s and 1950s" (M.A. dissertation, 1990).

Ziyad, Qassem, "An Arab Party: Yes or No?," *Al Hamishmar*, February 25, 1982.

——, "The Silent Voice of Freedom," *Al Hamishmar*, July 12, 1990.

Arabic

'Abd el-Fattah, "The Role and Position of the Palestinian Masses from within toward the Intifadah," *Ar-Rayah*, August 18, 1988.

'Abd er-Rahman, Muhammad, "The Arabs in Israel: New Directions in Identification with the Struggle of the Palestinian People," *Shuun Filastiniyyah*, no. 112 (March 1982).

'Asaqla, Hail, "Sindbad's Journey," *Al-Ittihad*, January 21, 1966.

Qabalan, Yusuf, "A Visit by Shamir with Sheikh Tarif Will Not Solve Our Problems," *As-Sinarah*, May 10, 1991.

Qassem, Samih el-, "No!" *Hadha al-'Alam*, May 5, 1966.

Salim, Naif Saleh, "We are the Root that Still Lives," *Al-Ittihad*, October 8, 1965.

Sarid, Yossi, "Meeting in Prison," *As-Sinarah*, December 14, 1990.

English

Mayer, Thomas, "The Islamic Opposition in Syria, 1961–1982," *Orient*, vol. 24 (1983), pp. 589–609.

Rosenfeld, Henry, "Change, Barriers to Change and Contradictions in the Arab Village Family," *American Anthropologist*, vol. 70 (December 1968).

Sharon, Moshe, "National Service for Arabs Can't Work," *The Jerusalem Post*, January 6, 1991.

Stendel, Ori, "National Service for Israeli Arabs: Should There Be a Law?", *The Jerusalem Post*, January 11, 1991.

——, "The Arabs of Israel: Between Hammer and Anvil," *Israel Yearbook on Human Rights*, vol. 20 (1991), pp. 287–308.

——, "The Minorities in Israel," *Israel Economist* (Jerusalem, 1973), pp. 10–13.

OFFICIAL PUBLICATIONS

Government of Israel, Bureau of Statistics, *Population Census*.
Government of Israel, Bureau of Statistics, *Statistical Abstract*.
The Hebrew University, Jerusalem, School of Social Work, *Survey of Graduates, 1961–1984* (Jerusalem, May 1985).
High Court of Justice, *Judgments*.
Israeli Police, *Annual Report*.
The Knesset, *Laws*.
Office of the Prime Minister, Bureau of the Advisor on Arab Affairs, *Review of the Events in the Arab Sector in Israel* (edited by Dr Yitzhak Reiter).

Democratic Arab Party, *Platform* (1988).
Government of Palestine, *Official Gazette*.
Government of Palestine, Department of Statistics, *Statistical Abstract*, 1944–1945.

NEWSPAPERS

Hebrew

Al Hamishmar; *Davar*; *Haaretz*; *Hadashot*; *Herut*; *Hetz* (quarterly on education and philosophy); *Kol Hair* (Jerusalem); *Koteret Kashit*; *Maariv*; *Yedioth Ahronoth*; *Zo Haderekh* (Rakah).

Arabic

Al-Anba; *Al-'Awdah*; *Ad-Diyar*; *Al-Fajr*; *Al-Ghad*; *Hadha al-Usbu'*; *Al-Ittihad*; *Al-Jadid*; *Kan'aan*; *Kull al-'Arab*; *Nida ash-Sha'b* (1947); *Ar-Rayah*; *Sada al-Jalil*; *Sawt al-Haqq wa-al-Hurriyyah*; *Ash-Sha'b*; *Shuun Filastiniyyah*; *As-Sinarah*; *As-Sirat*; *At-Tadamun*.

English

The Jerusalem Post; *New Outlook*.

Index